Plan of the Citadel Erecting at Calcutta in the Kingdom of Bengal

J P Losty

CALCUTTA
City of Palaces

A Survey of the City in the Days of the East India Company
1690-1858

THE BRITISH LIBRARY
ARNOLD PUBLISHERS

First published 1990 by
The British Library
Great Russell Street
London WC1B 3DG

Published in the Indian subcontinent by Arnold Publishers
AB/9 Safdarjung Enclave, New Delhi 110029

British Library Cataloguing in Publication Data
Losty, Jeremiah P
    Calcutta: city of palaces: a survey of the city in the
    days of the East India Company, 1690-1858.
    1. India. Calcutta, history
    I. Title   II. British Library
    954.147

ISBN 0 7123 0204 2 (cased)
ISBN 0 7123 0211 5 (paper)

Printed in England by BAS Printers Limited
Over Wallop, Hampshire

Designed by Alan Bartram
Typeset in Lasercomp Palatino by August Filmsetting
Haydock, St Helens

Contents

Preface / 7
Glossary / 9
The Trading Station 1690-1757 / 11
The Capital of Bengal 1757-1798 / 35
The Imperial City 1798-1858 / 71
Bibliography / 131
Index / 134

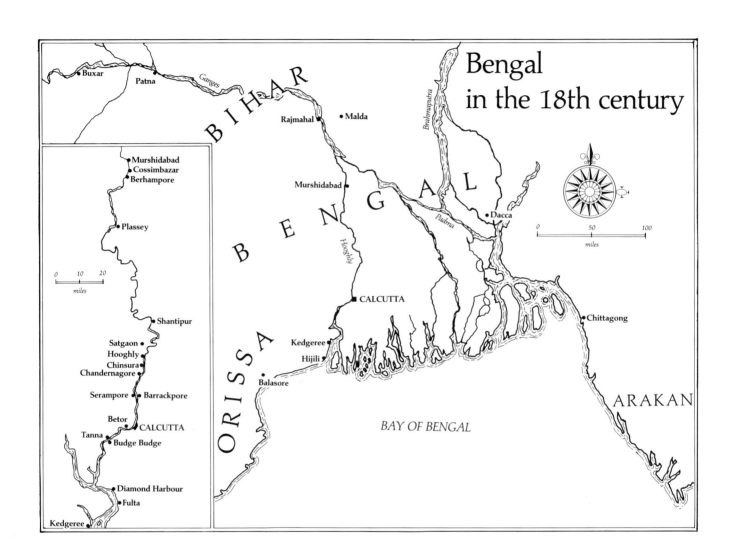

Bengal
in the 18th century

Main map labels:
Buxar
Patna
Ganges
BIHAR
Rajmahal
Malda
Brahmaputra
Murshidabad
BENGAL
Padma
Dacca
Hooghly
ORISSA
CALCUTTA
Kedgeree
Hijili
Balasore
Chittagong
ARAKAN
BAY OF BENGAL

0   50   100
miles

Inset map labels:
Murshidabad
Cossimbazar
Berhampore
Plassey
0   10   20
miles
Shantipur
Satgaon
Hooghly
Chinsura
Chandernagore
Serampore
Barrackpore
Betor
CALCUTTA
Tanna
Budge Budge
Diamond Harbour
Fulta
Kedgeree

Preface

CALCUTTA

Me the Sea-Captain loved, the River built
   Wealth sought and Kings adventured life to hold.
Hail England! I am Asia — Power on silt,
   Death in my hands, but Gold!

R KIPLING (from *The Song of the Cities*)

The village of Calcutta was in existence before Job Charnock made it the site of the English
East India Company's factory in 1690, but although its trading advantages may have enabled
it to grow into a flourishing town, it was Charnock and his successors alone who transformed
it into an imperial capital, a position it held from 1773 to 1911. This book, published to mark
Calcutta's 300th year, traces its growth from a trading station of mud huts into a city whose
beauty excited the admiration of all its visitors. Despite its importance, Calcutta has had few
studies of its topography, and none which made full use of the considerable visual materials.
There is a mass of material – plans, prints and drawings – which, when studied in the light of
the voluminous written records, both printed and manuscript, can be made to yield valuable
results. For the early period, the records of the East India Company are almost our only source.
These include the letters sent regularly between the Council in Calcutta and the Court of
Directors in London, and the Diaries and Consultations kept by the Council, of which copies
were sent to London for the Court's information. For the later periods, it is possible to use a
more extensive literature and wherever possible in this book, views have been enhanced
through the descriptions found in contemporary accounts. It must, however, be borne in mind
that these descriptions have been quoted for their period relevance rather than for their
accuracy. As the bibliography provides full details of the sources cited, it has not been thought
necessary to clutter the text with notes and references, the sources of which will already be
well known to historians of the period. The material is in fact so abundant that this study has
had to be restricted to the European part of the city in the age before photography, the
introduction of which into India almost coincides with the end of the Company's rule, thus
providing a convenient stopping-place.

   I have drawn particularly on the travel literature of the period, which from 1770 to 1830
provides one of the most delightful minor genres of English letters. With what elegance of
language and confidence in their own taste and judgement do these now largely forgotten
writers describe the appearance and customs of far-off places and peoples, which their fellow
countrymen could never hope to see for themselves. This literature forms a counterpart to the
volumes of engraved views, some of it originated by professionals but much of it based on the
work of amateurs, which brought the appearance of these same places before the British
public. Memoirs too from this period provide wonderful insights into the way the British
conducted themselves in such strange surroundings: indeed, the most important of this class
of material, the *Memoirs* of the lawyer William Hickey, is of a literary and historical interest far
exceeding the mining by historians of Calcutta to which it is normally subjected.

   Although references to the 'palaces' of Calcutta are found from as early as 1780, the epithet
'The City of Palaces' was first used by James Atkinson as the title of his poem published in

Calcutta in 1824, which sums up feelings expressed by many at this time. This will give the flavour:

> ... But we here behold
> A prodigy of power, transcending all
> The conquests, and the governments, of old,
> An empire of the Sun, a gorgeous realm of gold.
>
> For us in half a century, India blooms
> The garden of Hesperides, and we
> Placed in its porch, Calcutta, with its tombs
> And dazzling splendors, towering peerlessly,
> May taste its sweets, yet bitters too there be
> Under attractive seeming. Drink again
> The frothy draught, and revel joyously;
> From the gay round of pleasure, why refrain!
> Thou'rt on the brink of death, luxuriate on thy bane.
>
> I stood a wandering stranger at the *Ghaut*,
> And, gazing round, beheld the pomp of spires
> And palaces, to view like magic brought;
> All glittering in the sun-beam...

Atkinson goes on to compare the glittering European city with the surrounding squalor of the Bengali town, a contrast which became ever more obvious as the 19th century progressed.

Kipling's tremendous apostrophe quoted above encapsulates this ambiguous relationship between Calcutta and those who have attempted to describe it. His own epithet of 'The City of Dreadful Night' is now more famous, but what made it so dreadful to Kipling, that is, Eurasian whores in the back-streets of the Indian city, is a reflection on his philosophy of imperialism, and not on the city itself. It was, however, a prophetic epithet for the city in the 20th century, so that Calcutta has become a by-word in contemporary journalese for the horrors of a third-world megalopolis. But despite the prophecies of impending collapse, Calcutta still survives and, in its own way, flourishes.

Indian terms used in the text are explained in the glossary. For much of this period, the normal current rupee-Sterling exchange rate was roughly ten to the pound, and this may be used for calculating equivalents when not provided. There were, however, other rupees: *sicca* rupees are calculated as worth eight to the pound, while Arcot rupees were worth 3% less than *siccas*. Rupees are calculated in crores and lacks: a crore is 10,000,000 and a lack 100,000, thus a crore of rupees is worth a £1 million, and a lack of rupees is £10,000. It should also be noted that I have used, for brevity's sake, 'north', 'south' etc where 'north-east', 'south-west' and so on would be more accurate, when treating of directions in Calcutta, which is laid out along an axis running roughly north-east to south-west.

This book has been published to accompany an exhibition of the same name held in the British Library to celebrate the tercentenary of Job Charnock's founding of European Calcutta, drawing mostly on the resources of the India Office Library and Records. The Library is deeply grateful to those who have contributed towards the cost of the exhibition. I am grateful to all those colleagues in the British Library and in the India Office Library and Records who have helped me with both book and exhibition, as well as to John Ronayne and his team for their designing of the exhibition. My thanks also go to those institutions and collectors who have generously agreed to lend to the exhibition or who have allowed their material to be reproduced in this book, as well as to Robert Sykes and his staff in the British Council office in Calcutta for their help. I am especially grateful to my colleague Patricia Kattenhorn for relieving me of so many duties these past two years, thereby allowing me to concentrate on Calcutta. My deepest thanks go to my wife Kate for putting up with my absences and unpredictable hours so uncomplainingly, and for her unswerving support.

J P LOSTY

Glossary

anna	one-sixteenth of a rupee
banyan	Hindu trader, but in Bengal especially a broker or one dealing with the financial affairs of a European
begum	a Muslim lady of noble birth
bigah	Indian land measurement, about one-third of an acre in Bengal
bihishti	water-carrier, carrying water in a goat-skin
budgerow	a keel-less sailing barge, used for travelling on the rivers, over half of it occupied by a cabin with Venetian windows
chobdar	silver-stick bearer
chowkidar	watchman
chunam	prepared lime, used for fine polished plaster
cottah	one-twentieth of a bigah
crore	10,000,000
cutcha	poor quality, a building of mud and timber; contrasted with pucka
cutchery	administrative office of a magistrate
divani	power of revenue raising
durbar	public audience held by a ruler
Durga puja	autumn festival of the great goddess, especially popular in Bengal
faujdar	officer of the Mughal government in charge of the police and criminal jurisdiction in a given area
firman	order issued by letters patent from the Emperor
Gentoo	Hindu
ghaut	landing or bathing place on a river, normally with steps
godown	warehouse
hackery	bullock cart
lakh	also lack or lac: 100,000
madrassah	traditional Islamic college
maidan	open area, especially a grassy plain in British India
masnad	cushion or platform used by Muslim rulers in place of a throne
maund	Indian measurement of weight, standardized in British India at just over 82lbs
Mofussil	provinces, outside the Presidency capitals
mohur	gold coin, standardized in British India at 16 sicca rupees
morpunkhi	elaborately decorated boat, with a peacock prow
Mughal	the ruling dynasty of India from 1526-1858, and by extension all officials of their government
nautch	dance provided as an entertainment
Nawab	originally a Viceroy or Governor, and then the ruler of a province; in English a Nabob, also meaning one who made a fortune in the East
nullah	bed of a stream, usually dry apart from in the rainy season
ottur	essential oil of rose, which guests would be sprinkled with
palanquin	a travelling litter, with pole projecting fore and aft, carried by 4 men
parganah	sub-division of a district
parwanah	a grant or letter of authority, issued by the Emperor or by his subordinates
pottah	a lease of land
pucka	permanent, well-built, particularly a building of bricks and mortar; contrasted with cutcha
rupee	Indian unit of currency, worth 10 to the £ sterling, each divided into 16 annas
	sicca rupee, worth 8 to the £ sterling
	Arcot rupee, worth 3% less than a sicca rupee
sepoy	Indian soldier, normally working for the British
syce	groom
subah	province of the Mughal empire
subahdar	governor of a subah, appointed by the Emperor
taluqdar	in Bengal, a landholder paying rent to Government on inalienable royal lands, or one renting land from a zamindar
tamasha	entertainment or spectacle
topaz	half-caste Christian soldier
zamindar	in Bengal, an inalienable landholder paying rent direct to the Government

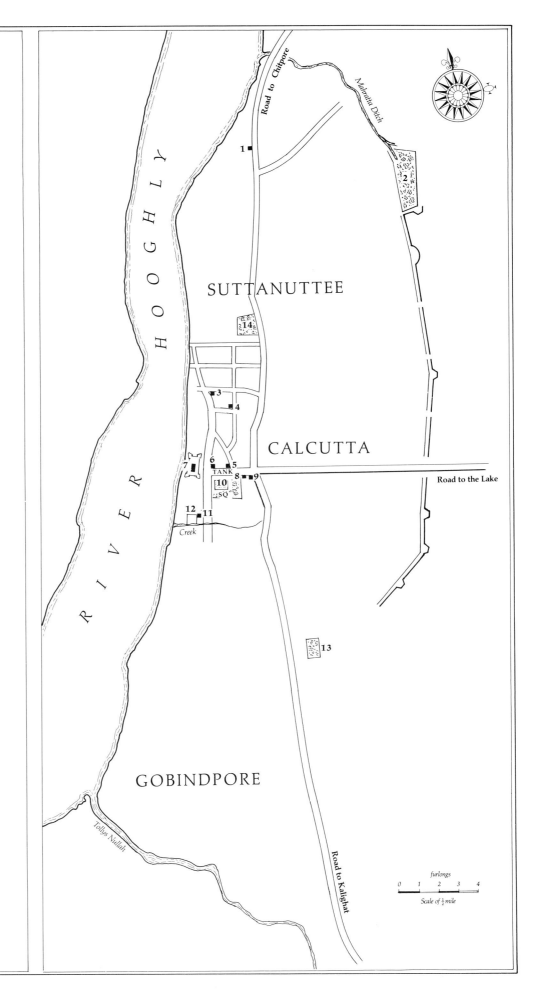

Calcutta
1690–1757

1 Black Pagoda
2 Gardens of Gobindram
   Mitter and Omi Chand
3 Armenian Church
4 Portuguese Church
5 Court House
6 Church of St Anne
7 Fort William and Factory
8 Theatre
9 Jail
10 Park and Tank
11 Hospital
12 Burial ground
13 Company's garden and
   fishpond
14 Garden of the Seths

Road to Chitpore

Mahratta Ditch

RIVER HOOGHLY

SUTTANUTTEE

CALCUTTA

Road to the Lake

TANK

SQ

Creek

GOBINDPORE

Tollys Nullah

Road to Kalighat

furlongs
0   1   2   3   4
Scale of ½ mile

The Trading Station
1690-1757

'August 24, 1690. This day at Sankraul ordered Capt. Brooke to come up with his Vessell to Chutanutte where we arrived about noon, but found ye place in a deplorable condition, nothing being left for our present accomodation & ye Rains falling day & night. We are forced to take ourselves to boats which considering the season of the year is very unhealthy.' With these depressing words from the first volume of the Fort William Factory Records, Job Charnock, the Honourable East India Company's Chief Agent in Bengal, recorded the third and final occupation of a foothold of ground in Suttanuttee within the confines of the modern Calcutta, and so begins the history of that city.

It was trade that sent the English and other Europeans to India, and it was obvious that the delta of the Ganges was the best place to establish a trading station. Bengal was the richest province in India, while downriver from the Ganges, Jumna and their tributaries came the goods of all of Hindustan. When the Portuguese arrived in Bengal about 1518, two great ports were already established there, Chittagong in the east (which did not control the Ganges trade) and Satgaon in the west, an ancient town originally on a branch of the river Hooghly (itself the westernmost branch of the Ganges delta) about 30 miles upriver from Calcutta. Satgaon's importance was diminished by the gradual silting up of its river, and about 1550 some of its Indian merchants, families of Bysacks and Seths, transferred themselves downriver to the site of the modern Calcutta, to the villages of Gobindpore on a slight eminence above the river, and Suttanuttee, where an important market for cotton, the principal trade of Bengal itself, was developing. The bend of the river just below was its last easily navigable stretch, and a temporary town at Betor on the west bank had sprung up to service the traders during the season. Further upstream the river shallowed, and the Portuguese used to send river boats to bring down the goods from Satgaon. About 1575, however, the Portuguese received permission from the Mughal Emperor Akbar to found a settlement at the town of Hooghly, and they were prepared to bring their ships further up while enjoying the Emperor's good will. Betor was largely abandoned and its trade transferred to Suttanuttee across the river. Akbar demanded in return that the Portuguese at Hooghly should keep the eastern seas free of the renegade Portuguese and Arakanese pirates from Chittagong and the Arakan who infested them. However, the tolerance of Akbar's successors for the presence of the European infidels was easily upset, and the Portuguese failure to fulfil their part of the bargain drew the vengeance of Shah Jahan upon them. In 1632 Hooghly was captured by the Mughals after a three month's siege, and its Christian survivors were transferred to Agra as slaves, ending all serious Portuguese economic activity in Bengal.

The first English East India Company had been founded by a group of merchants in London in 1599, and was given its first charter by Queen Elizabeth I in the following year. Its efforts to win trading rights for itself in India were made in the face of continued opposition first from the Portuguese and then the Dutch, who had by this time largely supplanted the former as traders throughout the eastern seas. The first English factory or trading station was established at Surat on the west coast in 1612, while Fort St George at Madras was founded in 1640. The English first established themselves in eastern India in 1633 in Orissa, at the port of Balasore (which later offered safe anchorage to ships waiting for favourable winds to take them up the Hooghly) and the inland mart at Hariharpur, but it was not until 1651 that they were able to establish themselves in the Gangetic delta, at the town of Hooghly. The Dutch meanwhile had established a factory at Chinsura close by in 1632. The two companies were bitterly hostile to each other, carrying on a fierce war in the East throughout much of the 17th century, until the accession of the Dutchman William of Orange to the throne of England in 1688.

No picture of this early English settlement survives, but one of the Dutch factory at Chinsura painted in 1665 by Hendrick van Schuylenburgh shows the general layout of such establishments (fig.1). The main building occupied three sides of a square, the principal part being two storeyed and forming the living quarters of the Director and the principal offices, while in the wings were warehouses for the valuable goods. Other warehouses were built round the inside of the perimeter wall of the compound. Fresh water and gardens were obviously of great importance. The whole was surrounded by a wall as yet unfortified. In van Schuylenburgh's painting, a Mughal official seems to have come to visit the Dutch Director. The diary kept by Streynsham Master during his tour of inspection of the English factories in Bengal in 1676 describes the Dutch factory as 'a large well built house standing by itself, much like to a Country Seat in England,' and records a visit to it: 'This afternoone Mr. Clavell with myselfe and others visited the Dutch at their Factory, which is very large and well built, with two quadrangles. The Directore was very obligeing, and shewed us the new built warehouses, which are three very large, that make one side of one of the Quadrangles next to the River side ... Alsoe he shewed us other accomodations of their Factory, their Gardens, which are very spatious, well kept, with Tarrass walks, and full of Lettice and good herbage. And adjoyning to their Factory, they have offices for all things needfull to them, as a carpenters yard with stores of good Timber brought from Batavia, a Coopers yard where they make many Casks for the Pork which they kill and Salt up and downe the river, a Smithes forge, a Grannary, an apartment for a great many weavers, where they have sett up Loomes for the weaving of saile cloth, and a feild to make ropes in.'

The English factories were all smaller in scale and even the largest of them at Hooghly, where resided the Chief and Council in the Bay, was terribly cramped, being ill-sited near the centre of the town and hence impossible to defend. In 1669 it contained 'but seven lodging rooms besides the Cheif and second lodgings and the writing office'. It was expanded in 1676 'to make the Factory capable of accomodating four marryed persons of the Councell, and alsoe to make a Penthouse to preserve the house to the Southward; and which are wanting the most necessary, an office, a Councell Chamber, and a place for the Registers to be kept in, out of two of the five upper roomes'. The new penthouse must have been an early form of verandah, to protect the southern aspect of the house from the fierce sun. Further expansion was authorised in 1679, both for the accomodation of the Company's servants and for warehouses: 'It is therefore ordered that both sides of the Quadrangle of this Factory be built to the gate, and divided into some lodging chambers with large ware houses for the fine goods ... and that offices for the Accomptant and the Secretary, a Councell chamber and a library roome, be built upon the new buildings or appointed out of the old upper roomes.' Master records the presence of 29 Company servants in Bengal in 1679, of whom nine or ten were stationed at the Hooghly factory, and among whom the older ones needed married accomodation.

As for the work carried out in the Factory, it consisted chiefly of ordering and checking goods, principally cotton and silk piece-goods, and later muslins, for the European markets, according to strict requirements laid down by London. The English had little contact with the actual weavers and depended on brokers or *banyans* to supply the lengths of cloth. Constant vigilance was required if they were to surmount the immense difficulties, both natural and man-made, and make a profit. There was little demand for European goods in India, so that most of what they had ordered had to be paid for in hard cash. Bullion had to be sent from London to India, where it was normally sent to the nearest imperial mint (at Rajmahal) to be converted into coinage, at rates which fluctuated wildly at this period. Good relations had to be maintained with the Mughal court, the *Subahdar* of Bengal based at Dacca, and a host of minor officials at different towns throughout the region, all of them wanting to exact their due out of the Company's profits. Much of the Company's diplomatic effort was devoted to obtaining *firmans* from the court allowing it to trade without paying custom dues, but imperial *firmans* were not too much deferred to in Bengal in the late 17th century. Because of the

Fig.1. Hendrick van Schuylenburgh,
The Dutch factory at Hooghly-
Chinsura, 1665. Oil on canvas;
203 × 316 cm. Rijksmuseum
Amsterdam, A 4282.

monsoon winds which regulated the trade of the Indian Ocean, ships could arrive and depart
only at certain times of the year, so that goods which were not ready on time would have to
wait an entire year, during which they would almost certainly spoil in the climate. And it was
only with great difficulty that the ocean-going ships could be got up so far as Hooghly itself,
as the main channel shifted course constantly; to get upriver so far, the ships depended totally
on a trained pilot service. In later years, no big Indiaman ventured further upriver than
Diamond Harbour, 40 miles below Calcutta, for the next reach of the river contained the
fearsome 'James and Mary' sands, named from the ship which was lost in the quicksands there
in 1694.

The Company divided its servants into ranks: 'Knowing that a distinction of titles is, in
many respects, necessary, we order that when the apprentices have served their times they be
styled writers; and when the writers have served their times they be styled factors; and the
factors having served their times be styled merchants; and the merchants having served their
times be styled senior merchants.' In the factories they lived a kind of collegiate life, with
meals taken in a common hall, seated in strict order of seniority, but apparently with groaning
tables before them, with arrack punch and Shiraz wine to drink. The Chief Agent and the
Second were allowed a palanquin each when they went out, while members of Council and
the Chaplain were allowed a parasol borne over them. Even this early, large numbers of
servants accompanied their every outing. Streynsham Master notes in August 1676 disputes
over the use of parasols at Masulipatam: 'There being an ill custome in the factory of writers
having roundells carried over their heads, which is not used or allowed by the Government of
the towne, but only the Governour and the next three principal officers, and to two or three
eminent merchants of ancient standing ... It is therefore ordered that noe person in this
factory have a roundell carried over them, but such as are of the Councell and the Chaplaine.'

Outside the Factory, where of course most of the work of securing trade was done, the
Englishmen adopted Indian ways – Indian wives, garments and eating habits. Their morals
became very lax, to the scandal of the inspectors sent out from time to time to report on them.
William Hedges, the Company's Chief Agent in Bengal from 1682-4, records bitterly in his

diary in 1682, when he was at Dacca petitioning the *Subahdar*: 'This morning a Gentoo [Hindu] sent by Bulchand, Governour of Hugly and Cassumbazar, made complaint to me that Mr. Charnock did shamefully, to the great scandall of our nation, keep a Gentoo woman of his kindred, which he has had these 19 years.' Mr Harvey, the Chief at Malda, 'regards nothing but to enjoy his little Seraglio of 6 Strumpets, and live at ease upon the Company's Expence'. Streynsham Master had attempted, it would appear unsuccessfully, to regulate the personal morality of the Company's servants through a series of orders to be read after divine service twice a year: 'We doe Christianly admonish every one imployed in the service of the Honble. English East India Company to abandon lying, swearing, Curseing, drunkeness, uncleanness, prophanation of the Lords Day and all other sinfull practices, and not to be out of the House or from their lodgings late at night, nor absent from nor neglect morning or evening prayers, or doe any other thing to the dishonour of Almighty God, the corruption of good manners, or against the peace of the Government.' Penalties were fines, or so many hours in the stocks in default, whereas persistent malefactors and those found 'guilty of Adultery, Fornication, uncleanness or any such crime, or shall disturb the peace of the Factory by quarrelling or fighting and will not be reclaimed, he or they shall be sent to Fort St. George, there to receive condigne punishment.'

Hedges had been sent out as Governor and Superintendent of the Company's affairs in the Bay of Bengal, after the experiment of having all the stations in Bengal subordinate to Fort St George had failed. The chain of command, however, within the councils of the various Bengal factories was not settled satisfactorily, and Hedges had too little power to put the Company's affairs in Bengal into order. Apart from his comments on personal morals, Hedges shows us a world in which many of the English factors indulged in private trade to the detriment of the Company, or who systematically filched from the Company's warehouses, from Indian traders and workmen depending on them, or worst of all (in the Company's eyes) who traded clandestinely with the various interlopers or private traders who were trying to break the monopoly of the London Company at this time. The interlopers and their backers in England forced the setting up of a rival Company in 1698, and there ensued bitter strife between the servants of the two Companies, until a preliminary union between them was enforced by Parliament in 1702 and a final one in 1708. The Mughal *Subahdar* in Dacca, Shaista Khan, exercised little control over the local governors, so that the Company's men were faced with constant demands for dues and bribes to allow trade to continue. Mughal officials were able to play off the old Company's agents against the increasing numbers of interlopers, who were prepared to pay customs dues to gain favour at the local courts. Worst of all was the quality of the Company's servants in Bengal, who quarrelled incessantly among themselves, and whom Hedges had not the power to subdue, since they appealed directly over his head to friends in the Company's headquarters in London. Shaista Khan complained that the English 'were a company of base, quarrelling people, and foul dealers'. Their official salaries were so ludicrously low that private trade had to be sanctioned in commodities not traded in by the Company, but they resorted to numerous other methods of increasing their income, all of them detrimental to the Company's interests.

Hedges and Job Charnock, the Chief at Cossimbazar, who had been far longer in India than any of these men sent out to govern him, were constantly at loggerheads. Charnock had been in India since 1655 or 1656. He spent most of this time as Chief of the station at Patna, where the trade was mostly in saltpetre, before being appointed Chief at the more important factory at Cossimbazar in 1679. Here was concentrated the silk-manufacture of Bengal, and its Chief was Second in Council in the Bay, that is, subordinate only to the Chief at Hooghly within Bengal, and with this post too promised in succession. This, however, did not actually fall his way until 1685, just at the time when the Company was prepared to sanction an open breach with the Mughal government in order to stop what they regarded as increasingly unjustified exactions, particularly from the local governors at Hooghly itself and Muxadabad. Charnock, like many of the English in Bengal, was convinced that a fortified factory was essential if the English were ever to trade free of the exactions of the local officials, realizing that *firmans* from Delhi were of little account in the changed circumstances of the Mughal empire. At this time the Emperor Aurangzeb was concentrating all his efforts on incorporating the

Deccan into his empire so that his local officials could openly flout imperial orders.

In 1686 the Company sent out a fleet of armed ships, whose purpose was to seize a convenient place at the mouth of the Ganges, fortify it, and stop all commercial traffic until the Mughals had reached a binding accomodation over customs dues. When the fleet arrived, however, they found Charnock besieged in the factory at Hooghly, as the Mughals had grown alarmed at the increased number of Company soldiers stationed in the factory at Hooghly, and preparing to withdraw from it completely. This Charnock managed to do on 20 December 1686, and by the end of the year he was encamped at Chuttanuttea (or Suttanuttee), on the site of modern Calcutta; here was the flourishing cotton market founded by Bengali traders who had abandoned Satgaon a century before. Charnock attempted to come to terms with Shaista Khan; but these negotiations came to nothing, and the English were driven from Suttanuttee too. They went downriver, took the Mughal forts at Tanna which had protected the upper river from the depredations of the Portuguese and Arakanese pirates, and then the island of Hijili in the swamps of the delta, which was important for its salt-works (a royal monopoly). Charnock used the island as a base, as he fortified it and then ventured out again briefly to take and sack Balasore. The unhealthy climate of Hijili more than halved Charnock's tiny army of about 300 men. Being compelled once more to negotiate by the Mughals' overrunning the island, Charnock and his men were allowed to return to Suttanuttee, which they reached towards the end of 1687 and where they remained for about a year. It is not clear under what terms they stayed there, as so many of the documents have not survived.

In the meantime the Court of Directors had sent out another squadron of ships under the command of one Captain Heath, with orders to seize Chittagong and fortify it, although they were worried – and this gives some idea of the fantasy world in which they lived – that it would 'be a very difficult thing for Capt. Heath and the fleet with him to get up the great Ganges as high as Chittegam without the aid of our pilots in the Bay.'

Captain Heath arrived in the bay in September 1688 and sailed upriver, where he found Charnock at Suttanuttee. Heath's instructions gave him the command of all the Company's servants in Bengal, but the impetuous Captain did not listen to those experienced in India; he entered into negotiations, but never stayed for answers. He took off the entire English company from Suttanuttee and set off for Chittagong, the Arakanese ports and eventually Madras: 'Then Capt. Heath, tripping from port to port without effecting anything, hath not only rendered our nation ridiculous, but hath unhinged all treaties, by which means the trade of Bengall will be very difficult to be ever regained.' This was written by an embittered Charnock and his Council in Madras, on 22 March 1689, whither the English had now retreated. A year later, overtures of peace came from the new *Subahdar* in Dacca, Ibrahim Khan, who offered to pay 60,000 rupees compensation for the goods plundered at Hooghly, while a new approach would be made to the Emperor for a *firman* for free trading. Charnock started back from Madras, and on 24 August 1690 established himself again at Suttanuttee.

Charnock's obstinacy in trying to settle in this place shows that he realised some at least of the strategic and trading importance of the site. Unlike all the other European trading stations on the Hooghly, it was on the east side of the river, and therefore well defended on the side that an imperial Mughal army might be expected to attack it, while English command of the river should in theory have prevented an army from crossing. On the east, it was also defended by the extensive Salt Lake and by swamps, and on the south, by an inpenetrable jungle, and it was therefore to some extent protected from an attack by the *Subahdar* in Dacca. As the furthest downstream of all the European stations, it was the furthest away from interference from the Mughal centre of power in western Bengal at Hooghly, while its guns in commanding the river could also control its European rivals' fortunes in future wars, news of which it would be the first to receive. The place was already an established trading centre, with the Suttanuttee Hat, or cotton-bale market, around it, while further north was the big village of Chitpore. The merchants who had abandoned Satgaon, the Bysacks and Seths, lived at Gobindpore, about a mile south of Suttanuttee on a slight eminence overlooking the river. Furthermore, ships of a greater capacity could be got up the river this far than could be got up to Hooghly and the Dutch and French factories. The place was besides on the north-south road linking Chitpore to the north with the temple of the Goddess at Kalighat a few miles to the south, a temple which by the time of Charnock's settling nearby was the most important in Bengal.

Between Suttanuttee and Gobindpore was another village, Calcutta, in 1690 the least important of the three, but destined to give its name to the whole city. The name Calcutta (Kalikata) has nothing to do with the temple at Kalighat, as is still often supposed, as the two were distinct places even in the 15th century, when both are mentioned by the Bengali poet Bipradas. No portrait is known of the founding father of this imperial city, but an entertaining if libellous description of him is found in Captain Alexander Hamilton's *A New Account of the East Indies* published in 1727. Hamilton had traded in the East Indies since 1688 as one of the 'Interlopers' so roundly condemned in the records of the old Company, and hence his remarks are decidedly biased against the latter and against its agent. Hamilton tells us that Charnock was supposed to have conceived the idea of setting up an English factory at this point when resting under a famous peepul tree, which is usually identified with a great tree to the east of Calcutta on the road to the Salt Lake. An alternative tradition has put forward the claims of a great tamarind tree in what became the old burial ground in Calcutta itself, which certainly seems preferable as it is much nearer the river. Wherever the tree may have been, tradition places Charnock beneath it, smoking his pipe and trying to decide on the best place to refound the principal English factory in Bengal. Although the strategic and trading advantages of Suttanuttee may have persuaded him to settle there, what his meditations failed to convince him of was its extreme unhealthiness, owing to the proximity of the swamps and the lake.

Let Hamilton's own account now tell us about Charnock and his choice: 'The English settled there [Calcutta] about the year 1690 after the Mogul had pardoned all the robberies and murders committed on his subjects. Mr. Job Channock being then the Company's Agent in Bengal, he had liberty to settle an emporium in any part on the river's side below Hughly, and for the sake of a large shady tree chose that place, tho' he could not have chosen a more unhealthful place on all the river; for three miles to the north-eastward, is a salt-water lake that overflows in September and October, and then prodigious numbers of fish resort thither, but in November and December when the floods are dissipated, those fishes are left dry, and with their putrefaction affect the air with thick stinking vapours, which the north-east winds bring with them to Fort William, that they cause a yearly mortality. One year I was there, and there were reckoned in August about 1200 English, some military, some servants to the Company, some private merchants residing in the town and some seamen belonging to the shipping lying at the town, and before the beginning of January there were four hundred and sixty burials registered in the clerk's book of mortality.

'Mr. Channock choosing the ground of the colony, where it now is, reigned more absolute than a rajah, only he wanted much of their humanity, for when any poor ignorant native transgressed his laws, they were sure to undergo a severe whipping for a penalty, and the execution was generally done when he was at dinner, so near his dining-room that the grones and cries of the poor delinquent served him for musick. The country about being overspread with paganism, the custom of wives burning with their deceased husbands is also practised here. Before the Mogul's war, Mr. Channock went one time with his ordinary guard of soldiers to see a young widow act that tragical catastrophe, but he was so smitten with the widow's beauty, that he sent his guards to take her by force from her executioners, and conducted her to his own lodgings. They lived lovingly many years, and had several children, at length he died, after he had settled in Calcutta, but instead of converting her to Christianity, she made him a proselyte to paganism, and the only part of Christianity that was remarkable in him, was burying her decently, and he built a tomb over her, where all his life after her death, he kept the anniversary day of her death by sacrificing a cock on her tomb, after the pagan manner; and this was and is the common report, and I have been credibly informed, both by Christians and pagans, who lived at Calcutta under his Agency, that the story was really true matter of fact.' The story of Charnock's sacrificing a cock on his wife's tomb, if true, seems related to the cult of the Panch Pir or Five Saints in Bihar, a cult observed there by low-class Muslims as well as by Hindus. Charnock was of course Chief at Patna in Bihar for many years.

On 28 August 1690, at another consultation, Charnock and his Council (Francis Ellis and Jeremiah Peachie) recorded: 'In consideration that all the former buildings here are destroyed, it is resolved that such places be built as necessity requires and as cheap as possible vizt. 1st A Warehouse, 2 A dineing room, 3 The Secretary's office to be repair'd, 4 A room to sort Cloth in, 5 A Cookroom with its conveniencies, 6 An Appartment for the Company's Servants, 7 The Agents & Mr Peachie's houses to be repair'd which were part standing & a house to be built for Mr. Ellis the former being totally demolish'd, 8 The Guard house, These to be done with Mudd Walls and thacht till we can gett ground whereon to build a Factory.' A letter from Fort St George to London in May 1691 describes these pioneers living 'in a wild unsetled Condition at Chuttanuttee, neither fortifyed houses nor Goedowns, only Tents, Hutts and boats with the strange charge of near 100 Soldiers, guard ship &ca for little or noe business, and a doubtful foundation wholly depending on the good Nabob's stay and favour'. Trade could not commence nor could a factory be built without the *firman* from the Emperor. This finally came that same year, allowing the English to trade free of all dues for an annual payment to the Emperor of 3,000 rupees.

Charnock, the founder of the city, died on 10 January 1693, and had done little to establish a permanent factory. He was succeeded by his son-in-law Charles Eyre as Agent, who built for his father-in-law in 1695 a grandiose mausoleum in the burial ground in Calcutta, which subsequently became St John's churchyard. Sir John Goldsborough, the Company's Chief Governor of all the settlements, visited Suttanuttee in 1693 after Charnock's death: 'When I came hither, I found the Agent and Councill had been Remiss in not marking out a place whereon to build a Factorie on, if we should hereafter be Libertized to settle here, and by that omission of theirs noe body knew where, or how to build, but everyone built straglinly where and how they pleased even on the most properest place for a factorie, and have dug holes and tancks that will cost the Company money to fill up agen, and the longer this Run The worss would be the Evill, Therefore I thought fitt to order the inclosing a peece of ground with a Mud wall whereon to build a factorie when we have a parwanna for it, which I meen to goe in hand to inclose in a day or two, this is all I know of this Matter.' Goldsborough's selected site for his factory had already been chosen for a Catholic church. However, 'I turned their priests from hence, and their Mass house was to be pulled Downe in Course to make way for the factorie when it shall be thought Convenient to build itt'.

If this extract from the records is to be taken as it stands, then it is to Goldsborough that the credit must go for shifting the nucleus of the settlement from Suttanuttee southwards to Calcutta itself, for the lines drawn by Goldsborough became the walls of the factory compound, within which the Agent was already living in 1695: 'There ariseing many inconveniences from the Right Honourable Companys ffactors and writers having lodgings out of the Right Honourable Companys Factory or compound which their Agent lives in . . . besides they are not at the call or under the Eye of the Agent, as youth ought to be. Tis therefore ordered that half a dozen Chambers of brick and mudd be built on the Northside of the Compound for them to live in.' The Company's servants had previously lived at Suttanuttee where Charnock's house was situated 'at a considerable distance from the ffactory'. Eyre took the opportunity in 1696 of a local insurrection to begin fortifying these same walls. This was the beginning of the first Fort William in Calcutta, christened under the name of the reigning king on 20 August 1700.

The Mughal government under Aurangzeb and his *Subahdar* in Bengal, now his grandson Azim ash-Shan, pursued policies varying between outright hostility and wavering support, always tempered by the knowledge of the revenues to be derived from trade with the foreigners. From the *Subahdar* in 1698 permission was obtained (in consideration of a gift to the prince of 16,000 rupees) to purchase the right of renting the three villages of Suttanuttee, Calcutta and Gobindpore, from the existing rent holders, a Majumdar family, who were compensated with 1300 rupees ('the best money that ever was spent for so great a priviledge'). The Company thought that it had bought the *zamindari* rights, giving it inalienable possession and the power to collect rents and revenues in return for an annual payment to Government of just under 1200 rupees, but since the land in question was part of the estate granted by the Emperor to the *Subahdar* in Bengal for his maintenance, it could not be

Deed of purchase of the right to rent Calcutta, 1698. A late-18th century copy. British Library Add MS 24039, no.39.

alienated in this way. What it seems to have bought were the lesser *talukdari* rights of rent-collecting on behalf of the *zamindar*, in this instance the *Subahdar* himself. However, the Court of Directors, unmindful of Mughal revenue practice, had already decided in 1695 that Suttanuttee should be its principal settlement in Bengal, and now in 1699 thought it was sufficiently strong to release it from subservience to Fort St George at Madras and elevate it to the rank of an independent Presidency under its first Governor, Sir Charles Eyre.

By every letter the Directors in London, fearful of chaos at the approaching end of the life of Aurangzeb and its effect on their profits, urged the complete fortification of the factory, although always with due regard to economy ('building being cheap in Bengall . . . We are not solicitous for the largeness so much as the strength of it, lest it create a vast Charge of many Soldiers to maintain it'). In fact the death of Aurangzeb in 1707 did not embarass the Company nearly so much as had the incursion of its rival the New Company, whose advent gave Mughal officials the chance to play one off against the other in terms of extracting cash payments, while the forcible union of the two in 1702 under a new title gave them the opportunity to declare all previous *firmans* and *parwanas* invalid. Although Aurangzeb's sons fought each other for the throne, the victory of Shah Alam was swift and by 1708 relative stability had returned; handsome presents to the new Emperor and his *Subahdar* in Bengal were enough to keep business going.

The Company's delight at being able to rent the land around the factory was owing to the money it would bring into its own coffers, from ground rents, taxes and various dues; the fortifications likewise offered security, for which the inhabitants of the three towns (as the Court now called them) would have to pay. By 1703 some of the English inhabitants had already built handsome houses, paying ground rent to the Company for their leases, but most money came in from the Bengali citizens. A survey undertaken in 1707 shows that the Company's lands consisted in total of 5077 *bigahs* or 1861 acres from the four divisions into which the three towns were divided, with Calcutta itself divided between the Town of Calcutta and Bazaar Calcutta (the boundary between the two being the east road to the Salt Lake). This survey apportions the area of each division between houses, gardens, crops, waste ground, and so on. Bazaar Calcutta was the most densely populated, with 400 out of its 488 *bigahs* given over to houses, as this division included not only half of the English settlement around the north of the Fort, as well as the Armenian and Portuguese areas further north, but also the Great or Bara Bazaar, the main Bengali area, which had already sprung up between the Christian part of the settlement and Suttanuttee itself. The other divisions were still sparsely populated, ranging from the 20% of the Town of Calcutta given over to houses to only 5% of Suttanuttee and Gobindpore. The maximum ground rent chargeable was three rupees per *bigah*, such as on houses in the Town of Calcutta, yielding a sizable revenue compared with what had had to be paid for the privilege of obtaining the renting rights. The Company's Calcutta accounts show an average monthly cash balance in 1707 of 885 rupees, representing nearly 10,000 rupees per annum, from a population probably of about 20,000 at this time. By 1711 the cash balances had practically doubled, and doubled again the following year, although these increases may reflect better methods of collecting or of accounting rather than rapid increases of population. The Court was especially desirous of increasing its revenues from the town, but not at the cost of oppression: 'Let your ears be open to complaints and let no voice of oppression be heard in your streets. Take care that neither the broker, nor those under him, nor your own servants use their patron's authority to hurt and injure the people. Go into the different quarters of the town and do and see justice done without charge or delay to all the inhabitants. This is the best method to enlarge our towns and increase our revenues.'

One of the members of the Council, Ralph Sheldon, was appointed in 1700 to be in charge of collecting the revenues of Calcutta, while he also acted as a magistrate with a police force under him for the native population. Hence he became the first Collector and Magistrate in British India, for which duties he needed the services of a so-called 'black collector' or 'black *zamindar*', figures who were, like their masters, notoriously dishonest in this early period by reason of the bad pay with which the Company rewarded them. From 1720 to 1756 the 'Black *Zamindar*' was Gobindram Mitter, who used his almost unassailable position of authority over the Bengali population to amass great power and a fortune. In theory, the Council had few legal powers, and all serious cases should have been referred to the Mughal *faujdar* at Hooghly; but the Company preferred to ignore its true legal position in Bengal, and even introduced into Calcutta in 1727, following a new Charter from the English King, a Mayor's Court with Aldermen to deal with important civil cases, and a Court of Quarter Sessions ('of Oyer and Terminer and Gaol Delivery') composed of the Governor and Council, to try all criminal offences, save only high treason.

The Company also needed a *banyan* or broker for its financial and commercial dealings concerned with the Indian trade and manufactories: their *banyan* was normally chosen from the Seth family which had been among the first to settle in Gobindpore in the 16th century. The Court in London consistently complained about the Seths, whom they imagined were cheating their Calcutta servants and themselves, and demanded that they be replaced by more subservient brokers and that the President should take more of the commissioning work into his own hands. To please their masters, the Council dispensed with the Seths for a while, but in the end had to reinstate them as no other brokers could deliver satisfactorily. The profits to be made all along the line in the East India trade were immense, but the Court of Directors fondly imagined that no body but they should make them. As an example, the fairly small ship *Sherborne*, which was taken captive by the French in 1712 just before the cessation of hostilities, carried goods loaded at Calcutta to the value of £43,000, but which were reckoned to be salable in Paris for not less than £150,000. Acts protecting the English cloth-manufacturers had recently been passed in Parliament prohibiting the import of Indian textiles except for re-export, but such was the demand that they were hurried across to the continent and shipped back again immediately.

The Council by this time consisted of nine men, each with individual tasks. The President was the Chief in Council, the Second and the Fourth were Chiefs at the two other English factories in Bengal at Cossimbazar and Dacca, the Third the Accountant, the Fifth Export Warehouse Keeper, the Sixth Import Warehouse Keeper, the Seventh Buxey or Paymaster, the Eighth Zamindar or Collector, the Ninth Secretary. The President and Chaplain were still paid a miserable £100 each (the latter £50 salary, and an equal amount as a gratuity if he satisfied the Council), the members of Council only £40. Below the Council were all the other merchants and writers undertaking the Company's business, who numbered 51 in Calcutta in 1711. Private trade was of course indulged in, and it was through this means that those fortunate enough to survive the climate were able to amass fortunes. Company servants were forbidden to trade in the goods in which the Company had a monopoly to Europe, but were able nonetheless to engage in the lucrative local trade, making use of the smaller ships which the Company kept in the East, to collect on their own account goods from Bengal and further upriver and send them round the coast of India or on to Persia. Some of the complexities of the trading situation in Bengal are indicated by Captain Hamilton in his description of Hooghly: 'This town of Hughly drives a great trade, because all foreign goods are brought thither for import, and all goods of the product of Bengal are brought hither for exportation. And the Mogul's Furza or Custom-house is at this place. It affords rich cargoes for fifty or sixty ships yearly, besides what is carried to neighbouring countries in small vessels; and there are vessels that bring saltpetre from Patana, above 50 yards long, and 5 broad, and two and a half deep, and can carry above 200 tuns. They come down in the month of October, before the stream of the river, but are obliged to track them up again, with strength of hand, about 1000 miles. To mention all the particular species of goods that this rich country produces, is far beyond my skill; but in our East-India Company's sales, all the sorts, that are sent hence to Europe, may be found; but ophium, long pepper and ginger are commodities that the trading shipping in India deals in, besides tobacco, and many sorts of piece goods, that are not merchantable in Europe.'

Although no records at this time give us even an estimate of the English population, it must have been considerably more than 51, for large numbers of free merchants, adventurers, traders and others, as well as their families, were already congregating in Calcutta. Hamilton's statement of 1200 English seems exaggerated, but perhaps half that number would be more accurate. Estimates for the total population vary wildly, as the records note only revenues received from the population, not the total numbers. For the beginning of the 18th century a total population of somewhere between 10,000 and 15,000, and for the middle of the century of upwards of 100,000, with 1000 Europeans, seem possible figures.

After his libellous account of Charnock, Captain Hamilton goes on to give an equally entertaining description of Calcutta. His book was published in 1727, but this passage seems to refer to the period about 1705-20. 'Fort William was built an irregular tetragon, of brick and mortar, called *puckah*, which is a composition of brick-dust, lime, molasses, and cut hemp, and when it comes to be dry is as hard and tougher than firm stone or brick, and the town was built without order, as the builders thought most convenient for their own affairs, every one taking in what ground best pleased them for gardening, so that in most houses you must pass through a garden into the house, the English building near the river's side, and the natives within land ... About fifty yards from Fort William stands the church built by the pious charity of merchants residing there, and the Christian benevolence of sea-faring men, whose affairs call them to trade there; but ministers of the Gospel being subject to mortality, very often young merchants are obliged to officiate, and have a salary of £50 per annum added to what the Company allows them, for their pains in reading prayers and sermons on Sunday. The Governor's house in the Fort is the best and most regular piece of architecture that ever I saw in India. And there are many convenient lodgings for factors and writers, within the Fort, and some store-houses for the Company's goods, and the magazines for their ammunition.

'The Company has a pretty good hospital at Calcutta, where many go in to undergo the penance of physick, but few come out to give account of its operation. The Company also has a pretty good garden, that furnishes the Governor's table with herbage and fruits; and some fish-ponds to serve his kitchin with good carp, calkops and mullet. Most of the inhabitants of Calcutta that make any tolerable figure have the same advantages; and all sorts of provisions, both wild and tame, being plentiful, good and cheap, as well as clothing, make the country very agreeable, notwithstanding the above mentioned inconveniences [that is, its unhealthiness] that attend it ... Most gentlemen and ladies in Bengal live both splendidly and pleasantly, the forenoons being dedicated to business, and after dinner to rest, and in the evening to recreate themselves in chaises or *palankins* in the fields, or to gardens, or by water in their *budgeroes*, which is a convenient boat, that goes swiftly with the force of oars; and, on the river, sometimes there is the diversion of fishing, or fowling, or both; and before night, they make friendly visits to one another, when pride or contention do not spoil society, which too often they do among the ladies, as discord and faction do among the men. And altho' the conscript Fathers of the Colony disagree in many points among themselves, yet they all agree in oppressing strangers, who are consigned to them, not suffering them to buy or to sell their goods at the most advantageous markets, but of the Governor and his Council, who fix their own prices, high, or low, as seemeth best to their wisdom and discretion. And it is a crime hardly pardonable for a private merchant to go to Hughly, to inform himself of the current prices of goods, altho' the liberty of buying and selling is intirely taken from him before.

'The garrison of Fort William generally consists of 2 or 300 soldiers, more for to convey their fleet from Patana, with the Company's saltpetre, and piece goods, raw silk and some opium belonging to other merchants, than for the defence of the Fort, for, as the Company holds their Colony in the tail of the Mogul, they need not be afraid of any enemies coming to dispossess them. And if they should at any time quarrel again with the Mogul, his prohibiting his subjects to trade with the Company, would soon end their quarrel ... In Calcutta all religions are freely tolerated, but the Presbyterian, and that they brow-beat. The Pagans carry their idols in procession through the town. The Roman Catholics have their church to lodge their idols in, and the Mahometan is not discountenanced; but there are no polemicks, except what are between our high-church men and our low, or between the Governor's party and other private merchants on points of trade ... The Company's colony is limited by a landmark at Governapore, and another near Barnagal, about six miles distant; and the Salt-water Lake bounds it on the land side. It may contain in all, about 10 or 12000 souls; and the Company's revenues are pretty good and well paid. They rise from ground-rents and consulage on all goods imported and exported by British subjects, but all nations besides are free from taxes.'

The first known pictorial view of Calcutta was painted about 1730 by George Lambert, showing the Fort from the west bank of the Hooghly (plate 1). It is one of a set of six paintings of its principal settlements in the East commissioned by the East India Company to decorate the newly refurbished Directors' Courtroom. The print-seller John Bowles published engravings of the set by Elisha Kirkall early in 1735. A second series of engravings by Gerard Vandergucht was published in 1736, from the inscriptions on which we learn of the involvement of Samuel Scott. Lambert doubtless painted the landscape and the buildings, but made over the sea and the ships to Scott, who specialised in marine painting. The Company paid 15 guineas per picture, as recorded in the Court Minutes of 1 November 1732.

Fort William (Hamilton's 'irregular tetragon') stretched 700 feet along the river front. Its fortifications were practically complete by 1712. The walls were 40 feet thick and 18 feet high connecting diamond-shaped bastions at the four corners, each mounting ten guns and sporting its own little pepper-pot of a watch-tower. The main gate on the east wall carried five guns. An additional lower curtain wall was built on the river side. Despite constant admonitions from London, no moat or ditch protecting the Fort was ever built. Within, a low building running east-west called Long Row divided the Fort. Here were originally the brick buildings put up for the residences of the young unmarried writers within the compound, as mentioned by Goldsborough in 1693. Long Row was built in 1715 to replace these delapidated earlier buildings, and a tower was added, probably in 1727 at a reroofing, but there is no record of its purpose. It is shown by Lambert protruding above the wall. The smaller part of the Fort to the north contained the magazine and armoury, also visible in the picture, while the main building in the southern part was the Factory itself, which served as the Governor's house, workplace and eating place. This was a grand structure (Hamilton's 'best and most regular piece of architecture that ever I saw in India'), resembling in plan the Dutch factory building at Chinsura. It formed three sides of a rectangle, the open side being to the east, with a raised cloister round the inner court (see plate 2). The principal public rooms were in the upper floor of the west range, while the Governor's apartments were in the southern wing. A portico in the centre of the west side gave access under a colonnade to the principal river gate, from which a wharf, usable at all states of the tide, projected into the river for the unloading of ships. Along the inner east wall of the Fort ran a row of rooms on each side of the main gate, and an open arcade was attached to their west sides. These rooms were used as barracks for the 200-300 soldiers, store rooms, and as a prison. By 1704 only the ground floor of the Factory had been built, so that the visiting President Sir Edward Littleton had to look for a house in the town. It seems to have been completed in 1709. Three years later the Directors wrote disapprovingly to Calcutta: 'We hear you make a very pompous Show to the Water side by high Turrets and Lofty Buildings which have the appearance but not the benefit of a Fortification. This if so is contrary to our Aim and Orders.'

Lambert's source for his Calcutta picture has not yet been positively identified, for of course neither he nor Scott visited India. The source cannot have been much earlier than 1730. Lambert's picture shows the spire of St Anne's church protruding over the Fort, and this was not completed until 1716, while the tower on Long Row does not seem to have been built before 1727. The letters and consultations between London and Calcutta make various references to plans of the Fort and its constituent parts being sent to London (every year between 1709 and 1714), and these may have been utilised by Lambert, but none seems to have survived. Clearly the Court's having to rely on hearsay in 1713 as to the appearance of the Fort shows that no drawing of the elevation had been received by then.

An embassy led by John Surman was sent by the Calcutta Council to the Emperor Farrukhsiyar in Delhi from 1714 to 1717, and was successful in trying to obtain the right to rent the 38 villages around the settlement (which together make up the modern city of Calcutta), as well as further privileges of free trade and the free use of the mint. Its success is traditionally attributed to the accompanying surgeon, William Hamilton, who cured the Emperor of an ailment when all his own doctors had failed. However, the privileges of free use of the mint (to turn the Company's bullion into coin) and of purchasing the rental of the villages, were not taken up owing to the unwavering hostility of the new *Subahdar* in Bengal, Murshid Quli Khan, an astute politician who, fully realising the significance of the foreign traders' positions, had transferred his capital from remote Dacca to Maxudabad on the river Hooghly, and

Fig.2. The Armenian Church of the Holy Nazareth, 1747. Detail of fig.6.

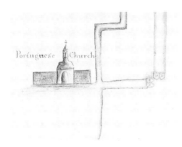

Fig.3. The Portuguese Church of the Virgin Mary of the Rosary, 1747. Detail of fig.6.

renamed the town Murshidabad after himself. Nonetheless, the privileges which were granted by Farrukhsiyar allowed the English settlement to flourish and trade to grow rapidly. The death of Aurangzeb in 1707 had marked the end of the great days of the Mughal Empire, and a succession of feeble Emperors, fatally weakened by the sack of Delhi by the Afghan Nadir Shah in 1739, allowed the great provinces of the Empire (Bengal, Oudh, the Deccan) to become independent in all but name. In central and western India, a new power was rising with the growth of the Maratha empire, while in Bengal, it was increasingly to the Nawab in Murshidabad that the English had to pay court rather than to the Emperor in far-off Delhi.

In addition to the English, the growing settlement had Portuguese, Armenian, Muslim and Hindu merchants. The term Portuguese is used in the literature of the period to denote not only descendants of the Portuguese inhabitants of Bengal, but also any native convert to Catholic Christianity, which had perforce to be tolerated by the English in India. The earliest Catholic church in Calcutta was, as we have seen, abruptly torn down by Sir John Goldsborough in 1693, and the priests were expelled. Another church was begun in 1700, and enlarged in 1720; this was on the site of the present Catholic Cathedral, to the north of the Fort. The Armenians too had pre-dated the English in Calcutta, and they had traded from Suttanuttee with the Portuguese. The oldest tombstone in the old Armenian cemetery in Calcutta, which is in the churchyard of the present Armenian church west of the Catholic one, is dated 1630, although there are no records of a continuous Armenian presence in Calcutta at this early date. The Company had indeed entered into a general agreement with the Armenians in 1688 to provide land for them to build a church wherever over 40 of them were present in one of the Company's settlements, and in 1690 a small chapel was erected for the Armenians. The present church, erected in the old Armenian cemetery in 1724, is the oldest place of Christian worship in Calcutta. The positions of both churches may be seen in the plans of 1742 and 1747 (figs.4 and 6), while in the latter plan occur vignettes of their elevations (figs.2-3).

The English themselves at first lacked a proper church, although they were provided with a chaplain, but in 1704 a site was provided by the Council outside the land gate of Fort William, and in June 1709 the church was consecrated and dedicated to St Anne, doubtless as a compliment to the reigning Queen. An anonymous painting, which seems to be contemporary with George Lambert's view of Fort William and is possibly also by him, shows the church in the foreground with the east side of Fort William behind, affording an excellent view of the three inner sides of the Factory building, of which that facing east has a colonnaded verandah on its upper storey (plate 2). The tower on Long Row is more clearly visible here. The flagstaff was situated between the armoury and the west curtain wall. The church of St Anne was situated within its own compound, on the north-west corner of the open area known as the Park. The nave of the church was about 20 feet wide by 80 feet long, with a slightly convex roof, terminating in an apse with five windows of full height. On each side were aisles, five bays long with pitched roofs, separated by pillars from the nave. The handsome and very tall steeple, apparently of wood sheathed with metal, was built to house the bell which was sent out by the Company in 1712, and this was finished in 1716. In 1724 the steeple was severely damaged by lightning, but was repaired and supported by the classical version of flying buttresses shown in this picture. It was finally thrown down in the great cyclone of 1737. North of the Fort may be seen the two large houses by the riverside which figure in the earliest plans of Calcutta, and were clearly already built. The earliest reference to the English 'laying out considerable sums of money in handsome buildings' is from 1703. In the picture the Governor is seen going in state on an important visit, preceded by a bodyguard of cavalry and by his *chobdars* or silver-stick bearers, while a guard of honour sees him off.

Calcutta in the early 18th century thus comprised the three villages of Suttanuttee, Calcutta and Gobindpore from north to south, three miles long by about one quarter-mile wide. A plan made in 1742 (fig.4) shows us the heart of the settlement, the Town of Calcutta and Bazaar Calcutta, huddling protectively around the Fort. Little change was made to the original street patterns observable in this plan until the 1770s, and most of them survived, especially in the northern part of the town, until the end of the next century. The English lived around the Park, whose beginning has been depicted by the painter of St Anne's. The Park stretched from the

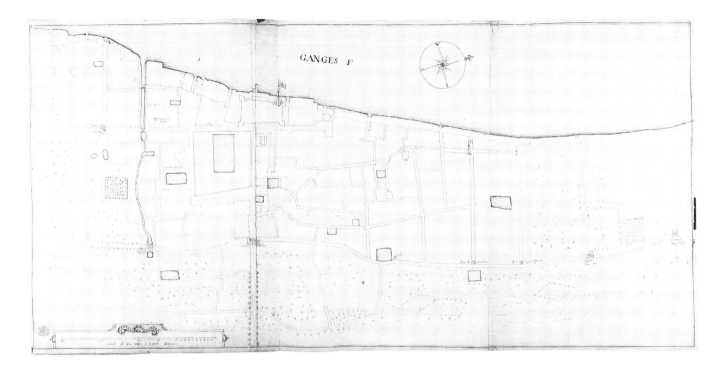

GANGES F

Fig.4. Theodore Forresti and John Ollifres, Plan of Calcutta showing the defences in 1742. Pen-and-ink and wash; 52.5 × 112.5 cm. British Library K Top.cxv 40.

land gate of the Fort eastwards to the street known as the Rope Walk, where the Company kept a field for the manufacture of ropes, and southwards to form a large rectangle. In the middle of the Park was the Lall Dighi or Tank, which in 1709 had been deepened and converted from a noxious pond into a reservoir of sweet water. The Fort was on the north-west corner of the Park, and we may note the presence of warehouses built in 1741 right up against the south wall of the Fort, whose presence seriously compromised the Fort's already limited defensive capacity. From the east gate of the Fort, past the Protestant church, ran the road already called the Lall Bazaar, which ran eastwards to the Lake, as far as which a raised road four miles long was made in 1710. The southern limit of Calcutta was the creek, where Hastings Street was later laid out, running eastwards eventually to the Salt Lake. On the north bank of the creek were the powder magazine (a huge domed structure built in 1733), the hospital founded in 1707 which Hamilton has told us about, and the burial ground containing Charnock's and other mausoleums. The creek marked the southern limit of Calcutta, but it is clear that building had already begun on the south side of the creek near the river. At the northern limit of 'Christian Calcutta' were the quarters inhabited by the Portuguese and the Armenians, around their respective churches. North again was the Bara Bazaar, here called the 'Gran Bazar', the most densely populated part of the town, where the majority of the Bengali merchants lived and did their business. That the 'Gran Bazar' in north Calcutta needed gates suggests it was already walled at this time. This area marked the northern limit of Calcutta, and beyond is Suttanuttee, which the plan shows with gardens and trees. The eastward limit of the town in this plan is the north-south Chitpore Road, a quarter-mile from the river. In consideration of the Seths' keeping the road to Chitpore in good repair, an abatement of their ground rent of eight annas in the *bigah* had been allowed them in 1707 for their great garden which they had established on this road, and along which they had planted trees, and the trees and garden noted as Zura Bari Bag are presumably those of the Seths.

Suttanuttee extended up to Chitpore, and besides the great garden laid out by the Seths, others had been planted further east by the banker Omi Chand, and by the 'Black *Zamindar*' Gobindram Mitter, which we can see marked in fig.5. Suttanuttee was dominated by the great temple built by Gobindram about 1731 on the Chitpore Road, near to the northern limit of Suttanuttee, by far the tallest building in the town (plate 3). To the south, Gobindpore was situated on the river bank separated from Calcutta by scrub with thick, tiger-infested jungle to its east and south, although the Council was at pains to lay out roads to the village from Calcutta. The southern limit of the settlement was the Kidderpore Nullah (a normally dried-up stream) which runs into the Hooghly south of Gobindpore. Its eastward limit was at this time the north-south road which connected Chitpore with the temple of Kalighat to the south. This famous temple owes its importance to its being the reputed site of the landing on earth of part of the dead goddess Sati. At her death, her grief-crazed husband Shiva took up her body and began a frenzied dance of destruction which threatened to destroy the world, until Vishnu with his discus cut up the goddess's body. The 64 places where the parts landed are especially sacred to this Goddess in one or other of her forms, and it is in her destructive aspect as Kali that she is worshipped at Kalighat (plate 4).

Between the construction of the Fort and the attack on Calcutta in 1756, the most eventful year was 1737, when a great cyclone passed over the town, of which the only surviving report in London is in abstract form. The storm 'levelled most of the Walls in the Town, shattered and threw down many of the Buildings and blew up the Bridges, the Tide some days after broke in upon and carried away some of the Wharfs, Slips and Stairs, the Places most Damnified are the Peers on the Factory Wharf, Wharf and Slips at Soota Loota [Suttanuttee], Walls round the burying place and powder magazine and the Factory Points, Church steeple was overthrown. Shall repair them in the most frugal and Secure manner its Deferred hitherto by Chunams [lime's] Dearness and Scarcity. A Sad Effect of the Hurricane was a Famine that raged all round the Countery best part of the Year, were obliged to forbid the Exportation of Rice the 5th June, which affected Private Trade, more particularly Mr. Elliott who had two Ships laden with Rice. Took off the Duty on all rice brought into the Town the 12th June, Hughley Government had done the Same. Rice was bought on the Companys Account Delivering it out in small Quantitys at the Buzar Rate, when Rice grew Cheap again, the Duty was Levied as formerly and Madrass was supplied with a large Quantity. Revenues were naturally Decreased hereby and the Impoverished Tenants were Indulged with Time to Pay their Rents, but when Famine was over revenues arose as Usual.'

In 1742 the Marathas under Raghunath Bhonsle were ravaging Orissa and Bengal. Since it appeared that Calcutta was directly threatened also, the Council at Fort William, having taken the advice of various military and engineering experts, prepared various measures for the defence of the town. The Council considered the building of a wall 30 feet high and six feet thick round the town, but this was rejected, unsurprisingly, as too expensive. The Council did, however, authorise the construction of a series of batteries on the approach roads to the north, east and south of the town. Their positions were noted on the plan of Calcutta drawn by the Italian engineer Theodore Forresti (who was summoned especially from Patna) and the variously named John Ollifres (Allifze, Aloffe), the Surveyor of Works, which we have already examined to show the layout of the town (fig. 4). This is the earliest known plan of Calcutta, and it survives – like a few other similarly early ones – only because copies were sent to King George III. All the many plans which were drawn at this time with a view to improve Calcutta's fortifications, and which we read about in the Consultations and Letters from Bengal as having been sent to the Court of Directors, were later destroyed. A southern battery was erected a short distance south of the bridge over the creek, and two eastern ones, one on the east road (the Lall Bazaar) where it was crossed by the Chitpore Road, and the other south of this where the latter road crossed the creek. Two other batteries were placed much further north on the same road at Suttanuttee.

Although nothing was done about the proposed encircling wall, the Consultations for 31 March 1743 record that the Bengali inhabitants of Calcutta had proposed to dig at their own expense a ditch round the whole of the town from the river north of Suttanuttee down to the battery situated at the Lall Bazaar, and wanted a loan of 25,000 rupees to begin the work, three of the Seths and Omi Chand engaging to repay the sum in three months. This is the origin of the famous Mahratta Ditch. A year later this had been completed, and a start made on completing the ditch towards the south-west and Gobindpore, but this seems never to have been finished as the threat from the Marathas disappeared. A plan engraved for the second volume of Robert Orme's *History of the Military Transactions of the British Nation in Indostan*, published in London in 1778, is our earliest source for the Mahratta Ditch (fig.5). This is based on an unknown original, not to be found even among the voluminous Orme papers in the India Office Library, which also served as the source for the plan of Calcutta in 1742 inset into Aaron Upjohn's map of Calcutta published in 1794. The Ditch began in the north at the divide between Suttanuttee and Chitpore, and, curving south-eastwards (with irregular

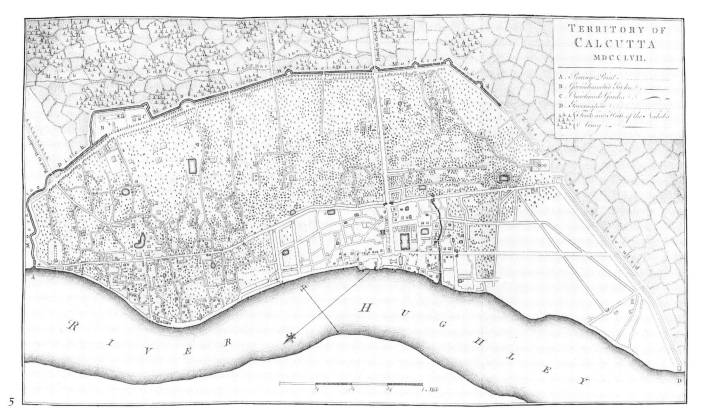

5

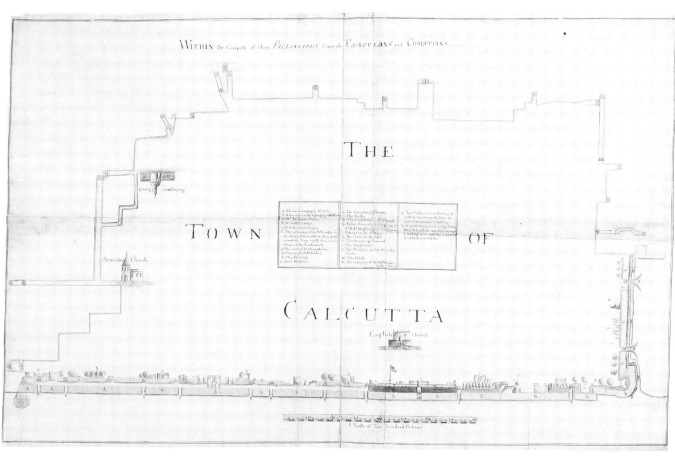

6

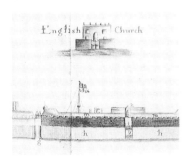

Fig.7. English Church of St Anne, lacking its spire, 1747. Detail of fig. 6.

extensions to take in the great gardens laid out by Gobindram Mitter and Omi Chand to the east of Suttanuttee) was meant to come back to the river south of Gobindpore. The south-westerly line suggested in this plan does not appear to have advanced very far, but other sources, not least Orme himself in a letter of 1754, indicate that in fact the Ditch had been dug nearly as far as the Kidderpore Nullah.

The Court of Directors and the Council in Calcutta were given a shock by the Maratha incursions into Bengal, as a harbinger of the anarchy into which India was sinking through the political weakness at its heart, and they became much concerned over the next few years with the state of the defences of Fort William. They were, however, never prepared to spend enough money to achieve effective improvements. Various plans were commissioned or suggested, but since it was clear that only the complete rebuilding of the Fort and the considerable strengthening of its garrison, together with the demolition of all the surrounding buildings which commanded it, would achieve any significant increase in its defensive capabilities, nothing serious was ever done. A report by Captain-Commandant Robert Hamilton of 31 August 1747 strongly recommended as a means of defending the town the construction of palisades all around it, and the Council on 3 September agreed to put the work in hand immediately. It is in this context that another plan in King George III's collection must be seen. This has been attributed to Forresti and Ollifres in 1742, but it obviously cannot be by them, as Ollifres had died in 1745, and the Court in London had ordered Forresti to be dismissed in 1744: 'Mr. Forrestie may be an Ingenious Skilful Engineer, but We dont see any Occasion that We have for him, such Persons have generally Expensive Schemes in their Heads, therefore he must be Discharged from our Service.'

In this plan, which is marked *The Town of Calcutta; within the Compass of these Pallisades live the Europeans and Christians*, the whole of the Christian portion of Calcutta is shown enclosed within palisades (fig.6). The palisades zig-zag south-eastwards from the river past the Armenian and Portuguese churches to the Chitpore Road (with extensions along certain streets to form gateways), where they turn southwards and run along the west side of the Chitpore Road, with gates again at the cross-streets and the main gate at the Lall Bazaar crossing. The palisades continue southwards to the creek, at which they turn westwards and run, somewhat irregularly, to the river, with an extension southwards over the creek to include the battery positioned there in 1742. The palisades were continued northward along the face of the river. Where the principal streets met the palisades there were gates, including those on the water-ways. The plan marks single palisades along the river front, from which the assumption must be that they were double all around the town. It is not clear to whose hand this plan may be attributed: Hamilton is unlikely to have drawn it himself, but equally unlikely is the hand of the Surveyor, Bartholomew Plaisted, who had succeeded Ollifres, as he is on record as vigorously opposing the usefulness of such palisades in the circumstances in which Calcutta found itself, and indeed was virtually dismissed by the Council for his opposition. The cost of erecting these palisades amounted to about 70,000 rupees.

This 1747 plan records the names of occupants for some of the buildings and includes some vignettes and elevations. The vignettes of the Armenian (viewed from the south) and Portuguese (viewed from the west) churches are our only records of the appearance of these churches in the 18th century (figs.2-3), while St Anne's is shown from the west without its spire and the upper part of its tower which fell in 1737 (fig.7). These churches are not drawn to the scale of the rest of the plan. The plan also shows the elevations of the buildings along the waterfront from just to the north of the Armenian church down to the debouchment of the creek (at Hastings Street) and also along the creek past the cemetery. Messrs Ross, Eyre, and Jackson owned houses along the river front opposite the Armenian church. Mr Griffiths' house we shall see in the plan of 1753 was situated where was later built the house lived in by Clive, on the bend in what became Clive Street north of the Fort. Mr Williamson's house is the large house immediately north of the Fort, of which the anonymous artist of St Anne's church (plate 2) has shown us a view from the other side. The depiction of the Fort is the earliest reliable first-hand evidence we have for its appearance: the Factory building protrudes over the west wall of the Fort somewhat less grandly than Lambert would have us believe. South of the Fort is the so-called Company's House, of which the earliest view is in Lambert's painting

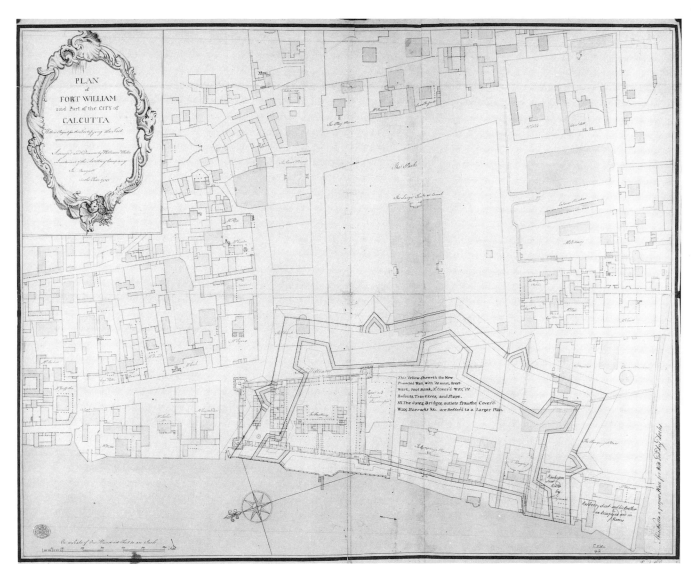

Fig.8. William Wells, Plan of Fort
William and part of Calcutta, 1753.
Pen-and-ink and watercolour;
68.5 × 84 cm. British Library
K Top.cxv 42.

of Fort William (plate 1), and which was purchased by the Council from the President, John
Stackhouse, on 27 July 1738. Stackhouse had been forced out of the Factory by the rebuilding
works necessary during 1733-5, and charged the Company the rent of a house in town at an
annual rate of 2,400 rupees, to the Court's consternation. Whether his rented house was the
one which he sold to the Council in 1738 for 16,373 rupees is not clear, but it may be surmised
that it was. This house had large godowns or warehouses attached to it, which the Council
needed for storage of goods. Subsequent Presidents took to living in this house, which took
the name of the Company's House. South again is the Dock and Banksall or marine yard at the
bottom of what became Hare Street. The Dock had been constructed about 1710, and could
receive two ships each of 400 tons for cleaning and tallowing. At the end of the elevation
along the river, two batteries were meant to command the river and the creek, continuing up
which are given the elevations of the towering tombs and obelisks in the burial ground as well
as the great dome of the powder magazine which was established here in 1733.

The Court's concern about Fort William's fortifications resulted in its sending a succession
(necessary because of a high death rate) of senior engineering officers out to Calcutta, with
instructions to draw up suitable plans for the proper defence of the settlement and the Fort.
Colonel Caroline Scott was one of these officers, who arrived in Calcutta in September 1753.
A tangible result of his visit is the detailed plan of Fort William and its environs drawn up by
Lieutenant William Wells of the Artillery Company, which was sent to London in January
1754 (fig.8). Wells was instructed to carry on Scott's work when the latter went to Madras in
March 1754, where he died in June. Scott's proposals for the fortification of Fort William as
shown by Wells's map involved the demolition of three-quarters of the old Fort as well as the

church and many of the buildings south of the Fort as far as the old burial ground, and the erection of the most modern fortifications in the shape of a half-octagon, with its radius along the river. The Court of Directors actually agreed to this, as well as to Scott's plan for the enclosing of the town, provided the President secured the permission of the 'Country Government', that is, the old Nawab in Murshidabad, Alivardi Khan. This the President, now Roger Drake, and Council thought most impolitic. Scott's scheme for the enclosing of Calcutta involved the digging of a ditch 36 feet wide and 12 feet deep from Gobindpore in the south round the whole town to Bagh Bazaar on the river north of Suttanuttee, making use where practicable of the exisiting Mahratta Ditch, together with large scale defensive works at the north and south entrances, the whole costing over 75,000 rupees. The Council remitted this to London to decide. Needless to say, both schemes were deferred on cost grounds.

This is the most detailed and accurate surviving plan of old Calcutta before its destruction in 1756, and as an added bonus it provides the names of the residents in the principal houses – Messrs Holwell, Douglas, Cruttenden, Tooke, Eyre, Watts, Griffiths, Bellamy, names which recur again and again in the accounts of the loss of Calcutta. The relationship between the powder magazine, the burial ground and the hospital behind them is made clear for the first time. We see where Omi Chand, the great banker, had his house, in which he was imprisoned during the siege, just east of the church. At the north-east corner of the Park stands the Court House. This was the building used for the Mayor's Court which had been established in 1727. This first met at the Company's house called the Ambassador's house (presumably because the Persian ambassador stayed there in 1712 on his way to Delhi), but this was sold in 1731 as it was too delapidated, the Council retaining however the ground and brick buildings on it for use as a jail. This building was at the end of the Lall Bazaar, on the south side, where the town jail remained until it moved to a site south of Gobindpore in 1783. The Council then rented at least part of the newly-built Charity School building on the north-east corner of the Park. We find the Council writing to London in 1729: 'Have set on foot a Charity School and for that purpose raised 23709 rs. 12a. 3p. & appointed the President & Council for the time being to be Trustees.' Eight boys were on the foundation and 40 other day-scholars, who were to be raised in the Protestant religion. Tradition associates the name of Richard Bourchier with this enterprise, at this time Second in Council. The spacious building with its flights of steps at front and rear which was erected was obviously too large for its purpose (compare its area with the private houses nearby and indeed the church), and was soon rented by the Council for the Mayor's Court, the Charity School being established elsewhere on the proceeds. Along the Lall Bazaar from the Court House is the Cutchery, where the Collector or *Zamindar* had his office, and on the opposite corner at the northern end of the Rope Walk is the Playhouse.

A Dutch engraver living in London, Jan van Ryne, produced in 1754 a new view of Fort William. Like the Lambert view, it is taken from across the river, but this time from further north and with reduced, virtually toy-like, ships, allowing a much better view of the buildings (fig.9). Unfortunately, no new first-hand source has been used. Although van Ryne has based his composition on Lambert's, and much of the rest of his composition is pure fantasy, it is worth examining in detail, as this view is often cited to show the appearance of Calcutta at this period. The Factory building is simply the Lambert one seen from a different perspective, while the tower of Long Row, which we know protruded above the walls, is absent. The Governor's private residence, the Company's House purchased from Stackhouse, is shown to the right of the Fort, with an avenue of trees leading down to the river, but what information the trees are based on is unknown. The house is shown as three-storeyed, like the other large houses in this view, a fact in itself to make us suspicious of the artist's sources, as such buildings were unknown in Calcutta until the 1770s. Other, more reliable, sources, such as the view engraved in Orme's *History* (figs.10–11), show no three-storeyed buildings at all, nor trees in front of the Company's House. Van Ryne is confused over the fate of the church of St Anne, and his confusion seems to have infected later writers.

Van Ryne knew that St Anne's steeple had been blown down in the cyclone in 1737, and he has depicted the top of the tower on which the steeple rested protruding behind the Factory building, in a position close to where it ought to be found when viewing the buildings in the

Fig.9. Jan van Ryne, Fort William from the opposite bank of the Hooghly, London, 1754. Line engraving; 23.5 × 38.5 cm.

Lambert painting from a different angle. The plan of the palisades around Calcutta in 1747 shows the tower of the church to be still steeple-less, but with urns erected on the parapet of the tower to disguise its nakedness (fig.7), and these urns are depicted by van Ryne. However, he has also included in the distance across the Park another church with a tower with a wooden bell-cote and a north-south orientation. There are no contemporary accounts of what if anything replaced the steeple of St Anne's, other than an application to the Court by the Council in 1750 to replace the steeple for the sum of 8,000 rupees, to which the Court assented in a letter of 23 January 1751. It is not known whether this work was carried out, or what form it took if it were, but it is unlikely that a depiction of it could have got back to London in time for van Ryne to use it. An anonymous plan for fortifying Calcutta sent to London before 1756, but included in the Correspondence Memoranda for 1757, suggests fortifying the church 'by opening portholes under the windows, which may be closed with Slight work to beat out occasionally. It is the strongest Edifice in Calcutta, and the beams being well underpropt, will compleat it a Cavalier of a double Tier of 3 and 4 pounders, besides there has been many years laid a foundation for a Steeple almost Solid. This should be carried up in the form of a Tower which will bear heavy Cannon, and the whole construction of that consequence as to command every part of the Fort'. No mention here of bell-cotes, and this church seems as pure a piece of invention by van Ryne as are his background hills.

We have now reached the time of the one great humiliation suffered by the English since the founding of Calcutta, namely the capture of the settlement by the Nawab of Bengal Siraj ud-Daula. The Nawab's grandfather Alivardi Khan had died in April 1756, and by June, his young and impetuous successor had gathered his armies and was marching on Calcutta. The impending war between France and England induced both Companies in Bengal to set about putting the defences of their forts in better order; this reaching the Nawab's ears, made him order both to desist, but Governor Drake's reply, suggesting that France and England might be carrying on their war in the Nawab's dominions, appears to have so enraged him that he immediately began to attack the English. On 7 June Cossimbazar under William Watts capitulated without a shot being fired, and Watts and his wife, the future 'Begum' Johnson, were taken prisoner to Murshidabad. Warren Hastings was at the time a member of the council at Cossimbazar, and he took shelter with his friend and counsellor Cantoo Baboo in his

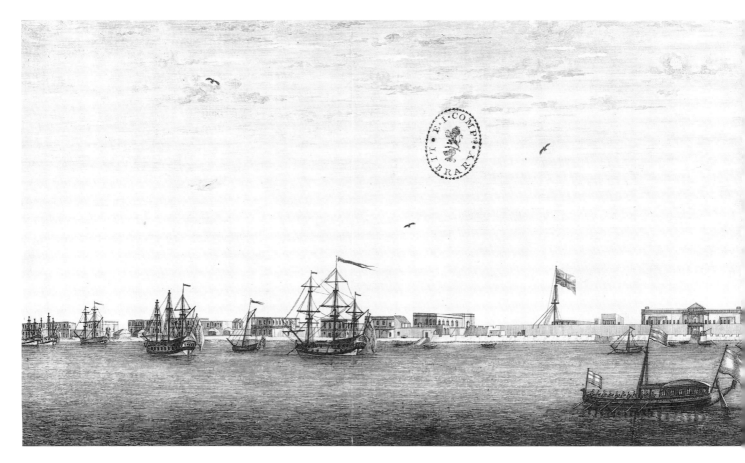

Figs.10-11. Anonymous view, *Calcutta as in MDCCLVI*. Line engraving, by Thomas Kitchin, from Robert Orme's *History*, vol.II, London, 1778; 20 × 71.5 cm.

nearby house. The fall of this factory was taken at last to mean in Calcutta that the Nawab was in earnest, and they began too late to attempt to put their fortifications and defences into order. The results of the Company's parsimonious policy were to be finally brought home to them. The Fort itself was, as we have seen, most ill-equipped for defence: warehouses had been built in 1741 up against its southern wall, it was commanded by the church and by various other houses around it, and its very fortifications were too weak to mount heavy guns upon, quite apart from the facts that the guns were in a deplorable state of readiness and that the number of reliable soldiers was tiny.

In Orme's *History* is published a view of the town along the river bank, based on an unknown original taken in 1756, showing the whole length of the European quarter (figs.10-11). The viewpoint is stationary, from opposite the Fort, while the houses to left and right of it are depicted receding accordingly. We can now link many of the names recorded in Wells's map to their actual houses. Fort William is seen just off centre, with the Factory building shown in its true appearance by an observer on the spot. The tower of Long Row is seen protruding over the wall of the Fort to the left of the Factory building proper, with beside it the Armoury. South of the Fort is the Company's House, depicted more realistically than in van Ryne's version with only two storeys, and no avenue of trees. Between it and the south wall of the Fort are the warehouses, while the pediment with statuary apparently in the distance must be the façade of the Playhouse across the Park. On the south side of the Company's House in the Dockyard, with behind it the houses owned by Messrs Holwell and Douglas. From our vantage point we can then see the burial ground with its towering obelisks and mausoleums along the north bank of the creek, which are actually behind the next group of houses which were owned by the Jain bankers the Seths. Beyond them is the debouchment of the creek into the Hooghly. This is the southern limit of the palisades marked in the 1747 plan, but obviously there had been continual building south of this line. North of the Fort, Wells's map enables us also to identify the houses. The large one nearest the Fort, which Mr Williamson had owned in 1742, is now owned by Mr Cruttenden (Second in Council), with Mr Tooke's beside it. Next is the house of Mr Watts with a colonnaded upper verandah. Beyond Watts's house is the saltpetre godown, while the next one set back is Mr

Griffiths' house, which is situated where the house lived in by Clive was built. Parts of the waterfront still appear to have their palisades, but most seem to have gone, which confirms Plaisted in his opposition to their being erected. Clearly, the steeple of St Anne's had been truncated so low that none of it in fact protuded above the skyline of the Fort.

It is to this ill-prepared settlement that the army of Siraj ud-Daula, consisting of about 50,000 men, advanced in June 1756. Estimates vary of the numbers available to defend Fort William: at the most just over 500, of whom half were the regular garrison and the remainder militia, but only just over a third of them were Europeans. Wells's plan shows us the settlement in all its nakedness. We have already seen from Orme's *History* the plan of the Territory of Calcutta in 1757, which shows the tiny English settlement huddled by the river within its outer ditch. A closer view comes from the same source, marking the positions of the three batteries rapidly thrown up to defend the Fort as well as earthworks on the roads leading out of the settlement made in 1742 (fig.12). A new battery position was constructed north of the Fort on the river between the saltpetre godown and Mr Griffiths' house, while the earlier battery positions erected in 1742 on the east at the Lall Bazaar by the jail, and on the south on the bridge over the creek at the burial ground, were reutilized. Also erected were four minor palisades which were meant to guard some of the streets leading towards the Park, two to the north of the latter and two to the south-east. It would have been far better to abandon the town entirely and retire with all the forces to the Fort, demolishing all the neighbouring houses, but 'so little credit was then given, and even to the very last day, that the Nabob would venture to attack us, or offer to force our lines, that it occasioned a generall grumbling and discontent to leave any of the European houses without them. Nay, the generallity wanted even to include every brick house in the place, Portuguese and Armenian, and thought it hard that any inhabitant should be deprived of protection against such an enemy.'

The resulting débacle has often been described, by eye-witnesses, by historians of the period and by later writers, and has been debated endlessly. Briefly, from 16-18 June, the Nawab's forces were occupied in forcing the various batteries and outstations erected round the settlement as shown in Orme's plan, none of which could be properly defended given the total number of men able and willing to bear arms. Once captured, the cannon were turned

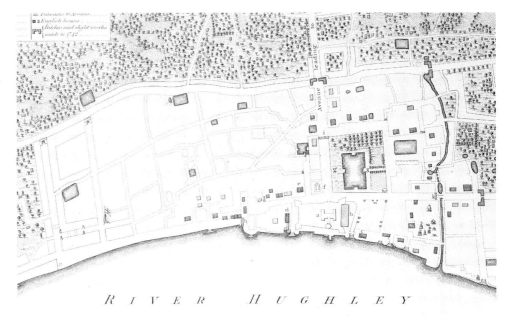

R I V E R   H U G H L E Y

against the besieged, and the earthworks were used for shelter when firing small-arms upon the Fort. By this time, the Nawab's forces had burnt the Great Bazaar to the ground, while the Bengali houses to east and south of the English part of Calcutta had been destroyed by the Company's troops. Most of the English women and children took refuge in the ships lying in the river, while into the Fort had crowded large numbers of Portuguese and Armenian women, some of whom also found refuge on the ships. By the evening of 18 June, the garrison had retreated to the walls of the Fort itself. Although the loss of the Fort before such an onslaught was at this stage inevitable, the resultant deaths of many of the defenders could have been avoided. However, the Governor, Roger Drake, with the military commander, Captain-Commandant Minchin, embarked on the ships still lying off-shore on the morning of 19 June, lost his nerve and gave orders for the ships to cast off and drop down river, leaving the remaining defenders to their fate. John Zephaniah Holwell, the Third in Council, became their leader, but after a vigorous defence, during which they were hoping in vain for some of the ships to come back up-river and pick them up (a not too difficult task in view of their superior fire-power), they were forced on Sunday 20 June to surrender. The Nawab entered Calcutta in triumph and held a durbar in the Factory. According to Holwell's account, the complete veracity of which many have questioned, all 146 of the survivors were herded into the Fort's prison, a small room of 18 feet square in the east curtain wall, south of the main gate. This prison had already become known as the 'Black Hole' before the night of 20 June 1756, which was the hottest and most sultry night of the year before the breaking of the rains. According to Holwell, only 23 emerged alive the next morning, when all but himself and three others were allowed to go free. Having plundered Calcutta, but being disappointed in the amount of loot realised (it being the wrong season for trade), the Nawab retired leaving a garrison in control of the town under Manik Chand.

Drake and his party, and those who had escaped downriver earlier, spent the rainy season on their ships at Fulta, where they remained in the most wretched condition with little shelter and few provisions. In Madras was a naval squadron under Admiral Watson, come out to the east when war with France seemed again imminent. Upon the news of the loss of Calcutta, the squadron sailed to Bengal, with Colonel Robert Clive as commander of the land forces, relieved the ships at Fulta and quickly recaptured Calcutta on 2 January 1757. The Fort was indefensible. Part of the east curtain wall had been pulled down to make room for a mosque, while the buildings within it were badly damaged. The church and Company's House, and most of the big houses around the Park, had been destroyed. Only Omi Chand's house near the church had escaped (he had been held prisoner by the English on suspicion of intriguing with the Nawab). Most of the native town was in ruins. In order to secure the Fort against any further attacks, the surviving houses around it were destroyed.

Plate 1. George Lambert and Samuel Scott, Fort William from the River Hooghly, c.1730. Oil on canvas; 78.5 × 117 cm. India Office Library F 45.

Plate 2. George Lambert (attributed), Fort William from the land side, with St Anne's Church, c.1730. Oil on canvas; 81.5 × 130 cm. Mafarge Assets Corp.

Plate 3. Thomas Daniell, Gobindram Mitter's 'Black Pagoda', c.1792. Coloured aquatint, plate 5 from *Oriental Scenery*, second series, engraved by T and William Daniell, London, 1797-8; 42 × 60 cm.

Plate 4. François Baltazard Solvyns, The temple at Kalighat, c.1795. Coloured etching, from his own *250 Coloured Etchings . . . of the Hindoos*, Calcutta, 1799; 34 × 50 cm. *Reversed from original.*

After a few more skirmishes, peace was agreed with the Nawab in a treaty of 9 February, which restored to the English all their former privileges of customs-free trading, as well as their factories, 'but only such of the plundered effects and monies as had been regularly brought to account in the books of his government', and permitted the fortification of Calcutta and the establishment of a mint. Here both sides would have been content to rest for a while, the Nawab to reflect on the value of trade to Bengal caused by the foreign presence, the English to recover their strength and gather reinforcements for their still very small forces, had not war been declared again between France and Britain. Clive and Watson opened hostilities in Bengal by storming Chandernagore. The Nawab, again enraged at foreign powers waging war in his dominions, sided with the French.

In the meantime, intrigues within the court at Murshidabad fomented by the Seths, whom Siraj ud-Daula had treated with contempt, and Omi Chand, who considered that the Nawab had to go but hoped to replace him with his own man rather than one favoured by the Seths, had suggested a way of disposing of the troublesome Nawab, whose efforts to rid Bengal of the foreigners caused the collapse of trade and hence their profits. It was proposed to elevate the Nawab's uncle Mir Jafar to the *masnad* of Bengal, and solemn treaties were entered into between Mir Jafar and the English, whereby the latter promised to assist him to the throne, in return for restitution money for the Company and for individuals who had suffered in the sack of Calcutta, to the amount of one crore, 77 lacks of rupees (£1¾ million), plus further donations to the armed forces of another £½ million and similar ones to the secret committee of the English leaders (Clive, Watts, Drake etc). In addition to the money, the treaty with Mir Jafar specified the restitution of all the Company's trading privileges, the complete exclusion of the French from trading in Bengal, and increases in the Company's *zamindari* land (by what amounted to confiscation from the existing *zamindars*, an injustice not remedied until Warren Hastings' time) to include the land south of Calcutta as far as Kalpi (what became the 24 Parganahs District). Finally, Calcutta ceased to be part of the *Subah* of Bengal: 'Whatever ground there is within the Calcutta Ditch belonging to the zamindars to be given to the English and 600 yards without the said ditch all round.' Omi Chand, on whom the English depended, but who saw that Mir Jafar was beholden to the Seths rather than to himself, consequently demanded 5% of the contents of the Nawab's treasury in return for his silence. Clive and the secret committee considered he was being too greedy and devised a means of deceiving him by the preparation of two treaties, one stipulating this condition and one without it. On the latter, Admiral Watson's signature had to be forged.

Clive, having sent the Nawab an ultimatum concerning the delayed restitutions promised in February and further hostile acts, marched from Chandernagore on 13 June 1757. The Nawab's army had remained encamped at Plassey, on the river 30 miles south of Murshidabad, since February, and here Clive's little army met it in battle on 23 June. The Nawab's army was so undermined by the conspiracies of the court that it offered little effective resistance; the Nawab himself fled, was captured and slain by Mir Jafar's son. Clive seated Mir Jafar on the *masnad* at Murshidabad on 29 June. The money in the treasury proving insufficient to satisfy the claims of the English, it was agreed with the Nawab's bankers, the Seths, that one half of the total sum of £2¾ millions should be paid immediately in coin and valuables and the rest in three annual instalments. The Seths were allowed 5% on the transaction. Omi Chand being informed that no commission was being paid to him, was reduced, according to Orme, to a state of imbecility from which he took to his bed and died some 18 months later. An alternative, and more satisfying, account goes to the effect that Omi Chand conspired with the new Nawab to deceive the English as to the extent of the Nawab's treasury (popularly supposed to contain £40 million) by concealing most of it in the harem. Great was the rejoicing in Calcutta when the news of the victory of Plassey reached it, and even greater when the stipulations of the treaties with Mir Jafar were made public. On 6 July, treasure to the amount of over 70 lacks of rupees was delivered to Clive and his committee in Murshidabad, and despatched downriver in 700 chests in 100 boats 'escorted' as Orme puts it 'by all the boats of the squadron and many others, proceeding with banners displayed and musick sounding, as a triumphal procession . . . Never before did the English nation at one time obtain such a prize in solid money; for it amounted (in the mint) to 800,000 pounds sterling'.

John Zephaniah Holwell. Platinotype from the painting attributed to Joshua Reynolds.

Robert Clive. Engraving by F Bartolozzi after Nathaniel Dance.

Calcutta
1757–1798

1 Black Pagoda
2 Armenian church
3 Portuguese church
4 Philip Francis' house
5 Orphan house for soldiers'
  children
6 Theatre
7 Steuart & Co
8 Old Fort/Customs House
9 Writers' Buildings
10 Old Court House
11 Magistrates' Court
12 Old jail
13 Persian Madrassah
14 Collector's Office
15 Mission church
16 Gen. Clavering's house
17 St John's
18 Francis Grand's house
19 Sir Robert Chambers'/
  William Hickey's last house
20 Edward Wheler's house
21 William Hickey's first house
22 New Court House
23 Justice Hyde's house
24 William Hicky's house
25 Accountant General's Office
26 Council House
27 Government House
28 Vansittart/Impey House
29 Great Burying Ground
30 New Jail
31 Col. Watson's dockyard
32 Richard Barwell's house/
  Orphan House for Officers'
  children
33 General hospital
34 Warren Hastings' estate
35 Belvedere House
36 Philip Francis' garden-house

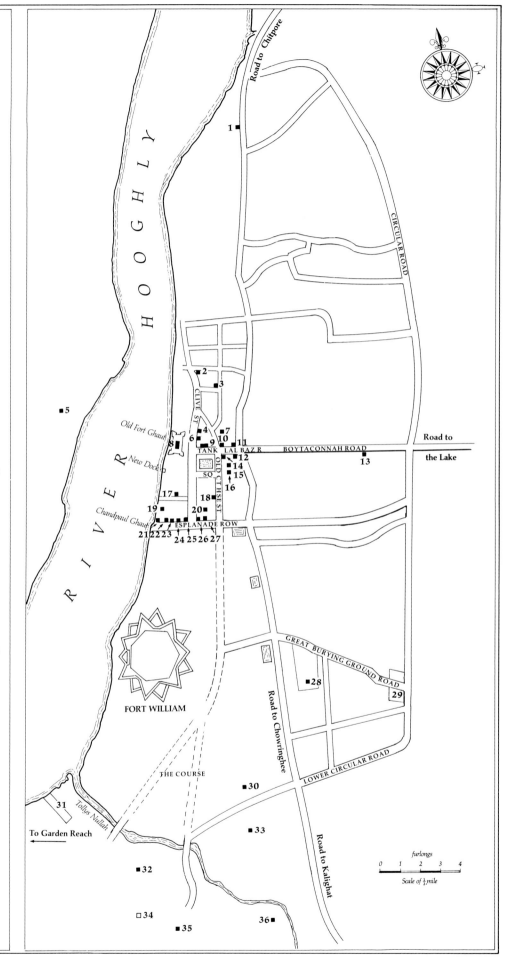

The Capital of Bengal
1757-1798

When Clive and Watson retook Calcutta in January 1757, they found the Fort and Factory partially destroyed, and the church and most of the English houses almost entirely so. Some of the surviving buildings round the Fort were now pulled down to secure a field of fire from the walls, which were not to be overlooked again. The Great Bazaar to the north of Calcutta had been burned down, although the Armenian and Portuguese churches seemed to have escaped. The restitution money from Mir Jafar was thus particularly welcome. The Company received 100 lacks of rupees (£1 million), the European inhabitants of Calcutta another 50, the Hindu inhabitants 20 and the Armenians seven, as part of the provisions of the treaty with Mir Jafar. In the words of the historiographer Orme: 'All the prosperities which had been imagined on the news of the battle of Plassey were now realized in Calcutta. A committee of the most respectable inhabitants were appointed to distribute the money received for the restitution of the losses of individuals, and executed the office with much discretion and equity. Commerce revived throughout the settlement, and affluence began to spread in every house.'

The new town which was built on the ruins was a very different place. The old Calcutta had huddled defensively round the Fort, and existed on the sufferance of the Nawabs of Bengal. This dependence was now reversed. The Nawab owed his throne to the servants of the English Company and was prepared to pay them handsomely for it: the Select Committee of the House of Commons investigating Lord Clive's conduct estimated in 1773 that in addition to the public donations, another £1¼ million had been given as private ones. Clive was appointed Governor of Bengal in 1758, and in the two years before he returned to England secured it against the Mughals in Delhi and against the French. In his absence, the Council in Calcutta was able to sell the throne of Bengal three times, to Mir Jafar's son-in-law Mir Qasim in 1761, who on showing signs of independence was dethroned in favour of Mir Jafar once more in 1763, and to the latter's son in 1765. The Nawab of Oudh and the Mughal Emperor Shah Alam declared in favour of Mir Qasim, but their forces were destroyed in the battle of Buxar in 1764, and Clive who had returned as Governor in 1765 extracted from the Emperor the *divani* or revenue raising powers of Bengal in return for an annual tribute of 26 lacks, leaving to the Nawab the shell of judicial administration and an annual payment of 53 lacks. Clive in this administration tried to destroy the monster his earlier acts had created by prohibiting servants of the Company from engaging in private trade and from receiving presents, at the same time as increasing their pay through revenue from the monopoly on salt (hitherto a prerogative of the Emperor), but his efforts here were not to bear fruit until the administrations of Warren Hastings and Cornwallis.

Although some plans were drawn up to build a new Fort in the middle of the English town, it was soon realised that, in the changed political circumstances, it was no longer necessary for it to be there, protecting the town's houses and inhabitants by its proximity. Captain Brohier, the Chief Engineer, chose instead Gobindpore, the southernmost of the three towns, for the new Fort's site. The original inhabitants of Gobindpore were compensated with land in Suttanuttee. Brohier laid out the lines of the new Fort William in August 1757, and work began in October. An Esplanade was formed out of the jungle surrounding the new Fort, extending northwards to a new road (now Esplanade Row) marking the southern line of the town, eastwards to the road leading to Kalighat, and southwards to a new road in continuation of the Mahratta Ditch, on a line more southerly than that suggested in Orme's plan (see fig.5). This whole area was cleared and levelled to form a great Esplanade, with an absolute

Plan of the fortifications of Fort William, *c.*1760. British Library, K Top.cxv 44.

prohibition on building thereon, so that the new Fort should not be dominated by the surrounding buildings as the old one had been.

The new Fort conformed to the very latest thinking in siege tactics. It was in outline an irregular octagon with seven gates, surrounded by most extensive defences, and was large enough to afford refuge to the entire population at the time or any then imaginable increase in it. The scale of the wholesale rebuilding going on in Calcutta meant that the new Fort was competing, often unsuccessfully, for scarce labour, so that, while the main construction work was completed within ten years, work on the fortifications dragged on until at least 1778. The whole cost £2 million. A Government House was built in the new Fort, but rarely occupied. The oldest barracks, the Royal Barracks facing the river, were completed in 1764, and the North and South barracks on either side shortly thereafter. Near the Water Gate is the Armoury built under the auspices of Warren Hastings in 1777 (see fig.59). The powder magazine, capable of holding 2,200 barrels of gunpowder and impervious at the time to any shot, was completed in 1778. From this same year the Treasure was also kept in the Fort. The great granary was begun in 1779, sufficient to contain 120,000 maunds of grain and rice; it was planned by Hastings as one of a chain of such places to alleviate the dreadful consequences of famines such as that which devestated Bengal in 1770. In 1780 it was completed and by 1782 over 70,000 maunds of rice and paddy were deposited in it. A bazaar was erected about 1787 with a complete range of shops. Although a church was planned, none was built until the 1820s.

The earliest view of the new Fort is probably that found as part of a panoramic view of Calcutta from the opposite bank of the river as it appeared in 1768 (fig.16), although this errs in omitting the half-mile of Esplanade between the southern limit of the town and the Fort. The scroll appears to be the work of Major Antoine Polier, who became Chief Engineer of the Bengal Army in 1762. In 1768 Polier was in Calcutta commanding the garrison and engaged in work on the new Fort William. Plans of the layout and the fortifications were sent to London, but these rarely show the buildings (actual or proposed) inside the fortifications, although Mark Wood's three maps of Calcutta and its environs of 1780-85 show the buildings which had then been completed, as well of course as the plan of the glacis and fortifications (fig.21). The earliest printed view of it is a view from the Esplanade engraved by William Baillie in Calcutta in 1791 (fig.13): a further three views appear in Baillie's set of 12 views of Calcutta published in 1794 (fig.31). New arrivals in Calcutta were much struck by the Fort, which, although of no great height, still dominated the scene as boats came upriver from Garden Reach, such as when John Prinsep made this journey in 1771: 'Next, the Fort opened to our view reminding me of Valenciennes, regular, majestic and commanding.' In 1780 Mrs Eliza Fay wrote: 'Our Fort is also so well kept and every thing in such excellent order, that it is quite a curiosity to see it – all the slopes, banks, and ramparts, are covered with the richest verdure, which completes the enchantment of the scene.' A French visitor in 1790, Louis de Grandpré, was even more struck: 'Le Fort William, la plus belle citadelle qui existe hors d'Europe, se présente d'abord aux yeux qu'elle étonne par sa grandeur et le luxe de ses bâtimens que l'on aperçoit pardessus ses remparts.'

Polier's panoramic view of Calcutta extends almost from the northern limit of the still village-like Suttanuttee (although it does not go as far as the 'Black Pagoda') to Fort William, and shows a long, low town strung along the river bank, with only one steeple, which is that added to the Armenian church in 1734 (fig.14). North of this church is the Great Bazaar. The European area extends southwards from the Armenian church, and the new buildings in this area are much grander than those shown in the similar view of 1756 engraved in Orme's *History* (compare figs.10-11). The large house with a pediment just to the north of the Old Fort is that reputedly occupied by Clive, on the site of Mr Griffiths' house in 1756, which we shall see again in a view by the Daniells (see fig.24). Those buildings which survived within the Old Fort (fig.15) were used as a Customs House, while the remaining part of the old Factory House, that is the northern wing with its verandah in front of it, was used as the Custom Master's house. One of the buildings visible just behind the river gate of the Old Fort, which appears to be the lower part of the south wing of the old Factory, has been given a new gabled roof, and this served the Protestant community as a replacement for St Anne's for

nearly 20 years. We shall be discussing this chapel more fully below. Behind the Old Fort may be seen the obelisk erected by Holwell in 1760 commemorating the Black Hole. The debouching of the creek into the Hooghly is now marked by a bridge, and the obelisks and mausoleums of the burial ground behind are more obscured.

There are a number of interesting descriptions of Calcutta at this period. Among them, that published in Mrs Kindersley's *Letters from the East Indies* in 1777, but in fact describing Calcutta in 1768, is the earliest. Mrs Fay's *Original Letters from India* was published in 1817, but her Calcutta description was written in 1780. The epistolary anonymous novel *Hartly House Calcutta . . . a Novel of the Days of Warren Hastings* was published in 1789 and describes Calcutta just before Hastings' departure in 1785. Mrs Kindersley's description is indeed exactly contemporary with the panorama. The enormous and totally unplanned growth of the city at this time is here made very clear. In fact, this building boom continued unabated for the best part of a century, and speculation in it was one of the most profitable sources of income for Company servants, as other avenues were gradually closed to them. Mrs Kindersley writes:

'I think I have never given you an account of the town of Calcutta; indeed, after Madras, it does not appear much worth describing; for although it is large, with a great many good houses in it, and has the advantage of standing upon the banks of a river, it is as awkward a place as can be conceived; and so irregular, that it looks as if all the houses had been thrown up in the air, and falled down again by accident as they now stand: people keep constantly building; and every one who can procure a piece of ground to build a house upon, consults his own taste and convenience, without any regard to the beauty or regularity of the town; besides, the appearance of the best houses is spoiled by the little straw huts, and such sort of encumbrances, which are built by the servants for themselves to sleep in: so that all the English part of the town, which is the largest, is a confusion of very superb and very shabby houses, dead walls, straw huts, warehouses and I know not what.

'About the middle of the town, on the river's edge, stands the old fort, memorable for the catastrophe of the Black Hole, so much talked of in England; it was in one of the apartments in

Fig.13. William Baillie, *View of Fort William in Bengal from the Government House at Calcutta,* Calcutta, 1791. Etching with aquatint, coloured; 18.5 × 28.5 cm.

it that the wretched sufferers were confined. The fort is now made a very different use of; the only apology for a church is in some of the rooms in it, where divine service is sometimes performed. In a different part of the town reside the Armenians, and the people called Portuguese; each of them have their own churches; and the Portuguese keep up the processions and pageantry of the Romish church, as far as they are permitted; but they are obliged to perform it all within their own walls. The chief connexion we have with these people is, employing some of the women as servants, or the men as writers, or sometimes cooks . . . Here is not, as at Madras, a black town near for the servants of the English to reside in; therefore Calcutta is partly environed by their habitations, which makes the roads rather unpleasant; for the huts they live in, which are built of mud and straw, are so low that they can scarcely stand upright in them; and, having no chimnies, the smoke of the fires with which they dress their victuals, comes all out at the doors, and is perhaps more disagreeable to the passenger than to themselves.

'The new fort, an immense place, is on the river about a mile below the town. If all the buildings which are intended within its walls, are finished, it will be a town within itself, for besides houses for the engineers and other officers who reside at Calcutta, there are apartments for the company's writers, barracks for soldiers, magazines for stores, &c. The town of Calcutta is likewise daily increasing in size, notwithstanding which, the English inhabitants multiply so fast, that houses are extremely scarce; as I have given you a description of the houses at Madras, I need only say, that these are much in the same stile, only they have not the beautiful chunnam [lime-plaster]; for although they have had the same shells brought from the coast of Coromondel, and have mixed them with the same materials, and in the same manner, it has not the least of that fine gloss which is there so greatly admired; this is owing to all the water in Bengal partaking so much of the salt-petre with which the earth is in every part impregnated. Paper, or wainscot, are improper, both on account of the heat, the vermin, and the difficulty of getting it done; the rooms are therefore all whited walls, but plastered in panels, which has a pretty effect; and are generally ornamented with prints, looking-glasses, or whatever else can be procured from Europe; the floors are likewise plaster, covered all over with fine matt, which is nailed down; for although carpets are manufactured in some parts of the country, they are such an addition to the heat, that they are seldom made use of; the rooms are few, but mostly very large and lofty; many of the new-built houses have glass-windows, which are pleasant to the eye, but not so well calculated for the climate as the old ones, which are made of cane.

'Furniture is exorbitantly dear, and so very difficult to procure, that one seldom sees a room where all the chairs and couches are of one sort; people of the first consequence are forced to pick then up as they come, either from the captains of Europe ships, or from China, or having some made by the blundering carpenters of the country, or send for them to Bombay where they are generally received about three years after they are bespoke; so that those people who have great good luck, generally get their houses tolerably well equipped by the time they are quitting them to return to England. Beds, or, as they are always called, cotts, are no very expensive part of furniture; the wood-work, which is exceedingly slight, is made to take in pieces; the furniture is either gauze or muslin, made to put on all at once; and people sleep on a thin mattrass or quilt; one sheet, and two or three pillows, complete the bedding; so that when it is taken in pieces the whole lays in a small compass, and is easily removed from one place to another; whenever people travel, they always carry their beds with them.

'In the country round the town, at different distances, are a number of very pretty houses, which are called garden-houses, belonging to English gentlemen: for Calcutta, besides its being a large town, is not esteemed a healthy spot; so that in the hot season, all those who can, are much at these garden-houses, both because it is cooler and more healthy. A little out of the town is a clear airy spot, free from smoke, or any encumbrances, called the *Corse*, (because it is a road the length of a *corse*, or two miles), in a sort of ring, or rather angle, made on purpose to take the air in, which the company frequent in their carriages about sun-set, or in the morning before the sun is up.'

Mrs Kindersley remarks on the 'apology for a church' being a few rooms in the Old Fort, this being the chapel of St John. The church of St Anne having been completely destroyed, no

attempt was made to rebuild it, and indeed in 1777 the consecrated ground on which it stood was built on. In January 1757, the Council, fearing that the Portuguese would side with their co-religionists the French in the war, was moved 'to interdict the public exercise of the Roman Catholic religion, and forbid the residence of their priests in our bounds'. They also confiscated their church, for use as the English church, and made some repairs to it and its church-yard that same year. But the Court disapproved of the proscription of the Catholic religion, and the Council 'taking into consideration the unwholesomeness and dampness of the Church now made use of, as well as the injustice of detaining it from the Portuguese – ordered the Surveyor to examine the remains of the gateway of the Old Fort, and report to us what it will cost to put it in tolerable repair and make it fit for a Chapel, till such time as the Chapel designed to be built in the New Fort be erected'. The cost of converting this building into a chapel was estimated at 2500 rupees. A chapel was ready in July 1760, and the Catholic church returned to the Portuguese. Whether it was in fact the gateway of the Old Fort that was used as a chapel is not so clear. Although the Consultations clearly state the intention of using the gateway for this purpose, the implementation of Council's orders is often not recorded, and it is to be suspected that another part of the Old Fort was converted for use as a chapel. Mrs Kindersley calls it 'a few rooms' amd Mrs Fay 'a room' in the Old Fort, and 'a great disgrace to the Settlement.' Sophia Goldborne, the heroine of *Hartly House*, describes the interior: 'It ... consists solely of a ground- floor, with an arrangement of plain pews; nor is the Governor himself much better accomodated than the rest; and of course the Padra, as the clergyman is called, has little to boast of; the windows are, however, [open to] verandas, which are pleasing to me in their appearance, independent of the blessing of air enjoyed through that medium.' None of these descriptions much recalls the Fort gateway, of which only the upper part, not the ground floor, could have been utilised. We shall try to locate this chapel more precisely when dealing with the Daniells' views. The chapel in the new Fort William did not in fact materialize until the 1820s.

The area round the Old Fort was still the heart of the English town, and it is here that Mrs Kindersley's strictures as to its haphazard appearance apply, although over the next decade newly developed areas such as the roads facing the Esplanade became more regular. English houses in India at this date were built on classical models, as may be seen in the panoramic view from the Hooghly, and some unsung genius had adapted the grandiose but useless porticos and peristyles of English classicism to incorporate verandahs. These were of great comfort and convenience as Mrs Kindersley notes: 'In all the good houses the apartments are upstairs, and all on one floor; the rooms are large and very lofty; most of the houses are built with a *varendar*, which is a terrace on a level with the rooms in the front, and sometimes in the back part of the house, supported by pillars below, and a roof above likewise supported by pillars, with rails round to lean on. The *varendars* give a handsome appearance to the houses on the out-side, and are of great use, keeping out the sun by day, and in the evenings are cool and pleasant to sit in.'

Mrs Kindersley mentions the garden-houses to which retreated all those who could do so in the hottest weather. These were in favoured suburbs, mostly south of the town, in Alipore, Kidderpore and Garden Reach, the stretch of the Hooghly below the town. Other favoured locations were north towards Barrackpore and Dum Dum. Garden-houses were originally bungalows, single-storeyed buildings with gabled roofs and verandahs, so called from their being developed from the Bengali or *bangla* vernacular style, and set in large gardens. However, some were becoming much grander affairs on two storeys, particularly those in Garden Reach. The Course mentioned by Mrs Kindersley (with erroneous etymology) was laid out on the Esplanade south of Fort William (Upjohn's map of 1794 shows it to be a triangle), and developed eventually into the race-course, for which a large elegant stand was built as early as 1816. In later writings the Course was the road crossing the Esplanade in southerly continuation of Old Court House Street.

The invaluable Mrs Kindersley also describes the routine of English life, as well as the servants necessary to sustain it, in these grand houses: 'As the morning and evening is cooler than the day, it is usual to rise early, and sit up rather late; for after the morning the heat is so intense, that it is difficult to attend to any business, and hardly possible to take any amuse-

Fig.17. Shaykh Zain al-Din, Lady Impey with her servants, c.1780. Watercolour; 45.5 × 53.5 cm. Private Collection.

ment. Ladies mostly retire to their own apartments, where the slightest covering is scarcely supportable. The most active disposition must be indolent in this climate. After dinner every one retires to sleep; it is a second night; every servant is gone to his own habitation; and all is silence: and this custom is so universal, that it would be as unseasonable to call on any person at three or four o'clock in the afternoon, as at the same time in the morning. This custom of sleeping away the hottest hours in the day is necessary, even to the strongest constitution. After this repose people dress for the evening, and enjoy the air about sun-set in their carriages, &c. The rest of the evening is for society. Living is very expensive on account of the great rent of houses, the number of servants, the excessive price of all European commodities, such as wines, clothes, &c. The perspiration requires perpetual changes of clothes and linen; not to mention the expences of palenqueens, carriages, and horses. Many of these things, which perhaps appear luxuries, are, in this climate, real necessaries of life. It is remarkable that those Europeans who have health enjoy a greater flow of spirits than in cooler climates. Except when parties are violent, which is sometimes the case, the society and hospitality is general; and there is no other part of the world where people part with their money to assist each other so freely as the English in India.'

As for servants, Mrs Kindersley devotes a whole letter to the subject. This is early evidence of the Anglo-Indian obsession with the servant problem and the caste system. 'The division of the Indians into *casts* is the cause of great inconveniences and expence to the English, as it obliges then to hire three times the number of servants which would otherwise be necessary;

for none of them, even on the greatest emergency, will perform the most trifling office which does not belong to their particular *cast*. The first servant is called a *Banian*; he is at the head of all the business, but if it is considerable, he has two or three *Banians* or *Sarcars* (a lower *cast* of *Banians*, so called) under him. The next is a *Butler Connah Sarcar*; his office is to take an account of all the money expended for provisions, to pay the butchers, bakers, &c. and answers to a clerk of the kitchen; the next is a *Consummah*, who is the house-keeper, he has under him a *compradore*, who goes to market; the *compradore* buys all small articles for the table, and gives his account to the butler *connah sarcar*; the next is a butler, who is an assistant to the *consummah*.' A delightful painting of about 1780 shows Lady Impey, wife of the Chief Justice of Bengal from 1774- 82, and one of the earliest British patrons of Indian artists, directing her household of servants (fig.17). Lady Impey joined her husband only in 1777, and they lived in the great house in the Park at what had been the outermost edge of Calcutta before 1756; its whereabouts may be seen in the plan of Calcutta published by Orme (fig.5), situated beside where his putative continuation of the Mahratta Ditch crosses the Chitpore-Kalighat road. It had served as Governor Vansittart's garden-house from 1760-64.

Mrs Kindersley continues: 'The other servants, who wait at table, or take care of a gentleman's cloaths, &c. are called *Kissmagars*. The *Peadars* usually called *Peons* run before your *palanqueen* and carry messages. The *bearers* are the chairmen, it is necessary for every person in a family to have six or eight of them, the lower casts of *bearers* take their turn to carry the *mussal* (a sort of torch) before the *palanqueen*; but the superior casts who are cleaner and more creditable will not condescend to touch it, therefore to every set of bearers it is necessary to have at least two boys of a low *cast* called *Mussal Chies*. The *bearers'* business, besides carrying the *palanqueen*, is to bring water to wash after dinner, &c; one brings an ewer with water, and pours it over your hands, another gives you a towel, but it must be a *Mussal Chie*, or a slave, who holds the *chillumchee*, for the *bearer* would be disgraced by touching any thing which contains the water after one has washed with it. A cook in a family will have at least one assistant, if not more, and every horse you keep must have a *sice* and a grass-cutter. The *hooker badar* will do nothing but dress a *hooker*, and attend his master while he smokes it. These servants are all men; and often the only woman in a family is the *Matrannee*, a *Hallicore*, who sweeps the rooms, and does all the dirty offices which the others will not condescend to. The servants who attend in a lady's appartment are generally slave girls, or Portuguese women; and all the nurses for children are Portuguese. The gardeners are called *Mollies*; like all the other people, many hands do but little work: the men who bring water for the gardens, and other purposes, are called *Busties*; they carry the water in large leather bags slung over their backs, at one corner of which there is a sort of spout, which they bring under the right arm; by that means they water the gardens, and throw it wherever else it is necessary. The taylors who make your linen are mostly servants; the slowness of these men can be equalled by nothing but their stupidity. All of the linen is washed by men, who are paid by the month. A *Derwan's* business is to stand at the outward door, to announce visitors; but they are not generally kept, as a *Peon*, or *Chubdar*, will do that office. *Chubdars* are men who carry a long silver-stick, and do nothing but go before a palanqueen, carry messages, or announce visitors. Keeping *Chubdars* is a piece of state allowed by the black people only to officers of dignity in the state; and by the English is confined to the council and field officers.

'The *Banian's* wages is the most considerable, and depends on the situation of his master. The wages of the other servants differ according to their quality: a *Consummah*, Cook, &c. have thirty, twenty, or ten *rupees* a month; the others less; and some of the lowest order not more than three or four *rupees*. None of the servants ever eat, drink, or sleep, in their master's house; nor will either *Hindoos* or *Mahomedans* eat of any thing which goes from their master's table. It is impossible to avoid this inconvenience of a multitude of servants; for if you lessen the number but one, they have a thousand tricks to distress you; and from your head *Banian* to the lowest *Mussal Chies* in your family, all are combined to oblige you to keep the number which they deem proportioned to your rank. As their master rises in life, they insist upon more Cooks, more *Peons*, more *Kissmagars*, more *Bearers*, &c... Most of the servants besides insist upon raising their wages in proportion to their master's rank. This they likewise tell him is *all time custom*, a favorite expression with the *Banians*; and, in their opinion, a sufficient reason for any thing.'

Fig.18. Fredrick Fiebig, Funeral monuments in South Park Street Cemetery, 1851. Salt-print from waxed paper negative, hand-coloured; 16.5 × 22 cm.

For an account of household expenditure and daily fare, we may turn to Mrs Fay: 'In order to give you an idea of my household expenses and the price of living here, I must inform you that, our house costs only 200 rupees per month, because it is not in a part of town much esteemed; otherwise we must pay 3 or 400 rupees; we are now seeking for a better situation. We were frequently told in England you know, that the heat in Bengal destroyed the appetite. I must own that I never yet saw any proof of that; on the contrary I cannot help thinking that I never saw such a quantity of victuals consumed. We dine too at two o'clock, in the very heat of the day. At this moment Mr. F[ay] is looking out with an hawk's eye, for his dinner; and though still much of an invalid, I have no doubt of being able to pick a bit myself. I will give you our bill of fare, and the general price of things. A soup, a roast fowl, curry and rice, a mutton pie, a fore quarter of lamb, a rice pudding; tarts, very good cheese, fresh churned butter, fine bread, excellent Madeira (that is expensive but eatables are very cheap,) – a whole sheep costs but two rupees: a lamb one rupee, six good fowls or ducks ditto – twelve pigeons ditto – twelve pounds of bread ditto – two pounds butter ditto; and a joint of veal ditto – good cheese two months ago sold at the enormous price of three or four rupees per pound, but now you may buy it for one and a half – English claret sells at this time for sixty rupees a dozen. There's a price for you! I need not say that not much of it will be seen at our table: now and then we are forced to produce it but very seldom. I assure you much caution is requisite to avoid running deeply in debt – the facility of obtaining credit is beyond what I could have imagined.'

Mrs Fay's description of the day's events echoes Mrs Kindersley's. However, after rising from the afternoon's repose 'next come the evening airings to the Course where every one goes, though sure of being half suffocated with dust. On returning from thence, tea is served, and universally drank here, even during the extreme heats. After tea, either cards or music fill up the space till ten, when supper is generally announced ... Formal visits are paid in the evening; they are generally very short, as perhaps each lady has a dozen to make and a party waiting for her at home besides. Gentlemen also call to offer their respects and if asked to put down their hat it is considered an invitation to supper. Many a hat have I seen vainly dangling in its owner's hand for half an hour, who at last has been compelled to withdraw without any one's offering to relieve him from the burthen.'

People exerted themselves in Calcutta society the more perhaps as their hold on life was so tenuous. Few things could dampen Sophia Goldborne's liveliness, but even she is reduced to melancholy by the massed ranks of the funeral monuments in the burying grounds (fig.18).

She describes the two main new cemeteries about 1785: 'Obelisks, pagodas, etc., are erected at great expence; and the whole spot is surrounded by as well-turned a walk as those you traverse in Kensington Gardens, ornamented with a double row of aromatic trees, which afford a solemn and beautiful shade: in a word not old Windsor Churchyard with all its cypress and yews is in the smallest degree comparable to them; and I quitted them with unspeakable reluctance. There is no difference between these two grounds, but in the expence of the monuments, which denote that persons of large fortune are there interred, and *vice versa*: whence in order to preserve this difference in the appearance, the first ranks pay five hundred rupees, the second three for opening the ground; and they are disjoined merely by a broad road ... Funerals are indeed solemn and affecting things at Calcutta, no hearses being here introduced, or hired mourners employed: for, as it often happens in the gay circles, that a friend is dined with one day and the next in eternity – the feelings are interested, the sensations awful, and the mental question, for the period of interment at least, which will be tomorrow's victim? The departed one, of whatever rank, is carried on men's shoulders ... and a procession of gentlemen equally numerous and respectable from the extent of genteel connexions, following.'

The old cemetery by the creek with its massive mausoleums and monuments was full by 1767. Alexander Hamilton's mortality rate of over 400 is perhaps exaggerated, but the sober records in the church burial registers cannot be gainsaid. In the epidemic of 1762, 241 burials are recorded in the English register, nearly 100 more than the previous year. A new cemetery was opened in 1767 near the Mahratta Ditch. This was at the end of the road which struck off south-eastward from the Esplanade opposite the Fort, past the Park in which was Vansittart's garden-house, as far as the Ditch. The road became known as the Burying Ground Road, but was later renamed Park Street after this same park round the house occupied by Vansittart and Impey. So far was it for the Chaplain to come from the church, and so often did he have to do so, that a separate palanquin allowance of 30 rupees per month was given him for his conveyance. The grim mortality figures ensured that even this one was soon filling up, so that others had to be established. By 1785 the cemetery on the north side of the Burying Ground Road was open, so Sophia Goldborne assures us. The Mission Church had its own special cemetery open beside them in 1773, while one for European Catholics was also established here by 1797 by Edward Tiretta. In 1840 the dead spread across the Mahratta Ditch, by then the Lower Circular Road, to a vast new cemetery.

British artists had been going to India since the early 1770s, lured by the apparent riches to be won. Originally portrait painters went, but in 1780 there arrived the first topographic artist of consequence, William Hodges, who intended not only to paint for local sale, but also to satisfy home demand by publishing engravings and aquatints on his return. His work was much admired by Warren Hastings, who acquired many of his pictures. On his return to London, Hodges published in 1786 his *Select Views in India*, the first great book of aquatint plates of India, and in 1793 an account of his travels, in which he describes his arrival in Calcutta in 1781, accompanied by an engraved version of a picture which he had painted for Hastings (fig. 19): 'The vessel has no sooner gained one other reach of the river than the whole city of Calcutta bursts upon the eye. This capital of the British dominions in the East is marked by a considerable fortress ... superior to any in India. On the foreground of the picture is the water-gate of the fort, which reflects great honour on the talents of the engineer – the ingenious Colonel Polier. The glacis and esplanade are seen in perspective, bounded by a range of beautiful and regular buildings; and a considerable reach of the river, with vessels of various classes and sizes, from the largest Indiamen to the smallest boat of the country, closes the scene.'

Raptures on first sight of Calcutta from the river are a feature of many accounts by newly arrived visitors. In 1771, John Prinsep describes his arrival in glowing terms: 'The stream seemed to widen as we proceeded and straight before us we beheld a stately forest of masts, vessels, an immense city and the bustle of commercial business.' In May 1780, Mrs Fay enthuses: 'The banks of the river are as one may say absolutely studded with elegant man-sions ... As you come up past Fort William [Calcutta] has a beautiful appearance. Esplanade-Row, as it is called, which fronts the Fort, seems to be composed of palaces: the whole range,

Fig. 19. William Hodges, *A View of Calcutta taken from Fort William*, 1781. Line engraving with etching by W Byrne, from Hodges' *Travels in India*, London, 1793; 13 × 19 cm.

except what is taken up by the Government and Council Houses, is occupied by the principal gentlemen in the settlement – no person being allowed to reside in Fort William, but such as are attached to the army, gives it greatly the advantage over Fort St George.' Other writers later recall their first impressions, such as William Hickey who in November 1777 was characteristically impressed in Garden Reach 'by a rich and magnificent view of a number of splendid houses, the residences of gentlemen of the highest rank in the Company's service', where his host Colonel Watson's house was situated 'upon an elevation... commanding a noble view of Garden Reach with all its palaces downward, and upward Fort William with the magnificent city of Calcutta, a sheet of water more than nine miles in extent, nearly two in breadth, covered with innumerable ships of different size'. Thomas Twining also, who arrived in 1792, recalls: 'Turning suddenly to the north, at the end of [Garden] Reach, the 'City of Palaces' with its lofty detached flat-roofed mansions and the masts of its innumerable shipping, appeared before us on the left bank of the Ganges. A range of magnificent buildings... extended eastward from the river, and then turning at a right-angle to the south, formed on two sides the limit both of the city and plain.' These writers are among the earliest to refer to the 'palaces' of the principal inhabitants, which give the epithet 'City of Palaces' to Calcutta, which we find for the first time in this full form in James Atkinson's poem *The City of Palaces* published in 1824.

Another artist who visited Calcutta at this time was the miniaturist and portrait painter Ozias Humphry, who spent two years in India from 1785 to 1787. In his sketchbooks are recorded some of his impressions of Calcutta, which lack sufficient detail to be of great topographic interest, except for a few individual studies of buildings, chief among them the Madrassah or Hindustani College (fig.20) which Warren Hastings established in 1781 'for the instruction of students in the Mahomedan law and in such other sciences as are taught in the Mahomedan schools'. The buildings round a quadrangle were completed by June 1782, and the revenues of certain villages amounting to 1200 rupees per month assigned to its support. It occupied a site on the south side of the Bow Bazaar, as the road to the east was now known

from beyond the Lall Bazaar, until it moved to the newly laid out Wellesley Square in the 1820s.

Clive had delivered eastern India to the Company, but his traditional system of revenue collection relied on corrupt native officials supervised by venal English masters. Further reforms were introduced by the great Governor-General Warren Hastings (1772-85) on the orders of the Court, which was determined to 'stand forth as Diwan, and to take upon themselves, by the agency of their own servants, the entire care and administration of the revenues,' in order to make Bengal pay for its own government and for the Company's investment in trade. Hastings appointed Company officials as the revenue officers or Collectors in each district, and reduced the role of Murshidabad by bringing the Bengal exchequer to Calcutta. He cut still futher into the allowance paid to the Nawab, while the tribute paid to the Mughal Emperor was abolished, as he was now in the hands of the Marathas, with whom it was increasingly evident there would have to be a final reckoning. The British Government's Regulating Act of 1773 created the post of Governor-General of Fort William in Bengal, and made the Governors of Madras and Bombay dependent on it, but at the same time circumscribed its powers by appointing a council of five members, on which the Governor-General had only a single vote and the right of a casting vote only in the event of an equal division. In addition to Hastings and Richard Barwell, who were already in Calcutta, the new members were General John Clavering (Second in Council and Commander-in-Chief), Philip Francis and Colonel George Monson. The Act also set up in Calcutta a Supreme Court, under a Chief Justice and three Puisne Judges, who were initially Sir Elijah Impey and Mr Justices John Hyde, Robert Chambers and Stephen Le Maistre. The court's jurisdiction was in criminal and civil cases in the town of Calcutta within the confines of the Mahratta Ditch, and as a court of appeal for Europeans, and those Indians choosing to submit to it, from the entire Presidency.

Calcutta had figured in some of the earlier more general plans of this part of Bengal in the 1760s and 1770s, but had no proper survey of its own attempted until 1780. However, in this year Government appointed Commissioners of Police for the administration of the city, the improvement of the drainage, and the disposal of filth and rubbish. Edward Tiretta was appointed Surveyor to the Commissioners and was 'required to survey the said Streets, Lanes and Passages and to report . . . whether any additional Drains and Sewers are wanted . . . and at the same time report the State and Condition of the Roads'. Likewise, in November 1780, 'a Rule and Ordinance had been passed for the Purpose of preventing Fires in the Town of Calcutta, for Disposing of the Town in Regular Streets, and for establishing such other Services and Improvements to it as greatly required', although there had been fierce objec-

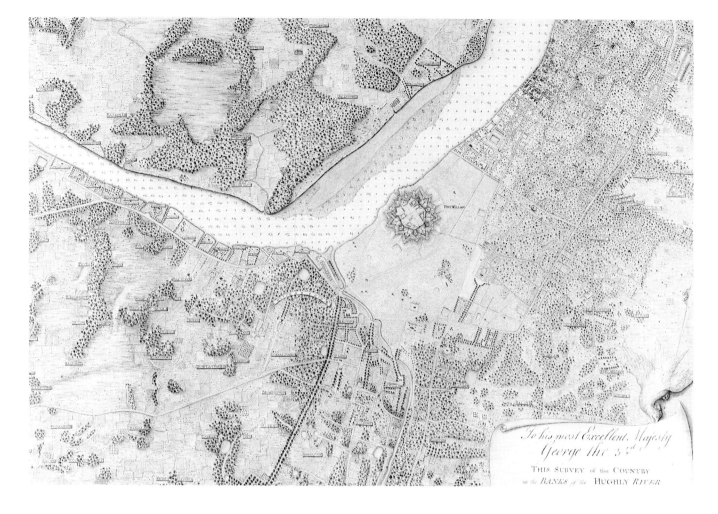

To his most Excellent Majesty
George the 3rd.

THIS SURVEY of the COUNTRY
on the BANKS of the HUGHLY RIVER

tions to this from various inhabitants both English and Bengali. This proposed survey of Calcutta had not materialised by 1784, when Captain Mark Wood was asked to 'prepare plan, survey and levels of Calcutta', work which was apparently completed by 1786, four engineers being employed for three years on this arduous project which showed every street, house and tank, on the scale of 200 feet to the inch. This has not survived, but a copy on a much reduced scale was engraved and printed in 1792 by William Baillie, which greatly disappointed Wood and the Council as it showed only the streets and not the houses.

Wood and his people also surveyed the Hooghly river and adjacent country from Chitpore down to Budge Budge, including Calcutta, between 1780 and 1784, as a result of a decision recorded on 30 March 1780, as to the great utility such a survey would be should Bengal be invaded by a European power. Three beautiful coloured maps are the result, which found their way into King George III's collection (fig.21). In these the detail of the town is not very great, but they do show the buildings within the perimeter of Fort William, as well of course as a plan of the fortifications. The buildings clustered by the Water Gate are the North and South Barracks and the Royal Barracks, while the isolated square building is the Government House. Invaluably, Wood notes the layout of the garden houses at Alipore and Kidderpore and along Garden Reach, as well as their owners.

There has been some controversy over the situation of the various houses at Alipore owned by Warren Hastings, who like his contemporaries found the housing market profitable. Wood notes the great house Belvedere, which Hastings like his predecessors Verelst and Cartier had previously owned but which by 1780 had been sold to Colonel Tolly. It is on the north-west boundary of the grounds of this house that Hastings and Francis fought their famous duel. Francis' own house is marked, which was in fact already sold to his friend George Livius in April 1780. Strangely, Wood omits to mark the large property in Alipore with two houses upon it retained by Hastings until after his departure in 1785, including the house in the background of Zoffany's famous picture of Warren Hastings and his wife, and which is

Fig.21. Mark Wood, *Survey of the Country on the Banks of the Hughly River extending from the town of Calcutta to the village of Ooloobareah*, 1780-84 (detail). Pen-and-ink and watercolour; 48.5 × 126 cm . British Library K Top.cxv 37.

Mrs Eliza Fay dressed in Egyptian costume. Engraving by J Alais after A W Devis.

described by Mrs Fay with her pen dipped in vitriol. A house which appears to have been on this estate is marked as belonging to Mr Auriol. This is James Peter Auriol, one of the Government's Secretaries, whose owning a house here contiguous to that one next marked, Richard Barwell's house at Kidderpore, is confirmed in the lists of the Calcutta Collectorate's deeds and leases. Barwell's house beside the Kidderpore or Tolly's Nullah subsequently became the Upper Military Orphanage (see fig. 34). Colonel Tolly constructed a canal suitable for country shipping out of the dried-up bed of the Kidderpore creek south of the Esplanade (or Maidan as it was now beginning to be called), which once brought the waters of the Hooghly to Kalighat, thereby linking the river with the Sunderbans or channels of the delta east of the Hooghly. On the south side of Tolly's Nullah, Colonel Watson, the Chief Engineer, constructed in his private capacity in 1776 his dockyard, with his house beside it. The names of the owners of all the garden-houses on the left bank of the Hooghly at Garden Reach are given. Beginning with Col Watson's house, they belong successively to Mr Petrie, Mr Reid, Mr Dacre, Mr Wheler, with Mr Stewart's inland, Mr Stark, Col Watson, Mr Vansittart, Col Pearse, Mr Hannay, Mr Charters, Mr Goodwin, Col Parker, Mr Murray, and Col Macpherson. Two other houses of interest marked are in Howrah opposite Calcutta, given to Mr Macpherson and Mr Levett. The latter's distinctively turreted house built originally as a distillery became in 1785 the Lower Military Orphanage (see fig.33).

The foundations of Calcutta topography, which allow us to see for the first time the appearance of a large part of the expanding city, were laid in the set of 12 views of the city which were published in Calcutta between 1786 and 1788 by Thomas and William Daniell. Thomas Daniell and his nephew arrived in 1786, hoping to be able to produce aquatints in India itself, and immediately set to work on their 12 views of Calcutta. These were engraved and coloured with the help of Indian artists, and finished by 1788. William Hickey mentions them in his *Memoirs*: 'I not only subscribed myself but procured many other names to a work they commenced upon of drawing and engraving in *aqua tinta*, twelve views of different parts of Calcutta; they completed them within a twelvemonth, but being the first attempt they proved very inferior to many subsequent performances.' William Hodges found in them not only excellent depictions of 'the mixture of European and Asiatic manners, which may be observed in Calcutta:- coaches, phaetons, single horse chaises, with the pallankeens and hackeries of the natives – the passing ceremonies of the Hindoos – the different appearances of the fakirs – [which] form a sight perhaps more novel and extraordinary than any city in the world can present to a stranger', but also commended them for their accuracy.

William Hickey himself redrew and annotated these views in October 1789, making use of the camera obscura which we know was among his possessions sold when he left India in 1808; he intended to send them to a friend in England, but instead, he seems to have presented them to Sir Robert Chambers, since they passed down within the Chambers family. The more interesting of these notes are quoted here. We shall examine the series from north to south, beginning with the 'Black Pagoda' built by Gobindram Mitter, the 'Black *Zamindar*', about 1731 (fig.22). It is a grand temple in the Bengali style near the northern end of the Chitpore Road, viewed from the south. The main tower is of the *pancaratna* or five-pinnacled type, with two subsidiary shrines each meant to be a *navaratna* or with nine pinnacles. Only one of these is complete in this view. Hickey calls it 'a place of worship built by a native of large fortune, but never completed. A part of it has fallen'. Whether he is referring to the absence of the pinnacles on the nearer subsidiary shrine, or to another part of the temple having collapsed, is unclear, but it is certainly not the case, as commonly found stated, that the main building was overthrown in the cyclone of 1737, as it is here still standing, and must have dominated the whole of northern Calcutta. A distant view in Solvyns' *Hindoos*, datable to between 1791 and 1795, shows the main tower still erect, but it collapsed sometime before 1813, the date of the earliest drawing showing it in a truncated state.

The other view from this set of the Indian city shows traffic on the river off the Bengali quarter, looking south, towards the Armenian church (plate 5), and is one of the most successful artistically of this set. Hickey comments: 'Description of this view must be short as it represents a part of the town entirely inhabited by natives . . . [It] takes in a space of about a mile and an half up the river, and goes very near to the Great Pagoda in the Chitpore road.'

Plate 5. Thomas Daniell, Views of Calcutta, 8. Traffic on the river off the Bengali quarter, looking south, Calcutta, 1788. Coloured etching with aquatint; 40.5 × 53 cm.

Plate 6. Thomas Daniell, Views of Calcutta, 12. St John's Church from the south-east, Calcutta, 1788. Coloured etching with aquatint; 40.5 × 53 cm.

Plate 7. Thomas Daniell, Views of Calcutta, 5. The new Court House, Calcutta, 1787. Coloured etching with aquatint; 40.5 × 53 cm.

Plate 8. Thomas Daniell, Views of Calcutta, 7. Houses on the Chowringhee Road, looking north, Calcutta, 1787. Coloured etching with aquatint; 40.5 × 53 cm.

The buildings show the influence of English classical taste on that of the wealthier Bengalis, which forms one of the most interesting but unexplored chapters of the history of the British in Bengal. This is the area in which lived Maharajah Nubkissen, the most influential Bengali in Calcutta until his death in 1797, and he and his family did much to lay out this area of the city.

Coming now to the European quarter, the Daniells provide views of three sides of what had been the Park, but was now known as Tank Square. Under Warren Hastings the Tank, which supplied the inhabitants of Calcutta with a great part of their water for drinking from a series of springs within it, had been squared off and embanked all around. A new street had been laid out some time before 1780 on the east side of the square running south from the Court House straight to the Esplanade, sweeping out of existence the buildings and the smaller tank in the south-east corner of the Park seen in Wells's plan of 1753. A visitor in 1790, Louis de Grandpré, was much struck with the square: 'Cet étang est entouré d'une pelouse renfermée dans un mur à hauteur d'appui, surmonté d'une claire-voie, dont chaque face a bien à-peu-près deux cent cinquante toises de longeur. Le tour de ce carré est décoré de maisons magnifiques, qui rendent Calcutta non-seulement la plus belle ville de l'Asie, mais même une des plus belles du monde.' The Daniells' view of the north side of Tank Square focuses on the Old Court House on its north-east corner (fig.23). The original building, which as we have seen was built by the Vestry of the parish as a Charity School, and was rented by the Council as a Court House, must have been partially destroyed in 1756; an enlarged building on two floors was planned in July 1762 by the Vestry, with a great hall for dancing on the upper floor, and a broad verandah on both floors at the front. 50,000 rupees were to be subscribed for this purpose, the subscription to be presented to the Charity School, and the latter was to let it out for a greatly increased rent for 'all the Public uses of the settlement, an Exchange for Merchants to meet at, a Post Office, Quarter Sessions, Public Entertainments and all the General

Fig.22. Thomas Daniell, Views of Calcutta, 4. Gobindram Mitter's 'Black Pagoda' on the Chitpore Road from the south, Calcutta, 1787. Coloured etching with aquatint; 40.5 × 53 cm.

Mrs Frances Johnson, the 'Begum' Johnson. Painted by Thomas Hickey, 1784. India Office Library, F 833 (Government Art Collection loan).

Meetings'. Although the sum realised was less than this, the various improvements were made, and presumably ready by 1767 when the Charity School was able to raise the rent to Government from 2,000 to over 4,000 rupees per annum. The new Supreme Court met in this building from October 1774. Here was held, in the sweltering heat of June 1775, the famous trial for forgery of Maharajah Nuncoomar, with the judges sitting in their heavy robes and full-bottomed wigs, for which Impey and Hastings were vilified, first by Francis and then by Burke and Macaulay, for allegedly arranging the judicial murder of a political opponent.

The court constantly required more space and, not being allowed by the Vestry to rent more of the building, as subscriptions had been sought for its enlargement as a place of public entertainment, was compelled to seek accomodation in adjacent buildings. However, the rent for the court was finally raised in January 1778 to 800 *sicca* rupees per month, although without any increase in the available space. Finally, in November 1780, the Council rented for the Supreme Court a large house on Esplanade Row. The Old Court House, as it was known thereafter, then became solely a place for public entertainment, until it became so ruinous that it was pulled down in 1792. Even so, Government still paid the rent of 800 rupees to the Charity School, and continued to do so even after the the land had been made over to build the Scottish church in 1818. Hickey notes on his copy that it was 'an immense building, being in depth thrice its front, of which only two thirds here appears'. Government House being so small, all grand occasions were celebrated in the upper rooms of the Court House, such as the King's Birthday celebrations described in Hickey's *Memoirs*, on which occasion the Governor-General always gave 'a dinner to the gentlemen of the Settlement, and a ball and supper to the ladies at night, at which entertainments everybody, *malgré* the extreme heat, appeared in full dress, with bags and swords'. Each of the numerous toasts was 'followed by a salute of twenty-one guns, from cannon drawn up for the purpose in front of the Court House'. Another view of the building from the south was painted by Francis Swaine Ward at about this time, and was published in William and Edward Orme's 24 *Views in Hindostan* published in London from 1802-05.

Occupying most of the north side of the square is Writers' Buildings: 'A range of buildings erected in 1777 by Mr. Lyon, and bought by Mr. Barwell soon after, from whom the Company have them on lease. They are given to Junr. Servants or those not receiving a salary of more than 300 rs. a month. This was the first building of three stories high erected in Calcutta. There are 19 houses, one excellent room on each floor, two gentlemen to each house, compleat offices behind. The situation airy and good, being about 50 yards to the northward of the Great Tank.' The *pottah* (land grant) granted to Thomas Lyon the builder on 18 November 1776 also included another parcel of land on the opposite side of the road, between the latter and the Tank itself, but Lyon came to an agreement with the Council not to build on it. Lyon seems to have been acting as a front-man for Richard Barwell, a member of Council. Government rented the buildings initially for four years at a monthly rent of 200 Arcot rupees per house, and allowed the occupants to live rent-free in them without deductions from their salary 'which we are well convinced is very unequal to their support'. In 1783 Lyon 'sold' the buildings to Richard Barwell, ostensibly acting for his young children. Barwell was another speculator in Calcutta's building boom, who had already left India; through the renewal of the lease on the buildings for the next five years at the same rent, 45,600 Arcot rupees per annum were paid into the account of Barwell's children. In the distance is the Holwell Monument, which we shall deal with in the next view ('in 1789 it was struck by lightning and much damaged, but was immediately repaired'), and beyond are the remains of the Old Fort. The building at its northern end, partly hidden by Writers' Buildings, is 'part of the Custom Master's house', part of the old Factory, which we have already seen from the other side in the Polier panorama. The gabled roof structure is the old chapel of St John which we have also seen there. It is to be noted that the roof is not over the principal gateway of the Fort, where the Consultations of 1760 would lead us to expect it. Hickey notes it as the 'Top of a building in the old Fort formerly used as a Chapel. It has within a few months been pulled down and a large house built on the ground for public offices', as the new church of St John had just been completed. Clearly then the chapel cannot have been in the old gateway. Some attempt at coping with the drainage of the town had been made by 1789, as Hickey says of

the grating on the extreme left that it was 'one of the common sewers lately compleated throughout Calcutta'.

The remains of the Old Fort still dominate the view of the west side of the square, in which the artist is standing looking north up Clive Street near the Fort's south-east bastion and turret (fig.24). Behind the curtain wall connecting the bastion with the principal gateway, half-way along, is the Black Hole prison. There is no sign of a gabled roof over the gateway, so clearly the chapel must have been set back from the east wall of the Fort. Just beyond the north-east bastion of the Fort is a house 'formerly Mr Middleton's', where Mr Cruttenden's grand house had stood in 1756. This may be the house, two houses north of the Old Fort, occupied by the Revd William Johnson and his wife, the 'Begum' Johnson, widow of William Watts, chief at Cossimbazar, who was taken captive in 1756, and whose reminiscences about the kindness with which she was treated by the old Begum, the widow of Alivardi Khan, Siraj ud-Daula's grandmother, must have earned her the nickname of 'Begum'. In 1774 she was married for the fourth time to the Revd Johnson, who with his wife's money (her previous husband having been a member of the Secret Committee which installed Mir Jafar on the *masnad* of Bengal) speculated profitably in building. We find him for instance in 1777 proposing to the Council to erect between his house and the river a landing-stage and warehouses, there being a great shortage of the latter in Calcutta. On his return to England in 1788, she elected to remain in Calcutta, until her death in 1812, when as the oldest and most respected of the English inhabitants of Calcutta, the old churchyard of St John's was opened especially in her honour. Her mausoleum still occupies the north-west corner of the churchyard. Her eldest daughter by William Watts was the mother of Lord Liverpool, the Prime Minister.

Opposite this house, the grand mansion in the centre is the house once reputedly occupied

Fig.23. Thomas Daniell, Views of Calcutta, 2. North side of Tank Square with the Old Fort and Holwell Monument in the distance, Writers' Buildings, and the Old Court House, Calcutta, 1786. Coloured etching with aquatint; 40.5 × 53 cm.

Fig.24. Thomas Daniell, Views of
Calcutta, 1. East side of the Old
Fort, Clive Street, the Theatre and
Holwell Monument, Calcutta, 1786.
Coloured etching with aquatint;
40.5 × 53 cm.

by Clive and then Philip Francis, Hastings' great enemy. Francis writes in one of his letters:
'Here I live, master of the finest house in Bengal, with a hundred servants, a country house, and
spacious gardens, horses and carriages, yet so perverse is my nature that the devil take me if I
would not exchange the best dinner and the best company I ever saw in Bengal for a breakfast
and claret at the Horn and let me choose my company.' Francis left Calcutta in 1780, and
Hickey tells us in 1789 that the mansion was occupied by the firm of Paxton, Cockerell & Co.
On the north-west corner of Tank Square is the Holwell Monument, an 'Obelisk erected to
the memory of the unfortunate sufferers in the Black Hole; upon a brass plate on the north side
(which is the opposite the one here in shade) are the names of all those who perished'. Holwell
in 1760 became Governor for six months after Clive's departure. During this time he put up
this monument in memory of those he claimed to have been in the Black Hole with him, on the
site of the ditch into which the bodies of the dead had been thrown. The monument bore 48
names only ('exclusive of sixty-nine, consisting of Dutch and English serjeants, corporals,
soldiers, topaz's, militia whites and Portugueze, whose names I am unacquainted with,' as
Holwell puts it in his *Genuine Narrative*). Beyond the monument is the end of the Writers'
Buildings. Between these buildings and Francis' house stands the single-storeyed old theatre,
which Hickey notes was 'built by subscription about 20 years ago'. In 1775, a *pottah* on this
site was granted to a large number of the leading citizens of Calcutta, including the Governor-
General and members of Council and the Judiciary, for the building of a theatre. Thomas
Lyon's *pottah* for his Writers' Buildings makes clear that the western boundaries of the latter
and the theatre were in a line. The theatre continued until 1808, when it was pulled down and
a block of shops known as the New China Bazaar built on the site. Here were also held for ten
years the grand dinners and balls to mark public occasions which had been held in the Old

Court House until 1792, as Calcutta lacked any other suitable hall until the opening of the new Government House in 1803.

Hickey tells us in his *Memoirs* that in the early 1780s the theatre had been riven by factions concerning the claims of the various gentlemen to the chief parts, so that it had become impossible to produce sufficient performers for any play, while extravagant costumes and scenery had rendered the theatre in debt to the tune of 30,000 *sicca* rupees. Finally, a Mr Francis Rundell, a man of no small theatrical talents, had taken over the entire management of the theatre, agreeing to give peformances once a week during the winter season, and charging one gold *mohur* admission, with eight *sicca* rupees for the pit. He undertook to pay off the whole of the debt and not come back to the proprietors for any further money. All that he had engaged to do, he did, and the theatre flourished exceedingly when Hickey returned to Calcutta in 1783: 'Mr. Rundell . . . finding that his emoluments far surpassed his most sanguine expectation. determined to send to England for some second-rate actors, both male and female, for thentofore all women characters had been filled by the male sex, and although there were two gentlemen, Mr. Bride and Mr. Norfar, who excelled in female parts, still the want of women was materially felt. He ultimately succeeded in getting three very tolerable female performers from London and some male understrappers.' To Grandpré such semi-amateur performances did not appeal: 'Tout auprès du vieux fort, se voit l'hôtel des spectacles, édifice qui ne répond pas à la beauté de la ville, et dans lequel on joue rarement, faute de sujets.'

The east side of Tank Square is viewed from the south side of the Great Tank (fig.25). The presence of Bengal sepoys is a reminder that the area south of the Tank had always been the training ground for the militia. Although a road now closed the east side of the square, little building had yet taken place on this side, as part of the land had been sold by the Company

Fig.25. Thomas Daniell, Views of Calcutta, 3. East side of Tank Square and the Old Mission Church, Calcutta, 1786. Coloured etching with aquatint; 40.5 × 53 cm.

with a prohibition against building, although a short-lived riding academy run by one Antonio Angelo Tremamondo had been based there from 1779 to 1784. This prohibition was not removed until 1806, and it allows as an uninterrupted view of the buildings in the street previously known as the Rope Walk, which after the construction of the Mission Church here became known as Mission Row. The Mission Church was built by Johan Zachariah Kiernander, a Swedish missionary who had attached himself to the Danish Mission in south India, but who came to Calcutta in 1758. He was maintained in Calcutta by the Society for Promoting Christian Knowledge at £50 per annum, and his missionary activities were principally among the Catholic Portuguese community. In 1763 Council made over to him the house formerly used as the Collector's office for use as a church and school. He built largely at his own expense, reputedly 60,000 rupees, out of his second wife's fortune, a 'Portuguese Protestant Church' for converts to Protestant Christianity from among the so-called Portuguese community. The foundation stone was laid in 1767 and the church consecrated in December 1770 under the name Beth-Tephillah, or House of Prayer. Asiaticus tells us that the architect was Martin Boutant de Mevell, a Dane.

In the grounds behind the church, Kiernander built in 1773 a Mission School, and later the Parsonage House between school and church, here apparently depicted to the right of the latter, but in fact set much further back. Kiernander actually opened his school in 1758, where in addition to Portuguese, Armenian, and Bengali boys, he also taught the 20 English boys maintained by the Charity School. The original rude church of 1770 had by the time of the Daniells' print been clothed in stone, while a spire was added in 1786. Like the Revd Johnson, Kiernander speculated in property, but failing health and the mismanagement of his affairs by his son drove him to financial ruin. In 1787 Kiernander sold for 10,000 rupees his church, house and school to Charles Grant, William Chambers and the Revd David Brown, the Fort Chaplain, who agreed to carry on his mission work. But in the following year Kiernander was declared a bankrupt and fled to the Dutch settlement at Chinsura, where he remained until it was captured by the English in 1795 and he returned to Calcutta. Asiaticus would have us believe that it was his church that was auctioned upon his bankruptcy, but in fact it was his garden-house. The church was much enlarged in 1835 with the addition of a south transept larger than the original church, while the spire was heightened. The latter hand to be taken down after the earthquake of 1897.

The house on the left is on the corner of Tank Square and the Lall Bazaar, and is identified by Hickey as 'occupied by an Attorney Mr. Raban (pity not o's)'. Raban is mentioned by Hickey briefly in his *Memoirs*, without any kind of disparagement, so presumably his comment here refers to Raban's and his own profession in general terms. Between it and the church are the backs of buildings on the Lall Bazaar, of which the one on the corner of the Lall Bazaar and Mission Row is the Old Playhouse – Calcutta's theatre prior to 1756 – while next door is the then Collector's Cutchery or office, which had been on the opposite side of the Lall Bazaar before 1756. The house on the right is identified by Hickey as 'the house in which Gen. Clavering lived and died, now Company offices'. Clavering was one of the new Members of Council and Commander-in-Chief who came out in 1774 with Francis, whose side he always took in the quarrel with Hastings. He died in 1777. The house belonged to the Company, and was leased by the Parish Vestry in 1790 to house the boys and (by this time) girls of the Charity School, as well as the children to be educated in the Free School, newly established in 1789, as it had become ever clearer that there were more destitute European children in Calcutta than the Charity School could maintain by itself. In 1795 a new building was erected at Jaun Bazaar south of the Dhurrumtollah for the combined schools, the two charities being amalgamated under the name of the Free School in 1800.

Moving now westwards to the river side of the Old Fort, the Daniells' set includes a view of its west face taken from slightly up-river (fig.26). When dealing with Polier's panorama (fig.15), we saw that the remains of the buildings in the Old Fort were turned into the Customs House, with import and export warehouses, while the surviving northern wing of the Factory building became the Custom Master's house, as Hickey notes here. As in the Polier version, what appears to be a two-storeyed verandah has been erected in front of the central windows for shade from the sun. The west river wall of the Fort had a whole range of

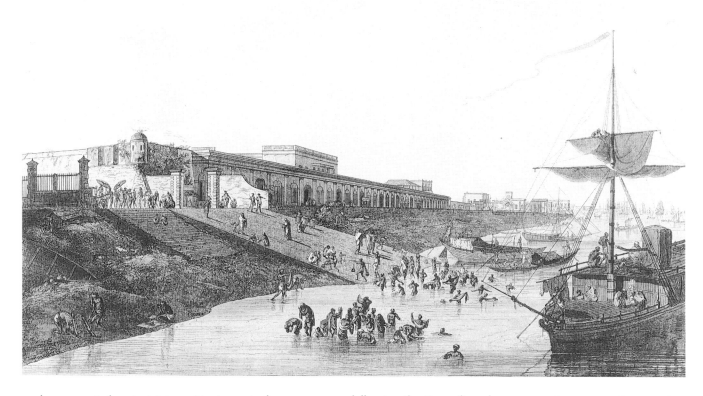

Fig.26. Thomas Daniell, Views of Calcutta, 6. Old Fort Ghaut and the west view of the Old Fort, Calcutta, 1786. Coloured etching with aquatint; 40.5 × 53 cm.

godowns erected against it in 1766, at a cost of 13,000 rupees, following the Council's order of 5 May for 'a Substantial Shed to be run up the whole Length of the Curtain with Brick Pillars and a Slight Terras covering for the conveniency of securing the Goods in case of Rain'. The gabled-roof building protuding over the wall Hickey notes as a 'house formerly used as a Chapel. It was lately pulled down'. Here then was the building used as St John's chapel, and from its site it must have been constructed out of the remains of some of the ground floor rooms of the south wing of the old Factory building, with a new roof put over them. Beside the old chapel the new building is 'a house of the Company's in the old Fort'. The slope which leads down to the river is the Old Fort Ghaut, much used by Hindus for access to the river for their ablutions. Thomas Twining landed here in 1792 and later wrote: 'Upon the custom-house wharf, extending from one end of the fort to the other, I saw immense piles of goods of various sorts, imports and exports... I quitted the boat at a spacious sloping ghaut or landing-place, close to the north-west angle of the old fort. The lower part of the slope went some way into the water and was crowded with natives, men and women, bathing with their clothes on.' Further down river Hickey points out what he calls 'a ship building' by a wharf, which is the dockyard noted in the plans of the 1740s.

The new church of St John was finished and consecrated when the Daniells were in the course of preparing this set (plate 6). The Revd William Johnson, Chaplain since 1770, was the prime mover in its erection. In March 1776, the Council had sent to London the Chaplain's petition for the building of a suitable place of worship, but it was not until near the end of Hastings' administration that a site was selected. This was the old burying ground, closed since 1767, where the mausoleums of Job Charnock and other Calcutta worthies stood, and the old powder-magazine yard immediately to its east. This latter had actually been auctioned by Government on 17 January 1774, being bought by the Maharajah Nubkissen; but he was persuaded in 1782 by Hastings to sell it to him in his private capacity for 10,000 rupees. Hastings made it over to a perpetual succession of trustees in trust for the building of a church. In fact no portion of the church was built on this part of the ground, which was rather built entirely within the burying ground. Some 35,000 rupees were promised by subscribers, while a lottery raised a similar sum. The architect was Lieutenant James Agg of the Bengal Engineers. The foundation stone was laid on 6 April 1784. Agg's design was of a hall-church with a portico and main entrance at the east end and a steeple at the west end, which found an early admirer in Grandpré: 'un superbe bâtiment d'architecture regulière, précédé d'un peristile dorique d'une belle proportion: la corniche et l'architrave simple décoré de ses triglyphes, sont d'un très-bon gout. En un mot, l'édifice est dans sa totalité un modèle de grâces et d'élégance.' Hickey comments less graciously that 'this building appears to advantage upon paper'. Immediately within were vestibules with staircases leading to the galleries used by society, the sexes being segregated. The altar at the east end was enclosed within an apse. The Court of Directors resolved to spend £1200 'towards the provision of communion plate, an organ, a clock, bells, and velvet for the pulpit, desk and communion table', but only the plate and the organ ever arrived in Calcutta. Johan Zoffany presented the church in April 1787 with a picture of the Last Supper as an altar-piece. All the faces in the picture are reputed to be based on those of the inhabitants of Calcutta, Jesus being based on Father Parthenio the Greek priest, while Judas was supposed to be Mr Tulloh the auctioneer.

The curious lay-out seems based on the need for the approach to the church to be from the east, as the west side must have seemed too cluttered with its tombs and mausoleums, as shown in the Daniells' view, to present a congenial approach. Only three of these grand mausoleums still survive, Charnock's, Admiral Watson's and the 'Begum' Johnson's, the latter not then built. Charnock's mausoleum is the octagonal one furthest to the right in this view, with the houses at the back of Hare Street beyond. Asiaticus writes that by 1802 'the Tombs in the Cemetery of Calcutta had fallen into a state of irrepairable decay, and to prevent any dangerous accident, which the tottering ruins threatened to such as approached them, it was deemed necessary to pull down most of them. The stone and marble tablets were carefully cleared from the rubbish, and laid against the wall of the Cemetery'. He then proceeds to give all the inscriptions on these tablets. Hickey notes Watson's monument, a tapering spire on a squared base, as the one visible between the columns of the portico; this was later moved near to Charnock's, presumably in 1802. He also notes of the mausoleum beside it that it was put up in 1738, which from Asiaticus' list would identify it as belonging to Sarah Bourchier, the wife of Richard Bourchier.

The church was finally consecrated on 24 June 1787 (the feast of St John the Baptist), before the assembled dignatories of Calcutta. William Hickey of course contributed his presence and his comments to this as to any other important event in Calcutta, when after a drinking sesssion lasting the entire night, he and a few of his cronies decided to attend the consecration: 'We accordingly remained pouring down claret until eight in the morning (Sunday) . . . At nine three carriages being announced ready, upon mustering the party no more could be prevailed upon to proceed than five . . . who all stepped into Mr. Keighley's coach and were rapidly conveyed to the church, the steps of which we were only able to ascend by leaning upon and supporting each other. It may easily be believed that in such a state we sadly exposed ourselves, drawing the eyes and attention of the congregation upon us as well as that of the clergyman, who took occasion to introduce into his sermon a severe philippic against inebriety, against indelicate behaviour in a sacred place and Sabbath-breaking, and directing those parts of his discourse pointedly to the pew in which we sat. I have often thought since of that profligate scene with shame and contrition.'

Moving now back to Tank Square, we have noted that a new street, Old Court House Street, had been laid out between the south-east corner of the Square and the Esplanade. The Daniells provide a view looking south from half way down, about where Larkins Lane comes in from the west (fig.27). Hickey picks out the interesting buildings, including the second house from the right 'belonging to Mr. Prinsep who married . . . Miss Auriol'. This is John Prinsep, who married the sister of J P Auriol, then Chief Secretary to Government, in 1783. The couple had seven sons who went to India in the early 19th century, some of whom we

Fig.27. Thomas Daniell, Views of Calcutta, 9. Old Court House Street from the north, Calcutta, 1788. Coloured etching with aquatint; 40.5 × 53 cm.

shall shortly be meeting. The large house further along the street is 'the house Mr. Francis made his entrée into which cost him 50000 Rupees'. Next is the house of 'Mr. Harding, one of the paymasters'. Behind these two houses may be seen the houses in Wheler Place, another cross street, behind old Government House. Further down is the range of 'stables and offices belonging to the Governor General's house', which ran along the east side of the old Government House compound. On the left, the first house is that of Mr Ellis the Surgeon General, while the large building with the apse on its side is the Library. The next two buildings down are 'Europe shops, that is where all Europe articles are sold', while the far house on this side of the street is a school.

Hickey's reference to Philip Francis refers to one of the great scandals of 18th-century Calcutta, when on the night of 8 December 1778, Francis, an inveterate ladies' man, was surprised in the house of Mrs Catherine Grand, the 16-year old French wife of Francis Grand, married but 18 months and reputedly the most beautiful woman in Calcutta. Grand was dining with his patron, Richard Barwell, so he tells us in his *Narrative*, when Francis climbed into his house with a bamboo ladder assisted by three friends, including Sir George Shee and Sir John Shore, a future Governor-General. The friends kept watch outside, while Francis gained access to Mrs Grand. In the meantime, Grand's servants had discovered the ladder, and secured Francis when he attempted to leave the house. He was able, however, to summon his friends, who assisted him to escape, but who were in their turn secured by Grand's servants until their master returned home. Since Francis refused to meet Grand in a duel ('conscious of having done me no injury, and that I labored under a complete mistake, he begged leave to decline the proposed invitation, and that he had the honor to remain my most obedient, &c. &c.'), Grand took him to court 'not without experiencing great difficulty, most of the complaisant Advocates of the Supreme Court having either been retained by him, or intimidated from

57

Philip Francis. Engraving by
H Adlard after John Hoppner.

acting'. The action was tried before Chief Justice Impey, and Judges Hyde and Chambers, who found for the plaintiff, with Chambers dissenting, that though no actual guilt had been proved, the damage done by Francis to Mrs Grand's reputation should be liberally compensated. Impey was delivering a judgement for 50,000 rupees, when interrupted, so Hickey informs us in his *Memoirs*, by Hyde: 'Mr Hyde, in a low voice, said 'SICCAS'. 'Aye, siccas, brother Hyde', added the Chief. This produced a roar of mirth from the auditors, at which Sir Elijah was greatly offended.' *Sicca* rupees were worth slightly more than the normal rupee. Grand returned his wife to her family in Chandernagore. She eventually made her way to Paris where, still beautiful, she married the Prince de Talleyrand.

Grand's own *Narrative*, when writing of events in 1777, states that he 'was then living at a garden house, a short distance from town, with my recently acquired consort', and evidently close to Warren Hastings' house at Alipore, in whose 'family' Grand had been. The notebooks of Mr Justice Hyde record that for ten months after their marriage, the Grands lived in the house of Robert Sanderson, Barwell's father-in-law, and this is presumably Grand's garden-house near town. However, there is no reason to suppose, as has usually been assumed, that the scandal 18 months later necessarily took place in this same house. Hyde's notes on this case also reveal that Barwell's dinner had been, not at his house in Kidderpore, but at the tavern kept by Francis Le Gallais in town. That the Grand house was in town is borne out by Hickey's account of the episode in his *Memoirs*, when he details the strategems to which he was reduced in order not to act for Grand, including having to leave town himself. The latter had wanted Hickey to act for him, which he declined to do on the grounds of his having been introduced to Francis by his friend William Burke.

At its south end Old Court House Street enters Esplanade Row, the street which runs across the northern limit of the Esplanade. On the west side of the junction stood the old Government House, which is viewed by the Daniells from the south-east (fig.28). Hickey notes: 'The Government house in which all the Governors of Bengal have resided since Lord Clive's time (He lived in the Council House). Since Lord Cornwallis's arrival it has been much improved . . . It belongs to Mahomed Reza Cawn. [Behind is] a private house built in 1781, and occupied by Mr. Wheler until his death, then by the Honble. Mr. Charles Stuart and now by Mr. Shore. It is situated behind the Council House.' The end wall of the latter building is on the left. Cornwallis succeeded Hastings in 1786. Edward Wheler, Charles Stuart and John Shore were members of Council, and in fact Shore, whom we have met before as a friend of Philip Francis, succeeded Cornwallis as Governor-General, retiring in 1798. The street behind Government House was named Wheler Place because of Mr Wheler's house there. Mahomed Reza Cawn was the Nawab of Chitpore, and an official of the Murshidabad court. Old Government House itself was built round three sides of a court, the wings containing offices being single storied. Its smallness aroused comment, such as from Grandpré: 'Quelque belle que soit cette maison, cependant elle est au-dessous de ce que devrait être la résidence d'un gouverneur de cette importance. Il y a des particuliers dans la ville aussi bien logés que lui. S'il voulait y déployer un grand luxe, le local s'y refuserait. Il s'en faut beaucoup que cet édifice soit aussi somptueux que le palais du gouverneur de Pondichéry.' In their letter of 15 March 1774, the Council inform the Court that 'in the month of June last Mahomed Reza Cawn made an offer to us of his large house next to the Government House for the use of the Company at the price of one lack of rupees . . . but as we were then renters of another house at the rate of 1000 rupees per month for the accomodation of the Secretary's and other public offices, we offered to hire Mahomed Reza Cawn's house at the same rate which he agreed to. The President has since chosen it for his own residence giving up the Government House for a council chamber and the offices of the Secretary, Select Committee, Accomptant, Persian Translator and Court of Appeals all which were accomodated in a much superior manner both as to room and convenience to what they were either in the former hired house or in the old Council House, which last we quitted in good time as it has actually since fallen down. We shall expect your orders as to the purchase of Mahomed Reza Cawn's house if it appears to you advisable.'

This house was therefore leased no earlier than 1773 as the residence of the Governor, but was not finally bought until the end of the century. However, Government already made use

Fig.28. Thomas Daniell, *Views of Calcutta*, 11. Old Government House from the south-east, Calcutta, 1788. Coloured etching with aquatint; 40.5 × 53 cm.

of it before 1773. We learn from J B Stavorinus, who accompanied the Dutch Governor of Chinsura on a state visit to Calcutta in 1770, that 'it was a very handsome building, provided with many and roomy apartments, all furnished in the European style, and hung with damasked silk. It was the property of the little nabob, or minister, Mahomed Rezachan, who had purchased it of an English gentleman for Rs.120,000, and always resided in it when he was at Calcutta; but as he was not now in the place, the English Government had made use of it'. In June 1779, two years after his marriage to the former Baroness Imhoff, we find Hastings complaining about this new Government House, of having to use it for his own accomodation and that of his 'family', and for government business, and the Council therefore proposing to rent a house owned by the late Col Fortnom on a one year lease for 1200 *sicca* rupees per month. This was the house at No 7, Hastings St, where Mrs Hastings held her receptions, while of course Hastings also had his various houses at Alipore. The new Government House could have been used then only for government offices.

The Daniells then move westwards and provide a view of the whole of the Esplanade Row between Government House and the new Court House (fig.29). Immediately beside Government House stood the Council House, where the Governor-General met his Council for the conduct of official business. Such an office had been necessary since the destruction of the Factory building in 1756, but the whereabouts of all but one of the earlier houses has been lost. This earlier one we know from an advertisement for its sale in March 1781, which fixes its location 'next door to the old Export Warehouse' in Koila Ghat Street south of the Old Fort. At a meeting there on 15 October 1764, the Council minuted: 'The present Council Room being from its situation greatly exposed to the heat of the weather and from its vicinity to the public office very ill-calculated for conducting the business of the Board with that privacy which is often requisite, it is agreed to build a new Council-room at a convenient distance from the offices'. This new Council House is the building in this view, which was designed by Colonel Fortnom the Civil Architect. It is a building of two storeys occupying three sides of a quadrangle, in this respect rather like the old Factory building. However, it cannot have been used for this sole purpose very long, for Hickey and other sources suggest that Clive lived in this Council House or at least used it for official purposes (for he is supposed to have lived in the grand house north of the Old Fort), as well as his successors Governors Verelst and Cartier. In the account by Stavorinus just cited, we have seen that the Governor of Chinsura was accomodated in the house owned by Mahomed Reza Cawn, but he was entertained officially by 'the English Governor [Cartier], who resided in the Government House, next to that in which we were'. Clearly then the building newly erected as a Council House was also used as a Government House, and only reverted to its true function when Mahomed Reza Cawn's house next door was officially rented for a Government House. In the meantime, many of the government offices continued in the old Council House, which we learn from a Consultation on 23 April 1773 was 'in so ruinous a condition that it was dangerous to continue the offices there. We were therefore under the necessity immediately of renting a large house belonging to Messrs. Keir & Co, at the rate of rupees 1000 per month, for the meetings of Council and the different offices immediately depending on it'. The newly rented house is no doubt the one further along Esplanade Row which was rented in 1780 for the accomodation of the Supreme Court. It was needed for Government offices for a short period only, as we have seen that on renting the new Government House, the Council and the offices dependent on it were moved into superior accomodation in the Council House. We have already cited a letter sent the following year which states that the old Council House had actually fallen down, but despite its ruinous condition, it was still put up for auction on 17 January 1774, described as 'a cutcha building in Calcutta. with a detached building for a godown, cook-room, etc., and a compound, part surrounded with a railing, containing 4 beegahs, 11 cottahs of ground'.

Hickey identifies the rest of the sights on Esplanade Row. On the left of the Council House is the entrance to 'Council House Street. It goes from the Esplanade to the Great Tank', running parallel to Old Court House Street. The spire of course is that of 'the new Church built by subscription finished in 1787', while the large house on the opposite corner with a colonnaded upper storey is 'a house used for public offices, built about 8 years ago by the Revd. Mr. Johnson, formerly inhabited by Sir Eyre Coote, then by Mr. Stables and lastly by Genl. Sloper, upon whose return to Europe the Company purchased it for a lack of rupees which was less than it cost building'. Johnson no doubt had to capitalize some of his assets in 1785, when his salary was cut by the Company from 1200 to 535 rupees per month as part of its wholesale retrenchments. The building subsequently became known as the Accountant-General's office and the Treasury. The house immediately to its left Hickey notes as 'the house I inhabited (*you see me looking out of the window*)', and indeed a man is certainly doing so: 'in Septr. 1788 I quitted it, when it was immediately pulled down, and a most excellent one erected in its place, which is just finished, and to which, when perfectly dry, I intend to return. It is now nearly as lofty as its neighbour and has eight good rooms on a floor.' From his note on the large private house north of the church in the view of St John's, we learn that Hickey's temporary home was close to it, and from his *Memoirs* that it was further up Council House Street (that is, to its right). In his *Memoirs*, Hickey writes about his new house: 'In March, 1790, my new mansion being finished and very handsome, I removed into it. I furnished it in such a style as gained universal approbation and acquired me the reputation of possessing great taste. The principal apartments were ornamented with immense looking-glasses, also with a number of beautiful pictures and prints, forming altogether a choice and valuable collection. The expense altogether was enormous, but as I looked only to pleasant times, having no idea I should ever be able to lay up a fortune, I was indifferent about the price of things, purchasing every article I felt any inclination for. When completed my house was pronounced to be the most elegantly fitted up of any in Calcutta, and, in fact, there was no one like it. Some of my facetious acquaintances christened it 'Hickey's picture and print warehouse'.' Hickey of course was an attorney, whose business often took him to the Supreme Court, living near which was most convenient for him; and 'notwithstanding I lived so dissipated a life in point of drinking

Fig.29. Thomas Daniell, Views of Calcutta, 10. Esplanade Row West with the Council House, Calcutta, 1788. Coloured etching with aquatint; 40.5 × 53 cm.

and late hours, no man laboured harder. I was always at my desk before seven in the morning, and with the break of half an hour for breakfast, never ceased work until dinner, after which, unless upon emergencies, I never took pen in hand'.

The next similar private house had been that of the advocate William Dunkin, who had lived a bachelor life in Calcutta as a great friend of Hickey, but who had gone back to England in 1788 to lobby for a seat on the Calcutta bench. He returned as a Puisne Judge and baronet with his family in 1791. The next big house is the Supreme Court judge 'Mr Justice Hyde's. He has tenanted this house from the time of his arrival [in 1774], and has paid rent to the amount of fifteen thousand pounds'. Behind the next unnamed private house comes, set back from Esplanade Row, that of Impey's successor as Chief Justice: 'Sir Robt. Chambers's. This is one of the most lofty houses in Calcutta situated immediately behind the present Court House. The entrance to it is from a cross street by the water side'. Hickey in fact rented this house in 1794, and built a verandah on two storeys in front of it, of which he was proud enough to include a drawing in his manuscript memoirs, no doubt because his earlier verandah-building exercise had come to grief (see below). The furthest building visible in this view is part of the Court House.

Further along Esplanade Row, contiguous to the last, stood the new Court House, a dignified but much abused building with an open colonnade along its south façade, which the Council had leased from Archibald Keir in 1773 for government offices, and again in November 1780 as the new Court House (plate 7). Here after certain additions and alterations, the Supreme Court met for the first time on 2 January 1782, and Hickey found it established when he returned to Calcutta in 1783, 'it being a noble pile of buildings, close to the edge of the river at Chaund paul Ghaut, and in which Sir Elijah, with his family, resided'. Impey had by this time given up his great house in the Park south of the Burying Ground Road, prior to his return to England. The Court House was the scene of the judicial labours of the great orientalist Sir William Jones, who arrived in Calcutta in 1783 to replace the dead Stephen Le Maistre, until his own death in 1794. Jones used to walk daily to the court along the river from his house in Garden Reach.

Hickey notes: 'The present Court House is the private property of Mr. Kear [Keir], to whom the Company pay a rent of near four thousand pounds sterling a year. The court is held in the east end, the judges' bench is in a recess under the dome [on the extreme right]. This house is delightfully situated upon the banks of the river, and quite open to the southward (the prevailing wind in this country). It is upon the Esplanade about a mile from the Fort. These views being taken with a camera [obscura] have the usual fault of greatly encreasing the distance, thus, from the appearance of the ships etc. you would suppose the river more than a mile distant, whereas the Court House is within an hundred yards of it . . . The land opposite to Calcutta [i.e. on the Esplanade itself] here gives you the idea of being hilly whereas it is as flat as a pancacke. It should be finished into trees.' Hickey notes that he himself occupied the last house visible in this view at the beginning of 1778. In his *Memoirs* Hickey tells us he set up house with his friend Augustus Cleveland at a 'house delightfully situated upon the Esplanade, open to the southward and eastward, and commanding an extensive view both up and down the river, to which it was close . . . The only reasonable objection that could be made was its being cutcha, that is built with mud instead of mortar. Formerly the greater part of the buildings of Bengal were of that description, whereas there is now hardly one to be seen throughout Calcutta, being replaced by well constructed solid masonry. For this house we agreed to pay three hundred sicca rupees, or thirty-seven pounds ten shillings a month. Pott exclaimed upon entering it at its unfinished state, and undertook to get it put into a proper condition for us, which he did, but at an expense of nearly one thousand pounds'. However, 'the sun striking upon the southern front made it intensely hot, to correct which I sent for a native builder, directing him to put up a matted verandah. My landlady, Mrs. Ogden, hearing this, came to me in the utmost alarm, expressing her fears that I should throw the house down, the walls not being sufficiently strong to bear a verandah.' Hickey after seeking advice from the builder Thomas Lyon, duly went ahead, only to have the entire new structure collapse in the first great north-westerly storm of the summer.

Chandpaul Ghaut, where Esplanade Row met the river, was the official landing place in Calcutta at this time for important arrivals and departures. Here the incoming Governors would land, to be received and conducted to Government House accompanied by the booming of the guns of Fort William. The most famous of these landings is undoubtedly that of the incoming members of Council and the Supreme Court on 19 October 1774, the atmosphere of which is memorably caught by Alexander Mackrabie, Francis' brother-in-law and secretary: 'Exactly at noon, a comfortable season for establishing the etiquette of precedency, the whole party are disposed in three boats, and both courts safely landed at the capital of their jurisdiction. The procession to the Governor's house beggars all description; the heat, the confusion, not an attempt at regularity. No guards, no person to receive or to show the way, no state. But surely Mr. Hastings might have put on a ruffled shirt. The ceremony of introduction gone through, the audience broke up, and we changed the scene though not the climate. At two the whole party, increased by this time to one hundred and fifty, met again at the Governor's house to dine. In such a company little order can be expected. We eat and drank and endeavoured at Society, but even wine in ale glasses cannot remove suspicion.' Macaulay discerns the origin of the discord in this reception: 'The members of Council expected a salute of twenty-one guns from the batteries of Fort William. Hastings allowed them only seventeen. They landed in ill-humour. The first civilities were exchanged with cold reserve. On the morrow commenced that long quarrel which, after distracting British India, was renewed in England, and in which all the most eminent statesmen and orators of the age took active part on one or the other side.' On Hastings' council, he was at the beginning in a minority with Barwell, against the majority of Francis, Clavering and Monson, although death intervened to even up the votes by removing the latter two in 1776 and 1777. The quarrels divided Calcutta society into the 'Minority' and 'Majority' or 'Franciscan' camps. The personal animosity between Hastings and Francis culminated in a duel fought at Alipore in 1780. Francis left

Calcutta the following year and set in motion in London the train of events which led to the impeachment of his adversary.

Retracing our steps past the buildings which we have just examined, wherein took place many of the most memorable incidents of the government of British India, and continuing eastward along Esplanade Row, the latter joins what was then the main north-south road through the city, leading to Chitpore to the north and Chowringhee to the south. The latter road runs for two miles along the east side of the Maidan, and became known as the 'road to Chowringhee' and then the Chowringhee Road. The name is usually derived from the Bengali for a square (*caurangi*), referring to the approximate shape of the area bounded by the Circular Road and the Maidan, but this can hardly be the real origin as the village of Chorangey was one of the 38 'towns' listed in Surman's embassy to Delhi in 1714, long before the road layout was thought of. Into this whole area from the 1770s the residential area of European Calcutta was gradually moved. Together with the buildings along Esplanade Row, the houses along Chowringlee Road framed the Esplanade itself and formed the backdrop to Fort William, creating a view sufficiently striking to have been exclaimed over by new arrivals to Calcutta.

Warren Hastings. Mezzotint by J Jones after J T Seton.

The Daniells' last view is looking north up the Chowringhee Road to the crossing with Esplanade Row, which can be seen in the far distance (plate 8). The houses in the foreground seem to be those between the side-streets off Chowringhee Road now named Lindsay Street and Sudder Street, opposite to the Manohardoss or Colinga Tank. Since this tank is actually immediately opposite the entrance to Lindsay Street, the northernmost of these two side-streets, beyond which even as late as the 1820s there was a considerable open space before the houses began again, it would seem that Daniell has for artistic reasons slightly misplaced the actual position of the tank. It is of these houses that Hodges writes: 'The line of buildings, surrounding two sides of the esplanade of the fort, is magnificent; and it adds greatly to the superb appearance, that the houses are detached from each other, and insulated in a great space. The buildings are all on a large scale, from the necessity of having a fine circulation of air, in a climate the heat of which is extreme. The general approach to the houses is by a flight of steps, with great projecting porticoes, or surrounded by colonades or arcades, which gives them the appearance of Grecian temples; and indeed every house may be considered as a temple dedicated to hospitality.'

William Hickey. Painted by Thomas Hickey, 1789. National Gallery of Ireland.

Hickey comments: 'This is a view of a part of Calcutta called Cheringhee; the whole has been built within the last twelve years; it extends a mile and a half further than this view, and all noble houses.' He carefully identifies the occupants or owners of the houses in October 1789. The nearest house belonged to the estate of the late Charles Short. The wide house with a pediment was owned by Capt Collins the Military Storekeeper, and lived in by Col Murray. The two tall narrow houses in the centre were owned by Col Wood, the one occupied by Mr Dawson, the other empty, while the lower house between them and obviously further north was Sir Charles Blount's. The next house was owned by Mr Hay the Secretary General and lived in by the Hon Charles Stuart; next a house occupied by Col Mordaunt, the brother of Henry; then one occupied by T Grant, Garrison Paymaster; and lastly on Chowringhee Road an untenanted house lately occupied by Jacob Rider.

The Daniells published a further set of six aquatints of Calcutta in 1797-8 in the second volume of their *Oriental Scenery*, based, they say, on views taken in 1792. Two of these views are of the Bengali part of town, one the great pagoda on the Chitpore Road built by Gobindram Mitter, seen here across its accompanying tank from a different viewpoint from the version published in 1787 and embodying one of the Daniells' grandest compositions (see plate 3). The other is of the Chitpore Road south of the great temple (plate 9). The text comments loftily, in a vein similar to that adopted by Hickey in his note on plate 5 above: 'In this view on the Chitpore road (taken in the Monsoon season) appears the house of a native Bengal merchant; the style of architecture in its ornamental parts is Mahomedan, except in the turret, which is an unsuccessful attempt at the Grecian, as introduced by the Portugueze. These incongruities very frequently occur in modern Indian buildings, whose owners have intercourse with Europeans.'

The remaining four views in this set are of the European part of town. The view westwards along Esplanade Row shows us practically all of the Council House, but omits the rebuilt

Fig.30. Thomas Daniell, Council
House and Esplanade Row, 1792.
Pen-and-ink and wash; 43 × 60 cm.
India Office Library WD 1294.

Fig.31. William Baillie, Views of
Calcutta, 9. *North View of the Water
Gate and Royal Barracks, Fort William,
Calcutta, 1794.* Coloured etching;
27.5 × 37.5 cm.

house of William Hickey, which his annotations of 1789 lead us to expect. It can be seen in William Baillie's view below (see fig.35), one of many occasions leading us to view with caution the pictures in *Oriental Scenery* as a completely accurate topographic record. A preparatory wash drawing of this view also survives (fig.30). Among their most beautiful views is one taken on the Esplanade, showing only the last two buildings on Esplanade Row but the river crowded with the shipping of many nations, while on the opposite bank stands the castle-like Military Orphan School for the children of British soldiers. The set also includes the north side of Tank Square viewed from the west rather than the east as in the earlier set, thus affording a close-up view of the Holwell Monument, and exactly the same view of the houses in the Chowringhee Road as earlier, even including the subsidiary figures, suggesting that the Daniells may not be entirely accurate in their memory of the original dates for their views.

We have seen how Mark Wood's survey of Calcutta of 1783-6 was engraved on a reduced scale and published by William Baillie in 1792, thereby greatly disappointing Wood. The engraved version included revisions undertaken in Wood's office 'as in the course of five years, Calcutta has undergone some considerable alterations', but its various deficiencies rendered a new map imperative. A new survey was undertaken in 1792-3 by Aaron Upjohn, who had been Baillie's printer, and was published the following year. This proved more acceptable than Baillie's map, and provides us with an up-to-date survey of the city. It has tiny vignettes of the churches in the appropriate places, including the Armenian and Portuguese churches which we have seen in the 1747 plan (figs.2-3), but additionally one of the Greek church across Amratollah Street from the Catholic church, showing it as a square, spireless building. This church was consecrated in 1781.

Another set of 12 views was engraved and published in Calcutta in 1794 by this same William Baillie who had engraved Wood's map. Baillie went out to Calcutta in 1777 as an infantry cadet, but in 1786 we find him engaged in setting up the *Calcutta Chronicle*, with Aaron Upjohn as the printer. He did not engrave any of his own work until 1791, when there appeared a view of the new Fort William taken from Government House (see fig.13). This is decidedly amateurish in its execution, but the 1794 set of coloured etchings is better. The new Fort appears in three of the 1794 views, including views from the north and from the south-west, and an interesting view of the Water Gate facing the river and of the Royal Barracks behind it (fig.31).

Other new views in this set include an unusual one of the west side of Tank Square, taken from one of the houses in Mission Row over the open stretch of ground between the Mission Church and the Square (fig.32). Baillie suggests that the wall of the Old Fort north of the east gate has been removed, but this did not actually happen until 1819. Within the walls of the Fort we can see the buildings erected for its new rôle as a customs' house. The Custom Master's house is on the right, made out of the north wing of the old factory, and on the left the other Company building noted by Hickey in his view of the west face of the Fort (see fig.26). Between these, the building behind the east gate must be the one erected (so Hickey tells us) on the site of St John's chapel. Behind the latter, and in fact on the other side of the river, is the Military Orphan School with its four towers. The old export warehouses still line the southern wall of the Old Fort, down what the Wood-Baillie map calls Takshall Street, now Koila Ghat Street. What the large house may be on the opposite side of this street is unclear, but it is possibly the building that used to be the old Council House next to the old export warehouse which we have mentioned before, presumably rebuilt since its collapse in 1773-4. South-west of Tank Square there seem still at this time to be few buildings other than the dockyard and associated marine buildings. Another view in this set is of the east side of the square taken from further back than the Daniells' view of 1786 (fig.25 above), showing the buildings actually on the east side of Tank Square, as well as the Mission Church across the vacant piece of ground.

The Military Orphan School in Howrah, opposite Calcutta, we have just seen from a distance, but Baillie also features it in another view in this set (fig.33). This was originally built as a distillery by a Mr Levett, and was taken over in 1782 by Captain William Kirkpatrick for the orphan children of British soldiers. Some 500 children had their home there when the Revd David Brown arrived in 1786 to be its superintendent, but he was dismissed from this

30

31

Fig.32. William Baillie, Views of Calcutta, 4. *View of Tank Square, Calcutta, from the East*, Calcutta, 1794. Coloured etching; 27.5 × 37.5 cm.

post in 1788 as the managers of the charity thought his other duties as Chaplain at the Fort William garrison and at the Mission Church left him too little time for this responsibility. In 1790, the chidren of officers were removed to a mansion in Kidderpore, south of the Maidan, once owned by Richard Barwell (fig.34). Officers in the Bengal Army through monthly contributions maintained the Kidderpore establishment, while the Company itself took on the maintenance of the one at Howrah, becoming, as Asiaticus puts it, 'the fathers of the orphans of their soldiers'. Grandpré speaks highly of this establishment where 'les enfans des deux sexes provenans du mariage légitime d'un de ses serviteurs, y sont reçus. On leur y donne une éducation et des talens utiles . . . Beaucoup de militaires établis à Calcutta, ou dans le voisinage, viennent y prendre pour épouses des filles dont ils ont souvent connu les pères. Ces mariages sont fort communs.' But times change, and Emma Roberts writes in the 1830s: 'Formerly it was the practice to give balls at the establishment at Kidderpore, to which vast numbers of beaux were invited; but this undisguised method of seeking husbands is now at variance with received notions of propriety, and the Female Orphan Asylum has assumed, in consequence of the discontinuance of these parties, somewhat of the character of a nunnery.'

The rest of Baillie's views duplicate much of what had already been published by the Daniells. The general views of Calcutta from the south give a better idea of the city as a whole, while his view of the Council House and Government House together shows the precise physical relationship of these buildings. The house which Hickey mentions as being rebuilt for him in 1789-90, omitted by the Daniells in their view of Esplanade Row in *Oriental Scenery* (see fig.30), is here beside the Treasury in Baillie's view (fig.35). This also shows us the large house of Sir Robert Chambers behind the Court House, into which Hickey moved in this same year.

Perhaps the most ambitious view of Calcutta to appear before those published in *Oriental Scenery* is of one of the premises of Steuart & Company, of which an aquatint version was

engraved and published in London by Francis Jukes in May *1795* (plate 10). This was a firm of coachbuilders situated behind the Old Court House, where they remained from *1783* to *1907*, and the original painting on which the engraving was based was done, so the inscription on the latter informs us, for the head of the firm, James Steuart. Besides coaches, for which because of the few suitable roads there was little demand, the firm made palanquins and other more exotic apparatus for getting about in India, including grand sets of elephant harness. The curious perspective of the main colonnade is caused by a misapprehension on the part of the engraver, for the original painting must have shown a curving colonnade. The demolition of the Old Court House in *1792* allows us a view down the street behind Writers' Buildings known as Lyon's Range, where in *1780* Thomas Lyon built on instructions from Richard Barwell, the owner as we have seen of Writers' Buildings, a 'range of boutiques' for letting for the benefit of his children's trust fund. This street leads to the walls of the Old Fort and the Custom Master's house within it.

The engraving was published with a key, which goes in great detail into the castes and occupations of the numerous figures in the foreground, the kind of detail which could have been contributed by an artist from Antwerp named François Baltazard Solvyns, who was in Calcutta from *1791*. Solvyns is also known to have painted the more elaborate palanquins made by Steuart's firm, and it has accordingly been suggested that Solvyns was the artist of the original picture. Undaunted by an inital lack of success, he began to prepare a huge compendium of *250* coloured etchings of the inhabitants of Bengal, illustrating the different castes, ascetics, trades and occupations. This was eventually published in Calcutta in *1799* (although one set at least has a *1796* imprint), and besides its pictures of the different castes and occupations, it also includes sets of the more exotic means of transport, boats, musical instruments, smoking utensils and festivals. The house of Steuart & Company is identifiable in the background of the print showing a box palanquin. A revised version was published in

Fig.33. William Baillie, Views of Calcutta, 5. *Military Orphan School, opposite to Calcutta, for the Children of private Soldiers*, Calcutta, 1794. Coloured etching; 27.5 × 37.5 cm.

Fig.34. William Baillie, Views of
Calcutta, 11. *North East View of the
Military Orphan House, near Calcutta,
for the Children of Officers*, Calcutta,
1794. Coloured etching;
27.5 × 37.5 cm.

Paris from 1808-12, with remade plates in a different order. All the plates in the Calcutta
edition are in mirror-reverse from the original drawings, presumably because of Solvyns' and
his Indian assistants' deficiencies in printing techniques. This does not of course matter in any
but the topographical views, but all have been corrected in the Paris edition.

Each of the various sections of the work begins with a double-page composition, and eight
of these are views of one kind or another in Calcutta, including views of the Hooghly when
one of the fierce north- westerly winds of the hot season had struck the city, and another when
the river was in the grip of its bore. There are several interesting views of the roads in the
Bengali city, but there are two which are of particular interest here. One of these is the
frontispiece to the section on servants, entitled *European Buildings*, and is a view looking
westwards along the Lall Bazaar from the crossing with the Chitpore Road (fig.36). In the Paris
edition Solvyns' text states: 'The view is taken from the meeting of four handsome streets.
The house of the justices of peace and the one remarkable for the extensive sale rooms which
it contains, forms a striking object.' After a general description of European houses in Calcutta,
he goes on: 'The roofs are always flat and accessible by a staircase; it is a great enjoyment to
breathe the morning and evening air upon these platforms. The walls are built of baked bricks,
and the mortar composed of lime and brickdust: this is covered first with a coat of sand and
lime, and afterwards with powdered shells which give a dazzling white colour. The platforms
[i.e. the roofs] are covered with pieces of wood, and afterwards with bricks of ten or twelve
inches, which are covered first with a layer of Sulky or pounded bricks, and then with one of a
finer Sulky mixed up with lime, Gour (sugar) and oil. After beating this composition during
several days, it is finally covered with a thin coat of fine lime, which forms a solid surface,
capable of resisting the temperature of all the different seasons.'

The auction rooms on the left were originally those of Burrell and Gould and subsequently
of Taylor & Company. The court of the justices of the peace on the right is on the corner of the

Fig.35. William Baillie, Views of Calcutta, 1. *View of Esplanade Row, Calcutta, from the River to the Council-House*, Calcutta, 1794. Coloured etching; 27.5 × 37.5 cm.

Lall Bazaar and the Chitpore Road, with on the opposite corner the old Common Jail. In this house as Hickey tells us 'previous to the establishment of a regular police in Calcutta it was customary for a judge to sit at chambers situate in the Lol Bazaar, for the purpose of transacting the daily business of the town, also of adjusting any little matters of dispute that might arise between the natives not of sufficient magnitude in itself, or the parties too poor to enter into a legal contest . . . The house wherein the judges thus sat in rotation to transact the police business in an evening was hired by the Company, the upper part being occupied by the clerk, who was also an attorney of the Court. From the crowd that daily attended these chambers, of the lowest order of people, the house had been facetiously christened 'Ragamuffin Hall''. The house on the corner of the Lall Bazaar and the Chitpore Road is normally claimed to be the site of the famous Harmonic Tavern, which flourished until 1791, when it became an 'academy', as a restaurant and place of public entertainment. Clearly Solvyns would seem to have disproved this claim. However, an advertisement in the *Calcutta Gazette* for 29 March 1787 for the sale of the old jail, states that the latter was 'facing the Harmonic and next door to Messrs. Burrell and Gould's'. The only solution to this dilemma is surely that the Harmonic must have been on the opposite corner, that is on the east side of the Chitpore Road, not the west.

The frontispiece to Solvyns' section containing ten prints of fakirs contains a unique view of the old Kalighat temple, before it was pulled down and replaced about 1809 by a much larger one (plate 4). The hall in front of the temple is incongruously built on English classical lines. Maria Graham, who visited Calcutta in 1810, notes in her journal for 24 October: 'This is the season of festivals; I hear the tomtoms, drums, pipes, and trumpets in every corner of the town, and I see processions in honour of Kali going to a place two miles off, called Kali Ghaut, where there has long been a celebrated temple to this goddess, which is now pulled down, and another more magnificent is to be erected in its place. In all the bazars, at every shop door, wooden figures and human heads, with the neck painted blood-colour, are suspended, refer-

Fig.36. François Baltazard Solvyns,
Lall Bazaar from the east, *c.1795*.
Coloured etching, from Solvyns'
own *250 Coloured Etchings . . . of the
Hindoos*, Calcutta, 1799; 33.5 ×
49 cm. *Reversed from original.*

ring, I imagine, to the human sacrifices formerly offered to this deity, who was, I believe, the tutelary goddess of Calcutta. Three weeks ago, the festival of Kali, under the name and attributes of Doorga, was celebrated. On this occasion her images, and those of some other divinities, were carried in procession with great pomp, and bathed in the Hoogly, which, being a branch of the Ganges, is sacred. The figures were placed under canopies, which were gilt and decked with the most gaudy colours, and carried upon men's heads. Several of these moving temples went together, preceded by musical instruments, banners, and bare-headed Bramins, repeating *muntras* (forms of prayer). The gods were followed by cars, drawn by oxen or horses, gaily caparisoned, bearing the sacrificial utensils, accompanied by other Bramins, and the procession was closed by an innumerable multitude of people of all castes. This feast lasted several days.'

The Imperial City
1798-1858

In 1798 Calcutta welcomed as its new Governor-General Marquess Wellesley, who set the British possessions in India on a new course with his expansionist policy. Having destroyed Tippoo Sultan in the south, he launched a campaign against the Marathas, the dominant power in the west and north, as a result of which nearly the whole of India apart from the west and far north-west either fell into British hands or entered into subsidiary alliances. As for his behaviour in Calcutta, Hickey as usual describes it eloquently: 'Marquis Wellesley was in no way sparing of the Company's cash. His Lordship's own establishment of servants, equipages, etc., were extravagant in the superlative degree, not only in point of number, but splendour of dress, the whole being put to the account of the chaste managers of Leadenhall Street. Not content with all this parade of suite, the newly created Marquis gave directions for various improvements and alterations to be immediatley carried into effect, not only within the town of Calcutta itself, but in the environs. One of the most marked and decided of these improvements was a new road sixty feet wide which was carried completely round the town of Calcutta, except towards the river Hooghly, to an extent of eight miles. A prodigious improvement it assuredly was, not only proving conducive to the health of the inhabitants in general, but likewise affording an agreeable morning or evening ride to those Europeans who were fond of exercise. His Lordship also determined upon building a palace suitable to his magnificent ideas, and such a one as would be proper for the residence of the British Governor-General of India. This he immediately caused to be commenced, partly upon the site of the old Government House, but taking in the Council House and about sixteen other handsome private mansions, many of them not having been erected above five years, the whole of which were pulled down, the ground upon which they had stood being cleared away to create a superb open square area, in the middle of which his meditated palace was to stand.'

The new road of course was the Circular Road beside the Mahratta Ditch, which although it had been usable to some extent before, was now improved. As for Wellesley's great palace, it was built to the designs of Captain Charles Wyatt of the Engineers, a relation of the well known English architect, on the site of the demolished old Government House and the adjacent Council House (figs.28-9). The land on which the latter stood was already owned by the Company, but the former had to be purchased from the Chitpore Nawab. Likewise, all the houses north of both the official houses were demolished, in order to provide a sufficiently grand enclosure on this side of the new palace, of which the northern limit was a new street in continuation eastwards of Hastings Street. These houses included the mansion which Hickey told us was lived in successively by Wheler, Stuart and Shore (fig.28), and all those on both sides of Wheler Place, which was swept out of existence. The eastward and westward limits were Old Court House Street and Council House Street. Building commenced in February 1799, and the new Government House was first used for official purposes in 1802. Not one rupee of the 15 lacks which it cost had ever been sanctioned by the Court of Directors, who were accordingly extremely irate. As Charles D'Oyly put it in his *Tom Raw the Griffin*, a satiric poem written in the early 1820s, describing the adventures of a new recruit to the Company's service in Calcutta:

> — that noble edifice
> The seat of government and Wellesley's pride,
> Type of the brains that fill that noble head of his,

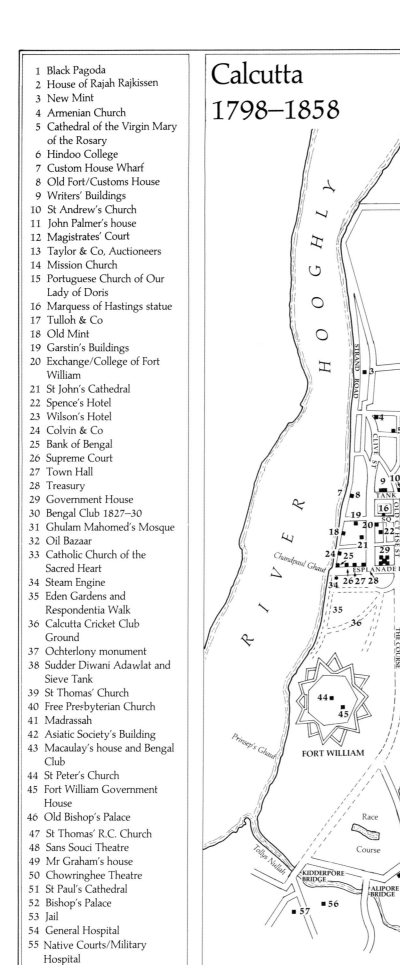

Calcutta
1798–1858

1 Black Pagoda
2 House of Rajah Rajkissen
3 New Mint
4 Armenian Church
5 Cathedral of the Virgin Mary of the Rosary
6 Hindoo College
7 Custom House Wharf
8 Old Fort/Customs House
9 Writers' Buildings
10 St Andrew's Church
11 John Palmer's house
12 Magistrates' Court
13 Taylor & Co, Auctioneers
14 Mission Church
15 Portuguese Church of Our Lady of Doris
16 Marquess of Hastings statue
17 Tulloh & Co
18 Old Mint
19 Garstin's Buildings
20 Exchange/College of Fort William
21 St John's Cathedral
22 Spence's Hotel
23 Wilson's Hotel
24 Colvin & Co
25 Bank of Bengal
26 Supreme Court
27 Town Hall
28 Treasury
29 Government House
30 Bengal Club 1827–30
31 Ghulam Mahomed's Mosque
32 Oil Bazaar
33 Catholic Church of the Sacred Heart
34 Steam Engine
35 Eden Gardens and Respondentia Walk
36 Calcutta Cricket Club Ground
37 Ochterlony monument
38 Sudder Diwani Adawlat and Sieve Tank
39 St Thomas' Church
40 Free Presbyterian Church
41 Madrassah
42 Asiatic Society's Building
43 Macaulay's house and Bengal Club
44 St Peter's Church
45 Fort William Government House
46 Old Bishop's Palace
47 St Thomas' R.C. Church
48 Sans Souci Theatre
49 Mr Graham's house
50 Chowringhee Theatre
51 St Paul's Cathedral
52 Bishop's Palace
53 Jail
54 General Hospital
55 Native Courts/Military Hospital
56 Upper Military Orphanage
57 St Stephen's Kidderpore

Plate 9. Thomas Daniell, *View on the Chitpore Road*, 1792.
Coloured aquatint, plate 2 from *Oriental Scenery*, second series,
engraved by T and William Daniell, London, 1797-8;
42 × 60 cm.

Plate 10. François Baltazard Solvyns (attributed), *View of a House, Manufactory, and Bazar, in Calcutta*, ie Steuart & Co, Coachmakers, *c*.1792-4. Coloured aquatint, engraved by Francis Jukes, London, 1795; 50.5 × 62.5 cm.

Plate 11. James Moffat, New Government House, c.1802.
Watercolour; 44 × 67.5. India Office Library WD 476.

Plate 12. Samuel Davis, *View of Calcutta from Fort William*, c.1805.
Coloured aquatint, engraved by C Duburgh after version by William
Orme, London, 1807; 48 × 64.5 cm.

Plate 13. Anonymous view of the north front of Government House, c.1820, with the Marquess of Hastings leaving it. Watercolour; 36 × 53.5 cm. India Office Library Add. Or. 3309.

Plate 14. James Baillie Fraser, *A View of the Scotch Church from the Gate of Tank Square*, 1819. Coloured aquatint, engraved by R Havell Junr, plate 12 from Fraser's *Views of Calcutta and its Environs*, London, 1824-6; 28 × 42.5 cm.

Plate 15. James Baillie Fraser, *A View of Government House from the Eastward*, 1819. Coloured aquatint, engraved by R Havell Junr, plate 3 from Fraser's *Views of Calcutta and its Environs*, London, 1824-6; 28 × 42.5 cm.

Plate 16. James Baillie Fraser, *View of Court House Street from near the South Eastern Gate of Government House*, 1819. Coloured aquatint, engraved by T Fielding, plate 14 from Fraser's *Views of Calcutta and its Environs*, London, 1824-6; 28 × 42.5 cm.

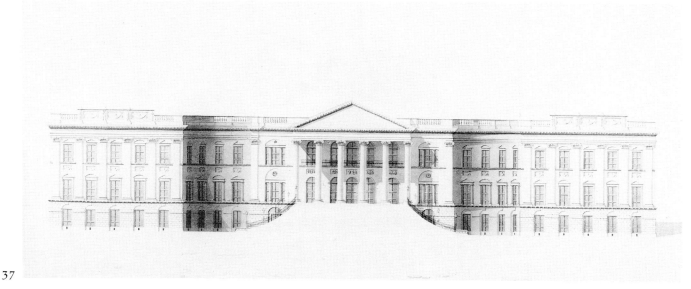

37

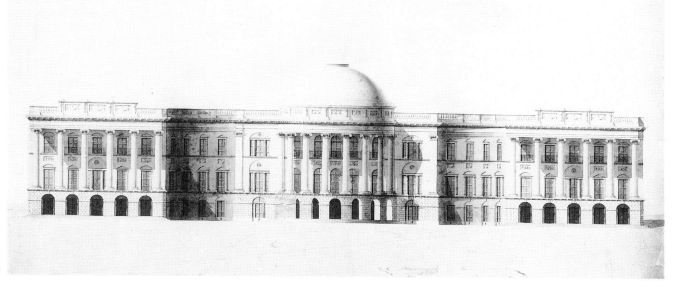

38

And the high horse he loved so well to ride.
'Twas built against the British powers allied,
When o'er the dams and banks of Leadenhall,
His grand munificence poured forth its tide;
Directors' tears cemented each fair wall,
And joint-stock sighs but firmer knit each rising hall.

In February 1804, Captain Wyatt left Calcutta for London bringing a letter of explanation from Wellesley, as well as plans and elevations of the new Government House, drawn by a draftsman in the Government's offices, James Best, to show to the Directors. Wyatt's designs have been criticised for the monotonous appearance of the elevations, but they performed their function admirably of ensuring a continuous flow of air through the building at all seasons. The otherwise uniform skyline was broken by the pediment on the north front (fig.37) and the dome on the south (fig.38), as well as by the Company's coat-of-arms placed on the parapet above each of the façades of the northern wings and the royal arms above the southern ones. The coats-of-arms were not shown on the drawings brought to London, and may have been afterthoughts. They were in position by 1810 when Maria Graham sketched them. On the south front the dome has often been regarded as an afterthought also, since it is just perched on top of the southern façade and is invisible from within. Clearly, however, Wyatt had planned for its presence, to add height to the south elevation as the pediment did to that of the north. The dome became the butt of witticisms such as in *Tom Raw*:

Fig.37. James Best, *Elevation of the North West Front of the New Government House, c.1803.* Pen-and-ink and wash; 44 × 73.5 cm. India Office Library WD 1319.

Fig.38. James Best, *Elevation of the South East Front of the New Government House, c.1803.* Pen-and-ink and wash; 44 × 73.5 cm. India Office Library WD 1320.

Fig.39. Sir Charles D'Oyly, *Tom Raw's Misfortune at the Ball*, showing the ballroom of Government House, c.1820. Coloured aquatint, plate 8 from his *Tom Raw the Griffin*, published R Ackermann, London, 1828; 11 × 19.5 cm.

One word about the dome, 'tis so superior
In every way to domes of brick or stone;
It covers naught below! – but ripens sherry or
Madeira; – a wood box, perched up alone
To aid proportion, and for dumpiness t'atone.

A drawing of the new Government House viewed from the south-east was made by James Moffat about this time and sent to London, where an aquatint based on it was published on 1 January 1805 by Edward Orme (plate 11). Moffat's drawing must have been taken as soon as the shell of the building was complete. His view of the house is accurate enough, but was clearly done before the dome was put up, as his is fanciful, while there is no sign of the four gateways and the railing is in the wrong position. The great ceremonial gateways, based on Adam's archways at Syon House, were already in place in April 1802, at each end of the carriageways running across the north and south façades. The southern gateways were built across Esplanade Row, the course of which was thus grandly interrupted. The north enclosure was cleared and laid out in the course of 1803, and surrounded by an iron railing. Two new roads were made on this side, one a continuation east of Hastings Street, linking Council House Street to Old Court House Street and forming the northern limit of the enclosure, another at right angles to this leading directly from the north entrance of the new building straight to Tank Square. On the south side, a much larger enclosure was formed out of the Maidan, continuing the lines of the streets flanking Government House and ending like an apse, but this was apparently done more gradually than the northern enclosure. Moffat's drawing must have been made in early 1802 at the latest, but may not have been brought to London until 1804 with Wyatt, with instructions to have it printed and disseminated, to strengthen Wellesley's case against his attackers in Leadenhall Street. The discerning public would already have known the Daniells' views of the two buildings which it had replaced, and could more readily admire the nobility of Wellesley's creation since they had nothing whatever to pay for it.

Maria Graham, in India between 1809 and 1811, provides in her published *Journal* a succinct description, together with an engraving, of the great house from the south: 'The lower storey forms a rustic basement, with arcades to the building, which is Ionic. On the north side there is a handsome portico, with a flight of steps, under which carriages drive to the entrance; and on the south there is a circular colonnade with a dome. The four wings, one at each corner of the body of the building, are connected with it by circular passages, so long as to secure their enjoying the air all around, from whatever quarter the wind blows. These wings contain all the private apartments; and in the north-east angle is the council-room, decorated, like the family breakfast and dinner rooms, with portraits. The centre of the house is given up to two rooms, the finest I have seen. The lowest is paved with dark grey marble, and supported by Doric columns of chunam, which one would take for Parian marble. Above the hall is the ball-room, floored with dark polished wood, and supported by Ionic columns of white chunam. Both these fine rooms are lighted by a profusion of cut-glass lustres suspended from the painted ceilings, where an excellent taste is displayed in the decorations.'

Marquess Wellesley. Painted by Robert Home, c.1803-05. India Office Library, F 2.

The lower of the two great halls, which was the state dining-room, was early called the Marble Hall, along the walls of which were ranged busts of the 12 Caesars, of uncertain and disputed provenance. The chandeliers were purchased from the sale of General Claude Martin's effects in Lucknow on 15 October 1801. In *Tom Raw* we find an engraving of the upper hall or ball-room with a ball in full swing and the state chairs at one end (fig.39):

Beneath a canopy, the chair of state
Reposes in magnificent array,
And on it sits — if the occasion's great,
The Ruler of the East, with princely sway...
But on festivities — a semicircle
Of chairs, below the throne, appears, where sit
On either side the chief — and with a smirk all
The Counsellers and Judges, as befit
The country's best support — its props to wit;
And as the parties come, their salutations
Are thitherward directed.

As for the ceiling paintings on canvas by an artist called Creuse:

... adorned with gods in many a string,
In imitation of basso-relievo-ing.
But classic taste gave way to the vile white ant ...
Thus in a few short years, they ate, outright,
What cost the Bengal Government between
Seventy and eighty thousand good rupees — I ween.

In the Throne Room at the south end of the Marble Hall was the so-called throne of Tippoo Sultan, captured from Seringapatam in 1799. The most important room in the wings was the Council Chamber, in the north-east wing on the first floor. Generally, the two southern wings were devoted to the use of the Governor-General's offices and family accomodation, and the northern ones to the offices (and quarters if unmarried) of his staff.

On 26 January 1803, the state rooms of Government House were lighted up for the first time for a grand ball to celebrate the Peace of Amiens. Lord Valentia arrived in Calcutta that same day and describes the occasion in his *Voyages and Travels*: 'At the upper end of the largest [room] was placed a very rich Persian carpet, and in the centre of that, a musnad of crimson and gold, formerly composing part of the ornaments of Tippoo Sultan's throne. On this was a rich chair and stool of state, for Lord Wellesley; on each side, three chairs for the members of council and judges. Down to the door on both sides of the room, were seats for the ladies, in which they were placed according to the strict rules of precedency, which is here regulated by the seniority of the husband in the Company's service... The room was not sufficiently lighted up, yet still the effect was beautiful. The row of chunam pillars, which supported each side, together with the rest of the room, were of a shining white, that gave a contrast to the different dresses of the company... About 800 people were present, who found sufficient room at supper, in the marble hall below, thence they were summoned about one o'clock to the different verandahs to see the fire works and illuminations. The side of the citadel facing the palace was covered with a blaze of light... The rockets were superior to any I ever beheld.

Fig.40. Henry Salt, View of
Chowringhee seen from the house
of Thomas Graham with the Maidan
and Fort William beyond, 1803.
Pen-and-ink and wash on proof
engraving, c.1809; 42 × 60 cm. India
Office Library WD 1297.

Fig.41. James Moffat, *View on the
Banks of the Houghly near Calcutta, the
Country Residence of William
Farquharson Esqr*, Calcutta, 1800.
Aquatint with soft-ground etching;
33.5 × 50 cm.

They were discharged from mortars on the ramparts of the citadel. The colours, also, of several of the pieces were excellent; and the merit of singularity, at least, might be attributed to a battle between two elephants of fire, which by rollers were driven against each other.'

The drawings of Henry Salt, whom Lord Valentia took with him as his secretary and draftsman, were used to illustrate Valentia's book, as well as Salt's own *Twenty-four Views* of 1809. The Valentia party stayed at the house of Thomas Graham in Chowringhee, a view of which from the house towards Fort William and the Maidan was published by Salt, for which a preliminary wash drawing also survives (fig.40). The Graham house was situated in the southern part of Chowringhee, and the view is towards the Maidan south of Fort William. A map in a field survey book of 1809-11 in the National Library, Calcutta, by C G Nicholls, identifies as Graham Street the road subsequently known as Harington Street, and this may be where Graham did indeed live. Graham, we learn from Hickey, was an old servant of the Company who expected a seat on the Supreme Council, yet who was also a partner in a great mercantile firm with John Mowbray, Robert Graham and William Skirrow, which failed in 1790. Graham himself seems to have survived the firm's bankruptcy quite well, and continued in his career, becoming in due course a member of the Supreme Council. However, Hickey tells us, he 'did not continue long in the station, the Court of Directors removing him from it under an idea that his commercial engagements and consequent connexions with many of the principal black people, to some of whom it was notorious he stood largely indebted, might induce an improper bias on his mind . . . But the worthy Cheesemongers of Leadenhall Street were never very remarkable either for their sagacity or even consistency; this remark they proved the justice of by placing him at the Board of Revenue upon turning him out of the Supreme Council, thereby putting him in a situation of all others the most objectionable, from the weight and influence it afforded him.'

Valentia devotes an entire chapter of his *Voyages and Travels* to his observations on Calcutta, many of them the obvious fruit of his conversations with the 'penetrating and expanded genius' of Lord Wellesley, such as his justification of the extravagance of the new Government House: 'I wish India to be ruled from a palace, not a counting-house; with the ideas of a Prince, not with those of a retail dealer in muslins and indigo.' As for the appearance of the city, 'on a line with [Government House] is a range of excellent houses, chunamed and ornamented with verandahs. Chouringee, an entire village of palaces, runs for a considerable length at right angles with it, and, altogether, forms the finest view I ever beheld in any city. The Black Town is as complete a contrast to this as can well be conceived. Its street are narrow and dirty; the houses, of two stories, occasionally brick, but generally mud, and thatched, perfectly resembling the cabins of the poorest class in Ireland. Twenty years ago, during a famine, the population of Calcutta was estimated at 500,000. I have little doubt that it now amounts to 700,000. The most remarkable sight of the kind I ever beheld was the throng that fills these streets in an evening. I drove for three miles through them without finding a single opening, except what was made by the servants preceding the carriage.'

There had been changes in eating habits since the days of Mrs Kindersley and Mrs Fay, as the tiffin or light lunch at twelve mentioned by Sophia Goldborne has now replaced the dinner at two, after which people retired to bed. 'The dinner hour is commonly between seven and eight, which is certainly too late in this hot climate, as it prevents an evening ride at the proper time, and keeps them up till midnight, or later. The viands are excellent, and served in great profusion, to the no small satisfaction of the birds, and beast of prey, to whose share a considerable proportion of the remains fall; for the lower order of the Portuguese, to whom alone they would be serviceable, cannot consume the whole; and the religious prejudices of the native servants prevent them from touching any thing that is not drest by their own cast. To this circumstance is to be attributed the amazing flocks of crows and kites, which, undisturbed by man, live together in amicable society, and almost cover the houses and gardens. In their profession of scavangers, the kites and crows are assisted during the day by the adjutant-bird, and at night by foxes, jackals, and hyenas, from the neighbouring jungles.'

James Moffat, the artist who first drew Wellesley's new palace, was an engraver based in Calcutta. His earliest, still amateurish, work was published in 1798 when he was 23, a set of six views along the Hooghly. Moffat seems to have learnt his art in Calcutta, growing as he

40

41

Fig.42. James Moffat, *General Hospital and Surgeons House near Calcutta*, Calcutta, 1800. Aquatint with etching; 33 × 49.5 cm.

matured more sophisticated but never losing a basic simplicity of composition and drafts-manship. Slightly later than those six views along the river is another one of Garden Reach published in 1800, showing the country house of William Farquharson, with the river, ship-ping, and a *morpunkhi* or peacock- prowed boat (fig.41). Farquharson was by this time a senior member of the civil service, who, we learn from Hickey, had bought Sir John Macpherson's country house which was 'a few miles down the river', on the latter's returning to England after his brief period as Governor-General between Hastings and Cornwallis. Lord Valentia, who landed here in 1803 to find Mr Graham's carriage awaiting him, describes it as 'about five miles from Calcutta'.

In 1800 Moffat published an aquatint view of the general hospital, which stood on the southern edge of the Maidan, facing Fort William (fig.42). A private house belonging to the Revd Johan Kiernander was purchased in 1768 for this purpose. Kiernander was a speculative builder, and he both altered this house and added two wings by 1770 to make it suitable for a hospital. The site was of course chosen to be as far as possible out of the city. This eventually became the Presidency General Hospital. Sophia Goldborne in *Hartly House* rhapsodizes about it: 'Near the Fort is the hospital I have already mentioned, erected for the reception of *all* indisposed persons, from whatever cause; throughout which, the wards or chambers are so neat and accomodating, that wretchedness reposes and malady is put to flight.- It is lighted and cooled by verandas, and every possible means are adopted to procure the free circulation of air, etc., etc., and it is allowed, by all who have seen it, to be superior to every thing under that appellation in the universe ... It was built by the united contributions of the Europeans of Calcutta, and the Company.- Yes Arabella, this blessed asylum owes its support solely to commerce ... To gain admittance into the hospital of Calcutta, there is no other interest or recommendation necessary, than being an European, and deprived of health.'

Another of Moffat's prints, this time appearing in 1805, is one of his most enchanting, entitled the *West View of Calcutta*, with a charmingly naive view of the shipping (fig.43). In Moffat's print, Chandpaul Ghaut at the west end of Esplanade Row is seen on the right. On

the corner is the building which was just about to become the Government Bank in 1806, and the Bank of Bengal in 1809. Behind it, the single storey building by the river is part of the premises of the shippers Colvin & Company, who gave their name to Colvin's Ghaut on the river here. Beyond and largely invisible is the Old Mint. We learn from *Tom Raw* that the street between the ghaut and Government House was called the Respondentia, presumably because here shipping insurance used to be arranged:

Fig.43. James Moffat, *West View of Calcutta*, Calcutta, 1805. Aquatint with soft-ground etching; 33.5 × 50.5 cm.

> Great Respondentia which, in pristine ages,
> Afforded petty merchants your assistance
> To calculate on gain – in all its stages,
> And settle policies, and ship's insurance;
> Now cleansed and beautified, you have th'assurance
> Boldly to rear your metamorphosed brow,
> Midst decorated piles, whose long endurance
> Thick walls and pucka roofs most amply shew
> As well's the reign of wealth, and grandeur's rapid flow!

Beyond is the colonnade of the Court House:

> A colonnade of most enormous length
> Amidst this splendid range the eye embraces;
> It is the court-house, provident in strength,
> But quite devoid of architectural graces . . .

One of Wellesley's most ambitious plans had been to embank the river all the way from the Fort up to the north of Calcutta, but none of this was attempted until much later. As for the shipping, Twining wrote of his arrival in 1792: 'Along the shore in front of the wharf, and to the north as far as I could see, were a great many ships, all manned with native sailors, but commanded principally by English captains, and chiefly belonging either to these captains or to British houses of trade established in Calcutta. These vessels, called 'country ships', were employed in the Indian seas exclusively, principally between Bengal, China and Bombay. never going, or being allowed to go, beyond the Cape of Good Hope, unless by a specific license from the East India Company, who possessed, by their charter, a monopoly of the trade to Europe.' The East Indiamen themselves lay 40 miles downriver, at Diamond Harbour, or, in the case of the larger ones, at Kedgeree, 30 miles further down. Here the passengers embarked and disembarked, using *budgerows* for the river journey between Calcutta and Diamond Harbour, and pinnaces thereafter for Kedgeree, while barges and country boats transferred the cargo up and down the river.

On Tom Raw's disembarking from his boat and mounting the slope up from Chandpaul Ghaut, the 'palac'd city' around the Maidan met his eye:

> And his bewildered vision wanders o'er
> This first bright promise of Calcutta's scope,
> The glance surpassing his most sanguine hope;
> For, here, in long perspective, he could trace
> Its finest works of art, that need no trope
> Rhetorical to magnify the grace
> Nor magic art of song to dignify the place.

The earliest view of the city showing the new Government House added to these 'works of art' is a watercolour view by Samuel Davis taken from Fort William about 1805, and now in the Victoria Memorial Hall, Calcutta. Davis returned to England in 1806 and must have brought this view back with him to London, as an engraved version with aquatint was published on 1 September 1807 by Edward Orme (plate 12).

It was not only Government House, Calcutta, that Wellesley sought to improve without the consent of his masters. At Barrackpore, 14 miles north of Calcutta, and a military cantonment, was a country retreat which had been purchased by Government as a garden-house for the Commander-in-Chief, and which Lord Wellesley had appropriated in 1801. Hickey again: 'Not content with having works of such magnitude and unbounded expence on foot, he at the same time commenced a second palace at Barrackpore, almost rivalling in magnificence the Calcutta one, which he intended as a country residence for future Governor-Generals as he could not expect it would be completed within his own reign. The grounds which of themselves were very pretty he laid out with extraordinary taste and elegance, upon different parts of which he erected a theatre, a riding-house, with probably the finest aviary and menagerie in the world, the two latter buildings being stocked with the rarest and most beautiful birds, and beasts equally uncommon, collected from every quarter of the globe.' Lord Valentia describes Barrackpore in 1803: 'The situation of the house is much more pleasing than any thing I have yet seen. It is considerably elevated above the Hoogly River, on a very extended reach of which it stands: directly opposite is the Danish settlement of Serampore: on the sides are pagodas, villages, and groves of lofty trees. The water itself is much clearer than at Calcutta, and covered with the state barges and cutters of the Governor-General. These, painted green, and ornamented with gold, contrasted with the scarlet dresses of the rowers, were a great addition to the scene. The park is laid out in the English style; and the house, at present unfinished, is well adapted to the climate, having a beautiful verandah on every side, and the rooms being on a very ample scale... Several of the bungalows belonging to the lines have been taken into the park, and are fitted up for the reception of the Secretaries., Aides-de-Camp, and visitors... At his Excellency's request, I left Mr. Salt behind me to take views of the place.'

The house described by Valentia, which may be seen in the drawing by Henry Salt published as a vignette at the head of Valentia's *Voyages and Travels*, was a new, temporary bungalow erected by Wellesley, who had pulled down the old one while his new palace was being built. This ambitious plan only got so far as the first storey before Wellesley was recalled. His temporary bungalow became the nucleus of Barrackpore House. When Wellesley left India, it consisted of three large rooms opening into a verandah, which Sir George Barlow, who acted as Governor-General from 1805 to 1807, enlarged by converting each corner of the verandah into a small room. This is the state of the house as seen in a watercolour

drawn in 1808 by Edward Hawke Locker, the civil secretary to Admiral Sir Edward Pellew, Commander-in-Chief in the East Indies 1804-09 (fig.44). The view is taken from the park. Lord Minto (Governor-General 1807-12) loved the simplicity of Barrackpore, and was very glad Wellesley's grand scheme came to nothing: 'It would have been magnificent, I have no doubt, but in perfect contradiction with every purpose of the place. It would have been to come from Calcutta to Calcutta again; and you must have had the same multitude of trouble-some attendants, and have lived the same full-dress, intolerable life at your country house as in town. I am extremely glad it has been stopped.'

From about 1820 comes a charming work by an anonymous Indian artist showing the north front of Government House with the Marquess of Hastings (Governor-General 1813-23) leaving for a drive attended by his bodyguard (plate 13). We obtain a good view of the coat-of-arms of the East India Company on each of the north wings, with their crossed flags. The inscriptions identify the house on the left, at the extreme end of Old Court House Street, as occupied by Bagshaw, Barlow & Company, one of the oldest mercantile firms in Calcutta and instrumental in setting up the Calcutta Chamber of Commerce in 1834.

We have reached a period in Calcutta's history in which amateur artists abounded, thereby adding vividly to our knowledge of the city. Musical and artistic talents were generally cultivated as part of the equipment needed in polite society. The Company's military officers were taught drawing at Addiscombe, the Company's military college, as part of their general military training, before embarking for India, and some of the most accomplished of the amateur artists of India entered the Bengal Engineers via Addiscombe. Talent abounded equally among many civilians stationed in India. The market which had been identified in Britain by Hodges and the Daniells for aquatint engravings of the exotic east, still flourished, and many of the amateur artists of the Indian scene had their works engraved and published. In Calcutta there was a lively musical and artistic circle under the genial leadership of Sir Charles D'Oyly, who spent much of his 40 years in India from 1798-1838 as a Company civil

Fig.44. Edward Hawke Locker. *The Governor-General's Villa at Barrackpore*, 1808. Watercolour; 29.5 × 41 cm. India Office Library WD 3856.

Marquess of Hastings. Engraved by
P Savignhac after George Chinnery.

servant stationed in Calcutta. From 1807 to 1825, the brilliant but wayward artist George Chinnery was based there, and around him gathered most of the amateur artistic talent in Calcutta.

The unpublished memoirs of William Prinsep, one of the seven sons of the before mentioned John Prinsep who found a career in India, furnish a lively picture of artistic circles in Calcutta at this time. Like nearly all his brothers, Prinsep had been well trained as an artist and musician, and soon moved in such circles on his arrival in Calcutta in 1817: 'I became very intimate with George Chinnery, the only painter we had in those days worth having. He was a man of extraordinary talent but entirely self-taught. He had come out to India from Dublin as a miniature painter, and his ivories of that day were beautiful. His eye for form peculiarly correct and minute and his sketches in pen and pencil perfect. As a colorist in watercolours he wanted delicacy, but his effects of light and shade were always good though sometimes heavy. His oil portraits of men particularly are excellent and he had always more work than he could get through being too fond of amusing himself and others by his small trifling individualities of landscape as he used to call them which he used rapidly to hit off by way of relaxation. I learnt very much from him as regards both form and colour. His conceit was ineffable but he had a good memory and much fun. We all found much amusement in his conversation. Many were the happy hours all lovers of the brush spent at the hospitable house of Sir Chas D'Oyly, himself an excellent artist, where Chinnery was a frequent and welcome guest.' D'Oyly devotes much of his fifth canto of *Tom Raw* to an account of Chinnery ('the ablest limner in the land') and his eccentricities. He lived in Garstin's Buildings on Hare Street north of St John's, which were built by Garstin out of the surplus of bricks required for the new Town Hall.

Chinnery's pecuniary embarrassments came to a head in the early 1820s, and Prinsep gives us a first-hand account of these events: 'In June of this year [1821] our amusing and instructive friend George Chinnery, the painter, fell into such distress from heavy pressure of his creditors, that he fled to the Danish settlement for protection, and took up his abode at Serampore... We all regretted the loss of his society and his brush from Calcutta, and upon enquiring into his position and getting from him a list of his creditors amounting to about 20,000Rs, John Palmer, Jas Silk Buckingham, Col. Jas Young and myself induced a few others to join us in advancing this sum and replacing him in his Calcutta studio taking as our security a formal lien on the public pictures for which he had orders in hand, many subscribed for and some of them begun. One of them being a grand portrait of Lord Hastings on horseback for the Townhall and for which he was to have 16000 Rs. He was heartily welcomed back and he resumed his active labors, not however upon our pictures, but upon fresh orders for which he got ready money. I had a most troublesome correspondence with him for it turned out that he had understated his liabilities full 10,000Rs and when I urged that it was unfortunately necessary that he should devote at least half of his day to the finishing of the works which were to repay his benefactors he used to meet my remarks with such words as these 'Chain Lord Byron to a rock, could he have written such poetry as his free spirit dictated? Place my brush under coercion, do you think you will ever get a picture worth looking at?' The unprincipled fellow never touched one of them, and when he ran away to China we found ourselves joint losers of more than 30,000Rs and the public pictures were most of them never painted at all.'

One of the earliest published fruits of this florescence of talent in Calcutta was James Baillie Fraser's *Views of Calcutta and its Environs*, a set of 24 coloured aquatints, which were published in London from 1824 to 1826. Fraser had arrived in Calcutta in 1814, hoping to engage in what he thought was the lucrative trade of the east. However, he found it easier to draw the city than to make a fortune from it, and in 1819-20 he was busy taking views, which he planned to have engraved in England, as he had his earlier *Views in the Himala Mountains*. Fraser had the benefit of expert tuition in Calcutta, from the long-resident artist George Chinnery, whose mannerisms in the depictions of Bengalis and their animals and houses, he like every other amateur artist in Calcutta, eagerly absorbed, as well as from the stay in Calcutta in 1817-18 of William Havell, who had accompanied Lord Amherst's embassy to China from 1815-17, and from whom Fraser learnt much in the depiction of landscape and

Fig.45. James Baillie Fraser, *A View of Barrackpore House*, 1819. Coloured aquatint, engraved by R Havell Junr, plate 10 from Fraser's *Views of Calcutta and its Environs*, London, 1824-6; 28 × 42.5 cm.

atmosphere. Fraser resolved to leave Calcutta in 1820, taking the overland route, and from his letter to his father of 25 March 1820, listing what he was sending direct to Scotland by sea, we learn that at this time the Calcutta views were not yet finished: 'The large portfolio contains my late labours, my sketches of Calcutta, in a very rough state indeed, but I have & shall have full materials to fill them up interestingly with figures and groups. You may shew such of all them as you think may do me no discredit recollecting to tell the unlearned that they are but sketches.' Fraser arrived home in 1823, and must have quickly added picturesque groups and figures in Chinnery's manner to people the streets of the city, as the first group was published in April 1824.

The aquatints based on the drawings, which do not seem to survive, have very rich colouring and atmospheric effects, but are not nearly as detailed as the Daniells' set of 1786-88. They are, however, a valuable source for the topography of the city about 1820, which had changed in some respects dramatically since the earlier set. Government House now dominates the heart of the city, and the series of great public buildings along Esplanade Row had been completed with the opening of the Town Hall in 1813. On the north-east corner of Tank Square, a new Scotch church dedicated to St Andrew had been built. Detailed information about the buildings and inhabitants of the city at this time is yielded by the Calcutta improvement map drawn by J A Schalch in 1824, whose full significance we shall shortly be discussing.

We shall follow the topography of the city from north to south as with the Daniells' views. Fraser includes two views at Barrackpore, one of the house itself, which the Marquess of Hastings had greatly extended, adding in 1814-15 a whole new storey (fig.45). On the left in Fraser's view is the Memorial Hall erected by Lord Minto to commemorate those who fell in the conquest of Mauritius and Java from the French and the Dutch respectively in the Napoleonic wars. Fraser also includes a view from Barrackpore Park (which Wellesley had of course landscaped in the English manner) across the river to Serampore. Bishop Heber was much impressed with Barrackpore on his visit to Lord Amherst, Hastings' successor, in 1823: 'The Governor-General has a very pretty country residence at Barrackpore ... offering as beautiful a display of turf, tree, and flowering shrub, as any scene in the world can produce ...

Fig.46. James Baillie Fraser, *A View of Writers Buildings, 1819.* Coloured aquatint, engraved by R Havell Junr, plate 6 from Fraser's *Views of Calcutta and its Environs,* London, 1824-6; 28 × 42.5 cm.

The house itself of Barrackpore is handsome, containing three fine sitting-rooms, though but few bed-chambers. Indeed, as in this climate no sleeping-rooms are even tolerable, unless they admit the southern breeze, there can be but few in any house. Accordingly, that of Barrackpore barely accomodates Lord Amherst's own family; and his Aides-du-Camp and visitors sleep in bungalows, built at some distance from it, in the park.' Heber was entertained by his host with a ride round the park on an elephant, a stable of them being kept there for the purpose, together with the suitable accoutrements and insignia for the howdahs. The elephants which enliven the Daniells' prints of Calcutta had long been banned from the city 'on account of the frequent accidents which they occasion by frightening horses'.

Moving south into the confines of the city itself, Fraser includes a view of the 'Black Pagoda' in the Chitpore Road, the appearance of which at this time we shall discuss below, when dealing with the watercolour view by Thomas Prinsep. Fraser includes five views of Tank Square. His view at sunrise from the west of the Writers' Buildings shows us a close-up of the Holwell monument to the Black Hole now in the last years of its existence (fig.46). It was taken down by order of the Marquess of Hastings in 1821, on the grounds of its increasing unsightliness. Built only of brick and plaster, it had also obviously become a kind of lounging place, where barbers plied their trade. An impromptu verandah has been added all along the façade of Writers' Buildings. At the far end of the square we catch our first glimpse of the new St Andrew's Church.

On the west side of the Square (fig.47), the gate to the Tank faces Koila Ghat Street, on the right of which is the old export warehouse built up against the southern edge of the Old Fort. Part of the latter was demolished in 1819 to build the new Customs House, which is further round to the right outside the present view. At the south-west corner of the Square, behind which the spire of St John's appears, Council House Street leads down to Esplanade Row. On the left side of Council House Street on the corner of the Square is the building where the first Public Exchange and Coffee House in Calcutta was situated, opened in 1788. This did not do very well, and the building was leased by Lord Wellesley for his College of Fort William. The College had by this date moved across the Square to Writers' Buildings, and the building had reverted to its original purpose as an Exchange and Assembly Rooms.

Hickey tells us about this College, another of Wellesley's grand schemes: 'He also proposed to establish a College, for the education of the junior servants of the Company on their first arrival, principally in Oriental languages, with a regular establishment of Provost, Vice-Provost, Professors of various descriptions and other officers similar to our Universities of Oxford and Cambridge... Until the intended College should be completed, Lord Wellesley took upon lease a very spacious mansion which a speculating dancing master named [John] Macdonald had planned and erected for a Public Exchange, in the most central part of Calcutta, but which speculation not answering the proprietor's hopes and expectations he was glad to let it on lease to such good tenants as the East India Company... This whole scheme was put a stop to, and the intended College done away with altogether, by the most preremptory orders from the Court of Directors, and which orders for a wonder the most noble Marquis thought proper to obey.' This College was planned by Wellesley to finish the often ignorant young writers' western education and to instruct them in the oriental languages necessary to govern those areas of India by then firmly under British control, as well as keeping the often riotous youths under firmer discipline. The order for outright abolition which came from London in 1803 was circumvented, and the College continued on a much reduced scale for teaching oriental languages. The Company set up its own College at Haileybury in 1806, through which those wanting to become its civil servants had to pass. A few oriental languages were taught at Haileybury, but instruction in the modern languages of India was continued at Fort William after the students' arrival at Calcutta. Wellesley instituted disputations in oriental languages at the annual prize-giving ceremony, which took place in great state at Government House before the Governor-General, judges and members of Council, as well as large numbers of Calcutta's inhabitants, and which were published annually along with a record of all the other proceedings. Maria Graham describes the 1810 session, by which time the College had crossed Tank Square to Writers' Buildings, of which she does not give us a very favourable impression: 'The writers buildings, to the north of the government-house, look like a shabby hospital, or poors-house; these contain apartments for the writers newly come from Britain, and who are students at the college of Fort-William, which is in the centre of the buildings, and contains nothing but some lecture-rooms.'

Fig.47. James Baillie Fraser, *A View of the West Side of Tank Square*, 1819. Coloured aquatint, engraved by R Havell, plate 22 from Fraser's *Views of Calcutta and its Environs*, London, 1824-6; 28 × 42.5 cm.

Fig.48. James Baillie Fraser, *A View of Tank Square from the West*, 1819. Coloured aquatint, engraved by R Havell Junr, plate 8 from Fraser's *Views of Calcutta and its Environs*, London, 1824-6; 28 × 42.5 cm.

Fig.49. James Baillie Fraser, *View of St. Andrew's Church from Mission Row*, 1819. Coloured aquatint, engraved by F C Lewis, plate 13 from Fraser's *Views of Calcutta and its Environs*, London, 1824-6; 28 × 42.5 cm.

As for the tank itself, Fraser has omitted in working up this view to draw in the balustrade which certainly surrounded it and which he includes in another view. Inside the gate, a ramp, crowded with those come to draw water, slopes down to the water's edge. The great tank in the Square remained the most important source of water for much of the city. Fraser also gives us the reverse view of the previous one with the air washed clean after rain (fig.48), in which we get a more distant view of the north side of the square from the south-west, as well as a view up Clive Street where the buildings of the New China Bazaar have replaced the old theatre. As always in his views, the Bengali inhabitants of the city add interest, with a group of *bihishtis* or water-carriers with their goat-skins for carrying the water slung over their shoulders. The turnstiles prevented the access of animals, and the sentry-box beyond the gateway was for the *chowkidars* or watchmen who prevented people from bathing in the tank.

Two other views in this set concentrate on the church of St Andrew newly built in the north-east corner of the Square, on the site of the demolished Old Court House. A congregation of the Church of Scotland was formed in 1815 by the Revd James Bryce, and money was raised both from the Government, who gave the site, and private sources to build a Kirk. In the meantime, the Exchange building across the Square was used. The Kirk was ready for worship in March 1818. Fraser's view from the eastern gate of Tank Square shows the Doric southern portico crowned by its handsome spire (plate 14). The steeple is taller than that of St John's, much to the dismay of Bishop Middleton, the first Bishop of Calcutta, who is supposed to have held that the Church of England had the monopoly of spires in all the British dominions. Bryce is thought to have added the cock weather-vane to be able to crow over his rival. Behind the church may be seen part of the colonnade of the premises of the coachbuilders James Steuart & Company. The large house on the right is that occupied by Dr Hare in Schalch's map of 1824, two physicians of this name, uncle and nephew, being much mentioned by William Hickey. This must be the house of the younger one. For his second view of the church, Fraser has moved to the east to the junction of Mission Row with the Lall Bazaar, showing the east façade of the church and the other Doric portico at the north entrance (fig.49). From Shalch's map of 1824 we may note the Oriental Library on the left corner of Fraser's view and St Andrew's Library opposite. Both were booksellers rather than libraries. Thacker, later Thacker, Spink & Company, was first established in the St Andrew's Library, and Colesworthy Grant's brother Harry established his Calcutta Depository in the Oriental Library.

Fraser provides us with two views of the Lall Bazaar, which was famous for its punch-houses and other places of entertainment, and which had otherwise been noticed only in one of Solvyns' etchings. From a little to the east of the junction with Mission Row, Fraser drew the view eastward down the length of the street (fig.50). The grand house dominating the composition is the house of John Palmer, the 'Prince of Merchants', which shortly after Fraser drew it was sold to the Government for a Police Station. Beyond it is the house which had served as a court for the Justices of the Peace, on the corner where the Chitpore Road comes in from the north. This is clearly the same house as that in Solvyns' view of the Lall Bazaar above (fig.36). Opposite Palmer's house (which has been rebuilt from the house shown by Solvyns) is the emporium and auction rooms now of Taylor & Company. East again was the famous Harmonic Tavern, as well as other places of entertainment, where Calcutta enjoyed itself. According to Mrs Fay 'the Harmonic was supported by a select number of gentlemen, who each in alphabetical rotation gave a concert, ball, and supper, during the cold season; I believe once a fortnight'. We have discussed the vexed question of the whereabouts of the Harmonic Tavern above, and it is clear from Schalch's map of 1824 that it cannot have been on the north side of the Lall Bazaar as there is simply no room for it; it must therefore have been east of the crossing with the Chitpore Road. As for Taylor & Company:

> The rooms themselves, as designated, prove
> Exceeding long – two hundred feet or more;
> And as, in India, colonnades we love
> A row of pillars cut their very core;
> Of every tasteful article a store,
> On tables heaped, reveal their varied charms,
> Porcelain from France and England glittering o'er

48

49

Fig.50. James Baillie Fraser, *View of the Loll Bazaar from opposite the House of John Palmer Esq*, 1819. Coloured aquatint, engraved by F C Lewis, plate 16 from Fraser's *Views of Calcutta and its Environs*, London, 1824-6; 28 × 42.5 cm.

Fig.51. James Baillie Fraser, *View of the Loll Bazaar and Portuguese Chapel from the Circular Road*, 1819. Coloured aquatint, engraved by R Havell Junr, plate 17 from Fraser's *Views of Calcutta and its Environs*, London, 1824-6; 28 × 42.5 cm.

With gold, and flowered patterns, call to arms
Th'extravagant, and even Prudence, self alarms ...
And from the ceilings droop stupendous lustres,
And girandoles and chandeliers, that vie
With wall shades stuck around in sparkling clusters,
Which Doorga, often, for her annual nautches musters ...
Here rich gilt, bronze, and di'mond cut epargnes,
And alabaster vases, meet Tom's view,
With plated dinner sets, and silver urns,
And strings of pearls, and shawls of splendid hue,
Boots, shoes, and cotton stockings, silks and laces,
Toys, walking sticks, and vermicelli too,
Milroy's neat hunting saddles — cues, and maces,
Preserves, pale ale, and hams, and jockey caps for races.

We are given a graphic description of the business of John Palmer at this time soon after the ending of the Company's trading monopoly to Europe in 1813, in the memoirs of William Prinsep, who was sent out to establish the Calcutta end of a raw silk business in 1817, using the firm of Cruttenden, McKillop & Company as a base. In 1819, Prinsep was asked by John Palmer to become a junior partner in the firm. 'Among my mercantile introductions, extending to the Alexanders, Colvins, and others I must not omit to mention the house of John Palmer in Loll Bazaar. He was the leader of that circle and called the Prince of Merchants from his unbounded liberality, amiability and wealth. He had married a very handsome woman of an Armenian cast of countenance of the name of Hampton. His house was always open and a dinner table for nearly 20 always spread and nearly always filled. No stranger arrived then in Calcutta without dining there as a thing of course ... I found that the firm possessed 16 ships actively employed to all parts of the world, particularly to Mauritius, China, America, Java, Sydney and the Cape of Good Hope, besides the regular trading to England and back. The ships' accounts kept by their Captains whom Palmer had in most cases made part owners had to be closely scrutinised for I found scarcely one honest man among them whose object was to hoodwink Palmer and keep whatever profit could be made by their voyage to themselves ... The correspondence with the agents who received and reloaded each of these ships at their various ports at once fell upon myself in addition to the daily correspondence with planters in the Mofussil of cotton, indigo, silk, coffee, piece goods, etc., etc., all requiring advances from such productions and each man seeking to overdraw his estimates. These came to examination, sale and shipment of the produce sent down, besides the receiving and attending to the wants of foreign supercargoes who were consigned to the house chiefly from America and France. Some faint idea may therefore be formed of the whirl I found myself in ... All the funds of both services passed through the hands of the six great agency houses. We were the investors for all funded properties and executors to all estates — in fact the only bankers except the Govt. Bank of Bengal, the business of which was limited to its small issue extending no further than the environs of the city itself. Not till many years afterwards was the credit of the Govt. sufficiently established to extend any issue into the provinces.'

Fraser then moved to the other end of the Lall Bazaar, which as one moved eastwards was named Bow Bazaar and sometimes Boytaconnah Street. At its eastern end, where it joined the Circular Road stood a Catholic church, with its northern façade on Bow Bazaar (fig.51). The Circular Road runs across the picture, while the tracks sweeping round from the left are those of carts heading eastwards to the Salt Water Lake. This is the church of Our Lady of Doris, begun in June 1809 and consecrated a year later, built by the munificence of Mrs Gracia Elizabeth. Bishop Heber comments on the Bow Bazaar church in November 1823: 'The Portuguese are numerous, and have two large churches here. The one I have seen, which is not however the largest of the two, is very handsome, exactly like the Roman Catholic churches of Europe, and as being something more obscure and shadowy in its interior, is both more solemn and better adapted to the climate than the Protestant places of worship.' None of the sets of views shows the principal Catholic or 'Portuguese' cathedral dedicated to the Virgin Mary of the Rosary, on the site of the old Portuguese church which was as we have seen first

50

51

Fig.52. James Baillie Fraser, *View of St John's Cathedral*, 1819. Coloured aquatint, engraved by F C Lewis, plate 19 from Fraser's *Views of Calcutta and its Environs*, London, 1824-6; 28 × 42.5 cm.

built in 1700 on the northern boundary of the European settlement. The new cathedral was built between 1797 and 1799 largely through the munificence of the banker Joseph Barretto, of the principal Portuguese family in Calcutta. The architect was Thomas Driver. It was aligned north-south, unlike the earlier church, and was built in a classical style rather like St John's, with a Doric portico at the south end and a spire at the north. The latter has long since fallen, and the south end has been remodelled in a more Iberian manner with cupolas.

Returning to the area south-west of Tank Square, Fraser has provided us with a new view from the north-east gateway on Council House Street of St John's, which has now become the cathedral of Calcutta (fig.52). Calcutta had been elevated to the dignity of a see in 1814. The first bishop was T F Middleton from 1814 until his death in 1822, when he was succeeded by the much loved Bishop Reginald Heber. Here is a lively view of the cathedral with a service going on inside and the conveyances and bearers of the worshippers outside. The variety of equipages used for conveyance to church is remarked upon by many visitors, and Fraser shows us sedan chairs and box palanquins as well as carriages and horses. In order to spare worshippers arriving by palanquin the climb up the steps to the door under the east portico, a ramp has been built, which sweeps round from near the south-east gateway, up to the level of the portico, and down again towards the north-east gateway. A palanquin is here being carried up it. The ramp must have been part of the improvements made in 1811-12, when in order to increase the interior space, the eastern vestibules and staircases were done away with, the apse behind the main altar squared, and new staircases for the galleries constructed at the west end. The order of the interior columns was changed from plain Doric to Corinthian, and new doors were provided in the east wall. The present colonnades on the north and south façades, the latter of which shields the windows from the sun and reduces the glare in the interior, were erected shortly after this view was taken, in 1823-4. They are often generally but erroneously stated to have been erected during the improvements of 1811 during Lord Minto's time. Further alterations to St John's include the transfer of the main entrance to the west end, with the addition of a palanquin ramp and a carriage porch, alterations already present in a photograph by Fiebig taken in 1851, and the further remodelling of the east end

Fig.53. James Baillie Fraser, *A View of the Town Hall*, 1819. Coloured aquatint, engraved by R Havell Junr, plate 11 from Fraser's *Views of Calcutta and its Environs*, London, 1824-6; 28 × 42.5 cm.

with a larger chancel, and a new apse for the altar constructed in the eastern portico. To the right of the cathedral in Fraser's view, we have our first sight of the monument, a pavilion of twelve pillars, to those who fell in the second Rohilla campaign of 1794. All the grand mausoleums and obelisks which may be seen in the Daniells' view of St John's have been swept away.

We can now deal with the buildings on, and streets running into, Esplanade Row. Starting at the west end, Fraser has a view of Chandpaul Ghaut where Esplanade Row meets the river, a closer view than the Moffat one of 1805. Still at this time the principal landing place for dignatories arriving in Calcutta, it is fast growing squalid, largely owing to the presence of a tank. Another of Fraser's views is along Esplanade Row, taken from this tank, showing the Supreme Court, the new Town Hall and Government House in succession. Fraser devotes a separate plate to the Town Hall (fig.53). The Old Court House in Tank Square had been used as a place of public entertainment, but its demolition in 1792 left Calcutta without any grand halls for public suppers or dances. It was resolved in February 1804 to erect a Town Hall for this purpose, and a lottery was proposed to raise the money. It was apparently already designed (by Colonel John Garstin of the Engineers) before Wellesley left Calcutta in 1805, but it was not completed until 1813 under Lord Minto. It occupies the site of the houses which were William Hickey's neighbours in 1789, those formerly occupied by the Supreme Court Justice John Hyde and the advocate William Dunkin. Beyond the Town Hall are Hickey's rebuilt house which he moved into in 1790, which Schalch tells us in 1824 was the Salt and Opium Department of Government, next the Treasury building and then Government House.

Tom Raw has much fun at the expense of the Town Hall's architecture:

... — that far-famed hall,
In which there of Graecia's school the traces,
But by its cracking predisposed to fall,
Till patched up, and well tried by many a festive ball.

A grand room with a double row of columns running the length of the upper storey ('how close they're jammed together' cries Tom Raw) was used for entertaining, and one of D'Oyly's amusing pictures for *Tom Raw* shows a ball in full swing:

> Against the rules of architect'ral art,
> The beams were all beneath the columns set,
> So that, when dancers danced, – with all their heart,
> They levers formed that did but bruise and fret,
> And crack the tough supports – and though displaced,
> When pillars bulged, and their foundations gave,
> And the great builder – (not to be disgraced,)
> Commenced anew, – folks still were heard to rave,
> And shunned its tottering walls, as one would shun the grave.
> Till, forced by splendid public fêtes – (no room
> Elsewhere), to venture its stability,
> Eight or nine hundred people risked their doom,
> And found – though much surprised – it's capability;
> And after that – they owned it shewed ability
> To bear their weight.

Garstin had to bear the cost himself of much of the reconstruction. William Prinsep describes the sort of entertainments that were put on there: '13 Dec. 1819. A great ball was given in the Townhall on the occasion of Lady Hastings' return to Calcutta from England with several young ladies under her charge. It was to be a fancy dress ball, and we [himself and his brother James, newly arrived in Calcutta] were both on the decorative committee. It was to be done regardless of expense. Between each pillar a shield was suspended by wreaths of evergreens with the name of some Indian victory on it. The ceiling was made to represent the interior of a tent by the tinted muslin festooned from the centre to the capitals of the pillars. At one end was a splendid tent of open drapery looped on to a group of tilting lances and a shield with the armorial bearings of the Loudoun and Moira arms. At the other end under the orchestra we made with the cheap white muslin of the country a temple to Hymen with fluted columns looking just like a Doric peristyle with flowers at the capitals, the only colour about it. It had a most elegant light appearance.'

Fraser devotes three plates to Government House, all of them along its eastern side. A view from the north-east, taken from the premises of Johnson & Company in Old Court House Street, shows the north front and the northern wings crowned with the Company's coat-of-arms (fig.54). Clearly the Governor-General Lord Hastings is about to set off for a drive, as his carriage and bodyguard await him. Here we can appreciate the layout of the grounds, surrounded by an iron railing upon a plinth interrupted by four triumphal gateways at both ends of the carriageways running across the north and south façades of the building. Beyond the far gateway of Government House, we can see part of the Treasury building in Council House Street, and the east wall of the Town Hall. Loudoun Buildings, named after the Marchioness of Hastings, who was Countess of Loudoun in her own right, was built shortly afterwards on the west side of Council House Street facing the north compound of Government House. The view from the eastwards shows one of these gateways in all its magnificence, the main arch crowned by a lion and the side gates by sphinxes, while in front passes Lord Hastings' carriage procession, preceded by his silver-stick and mace bearers and followed by members of his bodyguard (plate 15). The view up Old Court House Street, closed by St Andrew's at the further end, although not totally successful, as the perspective distorts the right-angle relationship between the south front of Government House and Old Court House Street, renders this same south-eastern gateway a veritable Roman triumphal archway (plate 16). Both these latter views show the more temporary nature of the balustrade round the southern compound commencing at the two southern gateways. The solemn adjutant-birds, standing stiffly to attention in their accustomed places, add to the picturesqueness of the scenes.

One of Fraser's most successful pictures is in a part of the Indian city which verged on the

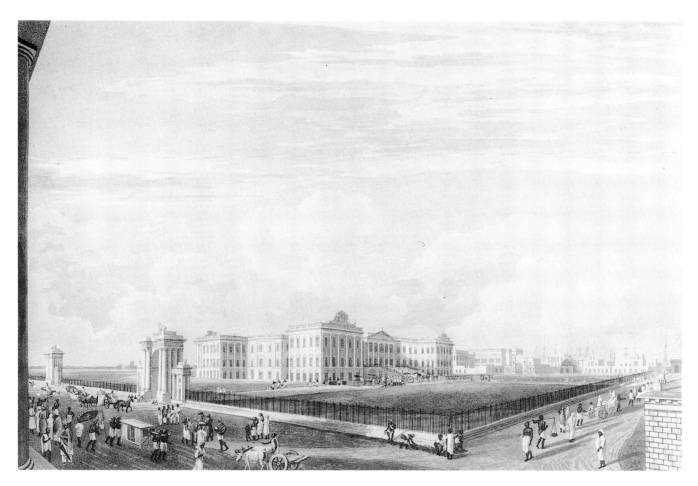

European area, in what he calls the view in the bazaar leading to the Chitpore Road (plate 17). At the east end of Esplanade Row, the European quarter continued if one turned at right-angles southwards down the Chowringhee Road. However, if one turned left up Cossitollah Street (named from its being the butchers' quarter originally), one began to enter the Indian city, and especially so when this road crossed the Lall Bazaar and became the Chitpore Road. It is not absolutely clear whether this view is of Cossitollah Street (which subsequently was renamed Bentinck Street) or the lower part of the Chitpore Road after crossing the Lall Bazaar. The street exhibits a bewildering mix of Indian and decaying Palladian architecture, but is very obviously a bazaar. Cossitollah Street itself had in it a large number of purely European businesses.

Finally from Fraser's set we shall deal with two of his lovely views including the river. One is taken from Shalimar Point opposite Kidderpore, where the river bends round to the west (plate 18). Here Colonel Robert Kyd, who persuaded the Company in 1786 to establish the great Botanic Gardens just downriver at Sibpur, and who became their first Superintendent, built his famous domed house called Shalimar. Hickey tells us that Shalimar had been sold by Kyd's son Colonel Alexander Kyd to Saadat Ali Khan, the brother of Asaf ad-Daula, the Nawab Vizier of Oudh, but who lived much at Calcutta, and who promised to return the house free of all charge to Colonel Kyd should he ever succeed to the throne of Oudh. When, contrary to all expectation, he did so in January 1798, he gave the house back to its purchaser, much to Kyd's surprise. The house figures in one of Moffat's views of the river of 1798, and also in one of D'Oyly's (see fig. 77). From here Fort William occupies the centre of the composition with the buildings of Esplanade Row and Chowringhee Road spread around it. And having followed the bend of the river round to the west and come up to the Botanic Gardens, we find the same view looking back upriver which Moffat had also engraved in 1798 of the Botanic Garden House on the left and the palatial country residences of Garden Reach on the right (plate 19). The house was the residence of the Superintendent of the Gardens, built in 1795 by Kyd's successor, the great botanist Dr Roxburgh.

James Fraser was also working in oils during his time in Calcutta. There are references in his

Fig.54. James Baillie Fraser, *A View of Government House from the Court House Street*, 1819. Coloured aquatint, engraved by R Havell Junr, plate 9 from Fraser's *Views of Calcutta and its Environs*, London, 1824-6; 28 × 42.5 cm.

diaries for 1819 to his submitting his oils to Chinnery for criticism, while the list of the contents of his trunks which he sent to his father on 26 March 1820 states: 'The small case contains several oil pictures, all painted by myself.' In the actual letter he writes that 'only the Calcutta view is fit for anything'. An unsigned view looking up Old Court House Street towards St Andrew's is almost certainly this Calcutta view in oils which Fraser refers to in his letter (plate 20). Two similar views looking towards the church of St Andrew occur in Fraser's published views, one from within Tank Square (plate 14), and the other from outside the south-east gate of Government House (plate 16). This view in oils is taken from an intermediate standpoint, north-east of the Government House enclosure, outside the entrance in Old Court House Street to the stables, cook-house and other out-buildings of Government House, which are the walls looming up on the left of the picture. On the right is a series of banks, auction houses, and shops. The triangular composition, the colouring, and the busy detail exactly complement Fraser's published views. The animated life of the city is similar in painting and prints, with their *bihishti* (water-carriers) based on Chinnery's prototypes, multitudinous methods of transport, and endless numbers of adjutant birds, although here their scavenging is carried further than with the more sedate birds in the engravings.

Of the greatest use in the study of Calcutta topography in the early 1820s is the plan of Calcutta drawn in 1824 by J A Schalch for the Committee of Improvements, of which the original version was sent to the Court of Directors. This immense work, the most detailed survey undertaken of the city since Wood's survey of 1784-6, is on the scale of 132 feet to the inch, and shows all the individual buildings in the city, many of which have their occupiers or functions noted. Lord Wellesley had set in motion various schemes for the improving of the city, of which the most important was the metalling of the Circular Road round the east and north of the city, as well as other schemes for the improvements of drains. Public hygiene was of course appalling, but probably no worse than in European cities of the time, except that the climate made the lack of it infinitely more dangerous. An Improvement Committee was set up, and devised numerous schemes, which only gradually were carried out during the periods of Lords Minto and Hastings, with much of the money raised from lotteries organised by the Lottery Committee. The church of St John and the Town Hall had been constructed with the proceeds of such lotteries, and during the next 20 years numerous roads were laid out or straightened and tanks dug. The Salt Lake was drained by a canal which was cut round the east and north of Calcutta falling into the Hooghly at Chitpore, and this Circular Canal also took much of the city's drainage. As D'Oyly puts it in *Tom Raw*:

> Here we might moralize on public lotteries,
> And wail the gambling spirit of the times,
> But, when we think the upshot of the matter is
> To clear Calcutta from unwholesome slimes,
> By making drains – important in these climes,
> And other works that cost so many lacks,
> We waive the playful impulse of our rhymes.

Schalch's map of 1824 shows many more new roads made since Upjohn's map of 1794. The most important of these was a long north-south road east of the Chitpore-Chowringhee Road axis which was named College Street-Wellington Street-Wellesley Street-Wood Street, linking the north-east and south-east portions of the city. College Street was later extended further north under the name of Cornwallis Street. Three squares with central tanks were laid out on this line: College Square, where the Hindoo College was built in 1824, Wellington Square, where this new axis crossed Dhurrumtollah Street, and Wellesley Square, where the Madrassah founded by Warren Hastings was moved in 1827. To the east of Wood Street a whole new quarter was laid out with street names derived from the various titles of Lord Hastings and his wife. The Strand, the road along the river front, had also been constructed from Chandpaul Ghaut northwards, thus beginning Lord Wellesley's great scheme for the embankment of the river. The plan with all its inscriptions was engraved the following year in Calcutta by E de la Combe, with the additions of more of the southern suburbs as well as Garden Reach.

In 1823 Bishop Reginald Heber arrived in Calcutta, and his *Narrative* gives us some interesting pictures and impressions of the city. After the by now familiar encomiums on the approach to the Fort and the city, he opines that the view from the Esplanade was 'so like some parts of Petersburgh, that it was hardly possible for me to fancy myself any where else. No native dwellings are visible from this quarter, except one extensive but ruinous bazaar, which occupies the angle where Calcutta and Chowringhee join. Behind the esplanade, however, are only Tank-square, and some other streets occupied by Europeans, – the Durrumtollah and Cossitollah are pretty equally divided between the different nations, and all the west [north] is a vast town, composed of narrow crooked streets, brick bazaars, bamboo huts, and here and there the immense convent-like mansions of some of the more wealthy 'Baboos' (the name of the native Hindoo gentleman, answering to our Esquire) or Indian merchants and bankers... I was introduced to Lord Amherst; and afterwards went to the Cathedral, where I was installed. This is a very pretty building, all but the spire, which is short and clumsy. The whole composition, indeed, of the Church is full of architectural blunders, but it is still in other respects handsome. The inside is elegant, paved with marble, and furnished with very large and handsome glass chandeliers, the gift of Mr M'Clintoch, with a light pulpit, with chairs on one side of the chancel for the Governor-General and his family, and on the other for the Bishop and Archdeacon... Calcutta stands on an almost perfect level of alluvial and marshy ground, which a century ago was covered with jungle and stagnant pools, and which still almost every where betrays its unsoundness by the cracks conspicuous in the best houses. To the East, at the distance of four miles and a half, is a large but shallow lagoon of salt water, being the termination of the Sunderbunds, from which a canal is cut pretty nearly to the town, and towards which all the drainings of the city flow, what little difference of level there is, being in favour of the banks of the river.'

Bishop Reginald Heber. Painted by Thomas Phillips, 1822. India Office Library, F 97.

Lord Amherst had succeeded Lord Hastings in 1823. He and his wife, the widow of the fifth Earl of Plymouth, took two of their children with them to India, Jeffrey, their eldest son, as Military Secretary and ADC , who died at Barrackpore, and Sarah Elizabeth. The latter was already an artist of some accomplishment, and obviously took lessons from Chinnery until he fled to China in 1825. To her brother still in England she sent in August 1824 five drawings with descriptive notes of the layout of Government House and its gardens. The Amhersts were the first occupants of Government House to attempt to create any kind of a garden in its spacious compound. On the west side was laid out a flower-garden of which 'one part resembles the parterre before the conservatory at Oakly Park [the seat of the Earls of Plymouth]. This is on Mama's side and the beds are full of beautiful shrubs and flowers and creepers raised on bamboo baskets. On Papa's side there are larger flowering shrubs dotted about on the grass, and in front [that is, the north side] large clumps... On the south side of the house, the circle only is planted and the large field of grass left untouched, and beyond it we look over a fine plain of grass enlivened with numerous flocks of cattle to the Fort and the river on the right, and the whole of Chowringhee to the left... The handsomest part of Calcutta lies on the Govt. House side of the town, and along the banks of the river, where several public buildings are erecting and a new wide road and embankment making. The bazar streets are all composed of the low native huts, and are mostly narrow, dirty and very crowded. There are neither trottoirs nor pavement in the streets, and the road is made of bricks broken small, the only material in this part of the world for roadmaking. Tanks or reservoirs of water occur in every part of the town, and are filled by the rain, so that all drinking water is purified by artificial means, but it is extremely good and tasteful.'

Sarah Amherst's drawing of the south side of Government House (fig.55) is she tells us 'copied from the view in Mrs. Graham's book... The wing No. 1 [S E] contains Papa's sitting rooms and a dressing room, which saves him the trouble of going upstairs at dinner time. Above are spare rooms for visitors. The breakfast and tiffin room is the gallery under the circular veranda, and the same gallery upstairs serves as a ballroom when there are private parties. We dine in the large Marble Hall. The wing No.2 [S W] contains Mama's sitting rooms and above stairs under the veranda his and Mama's bedrooms. The 5 windows in shade are my bedroom [facing westwards]... Wing No.3 [N W] is the other side of Dr. and Mrs. Abel's rooms [the Amhersts' physician] and Jeff's underneath on the same floor with Edward

[Hale, the Private Secretary]. The stone posts and chains have been put up since our arrival, before there were only old decayed wooden ones, also the balustrade round the compound has been added. The posts come from a place called Chunar some hundred miles up the country, as there is not a bit of stone, not a pebble down here. For the same reason all the ornaments of architecture are done either in brick or cast in chunam, and the balustrade so much in use and which makes such a handsome appearance, is only pottery, washed over with chunam. The grasscutters inserted in the foreground have enough to do at this season of the year, when the grass sprouts faster than they can mow it. When cut, they scratch it up together with their hands, tie it in tall bundles, and carry it away on their heads. On the southern or Britannia's side of the house, the wings are surmounted by the King's arms, but to the front they are the Company's. The colour of the building is a lightish yellow and the venetians are painted green.'

The circular bed already existed in 1810, as it occurs in the view by Mrs Graham which Sarah Amherst copied. The stone posts running across the south and north fronts of the house replaced in 1823 the earlier wooden ones seen in Mrs Graham's view. The plastered balustrade around the southern compound replaced the wooden palings and chain seen in Fraser's view of the south-east gateway (see plates 15-16). The dome on this side was renewed in 1824 and the figure of Britannia (or Minerva, it seems unclear which) placed on top of it – this is the first known view of it. It aroused D'Oyly's mirth:

'Twas first suggested that a marble hero,
Sculptured by Bacon, should be placed to serve as
A vertex; but somebody, seeing clearer,
Thought it might fall, and cried, 'the Lord preserve us!'
So Pallas came – in wood – the clumsiest of Minervas.

The 'marble hero' is the colossal statue of Lord Cornwallis by John Bacon in the Town Hall.

The most entertaining of Sarah Amherst's views is taken across the north front of Government House (fig.56), looking towards the Council Chamber on the first floor of the north-east wing, showing the pomp which attended every moment of her parents' movements. 'It is not customary for anyone to go down the great steps but the Governor General and his family, and this is supposed to be evening, when His Lordship and Her Ladyship, the first ADC and Mily Secy, with your humble friend the artist, attended by the two ADCs in waiting, are going to take the air. His L. ship's and Her ladyship's two head servants, the Nazer and Jemadar are following them, and the rest of the Swarry or retinue, who have preceded them carrying silver sticks and clubs, have arranged themselves on the steps for them to pass between down to the carriage. The buggy behind is for the ADCs. A small detachment of the Body Guard is drawn up and carrying arms, two troopers precede the carriage and the rest follow. The foot guard are presenting arms, and the drummer and fifes playing a wretched imitation of the Grenadiers' March, with which they salute our ears whenever we go out or return home and generally frighten some of the horses, as you will see portrayed. The area before the house is quite filled at airing time with buggies and horses, but I have only inserted a few to avoid confusion; it is the custom to have all the vehicles and horses in readiness that their masters may take their choice. When we are fairly underweigh and through the gateway, which is in sight, we turn to the right to go to the Course.' We obtain a glimpse here of the layout of the 'large clumps' in front of the house, an extraordinary arrangement of circular flower beds at regular intervals, which are seen more clearly in her view of the north front.

She continues with one of the best of the many descriptions of the Adjutant birds, which we have seen almost dominating Fraser's views: 'The large birds on the top of the house are called Adjutants, most huge clumsy creatures but rather ornamental than not to Govt. House as they arrange themselves like statues at regular distances on the balustrade and on the most conspicuous points of the building, and remain motionless for hours in a musing posture. They have a long bag which they can contract or dilate at pleasure, but they do not use it for provisions or any particular purpose. They are so useful as scavengers that there is a fine for killing them, however in the Fort where they abound, the young Cadets play them sad tricks, such as throwing out a leg of mutton tied to a large stone, so that when the Adjutant has

55

56

Fig.57. Lady Sarah Elizabeth
Amherst, View across the south
front of Government House
towards Chowringhee Road, 1824.
Pen-and-sepia ink; 20.5 × 32 cm.
India Office Library WD 3904.

gobbled it up, he finds himself anchored – putting out meat smeared all over with mustard and
pepper – and there is a story in the house that to satisfy Lord Hastings' own eyes, a calf's leg
with an iron shoe on the hoof was thrown out and immediately swallowed whole by an
Adjutant, they are so greedy. The buildings outside the iron railing are part of the town of
Calcutta, the large house is a great warehouse and shop [Messrs Croll and Collier according to
Schalch's map], and to the left of it is the end of the range, which are the godowns or offices of
Govt. House, the cook house, etc.'

Wellesley had instituted his great love of ceremony into the routine of his new palace, with
bodyguards, silver-stick bearers, club-bearers, fan-wavers and the like, attendant syces or
grooms, and sentries everywhere. His successors Cornwallis and Minto could not bear any of
this, but the ceremonial returned with Hastings and Amherst. Lord and Lady Hastings tried to
introduce a rigid etiquette and formality 'probably modelled on that of the Castle at Dublin' as
William Palmer complained in a letter to Warren Hastings, while Emma Roberts tells us in her
Scenes and Characteristics of Hindostan, that Lady Hastings had tried to introduce court plumes.
The consequence was 'a dearth of ostrich feathers, the whole of the supply being speedily
bought up; and as it was not considered allowable to substitute native products, there was no
alternative but to remain at home'. Lord Amherst, we learn from Henry Thoby Prinsep, 'never
moved from one room of Government House to another without a long train of *chobdars* (*ie*
servants with silver maces) preceding him. When he rode out with Lady Amherst, it was a rule
that she should never advance beyond his horse's quarters; and in all things he required similar
formal observances'. With Amherst's successor, Lord William Bentinck, Governor-General
1828-35, there is a return to the hatred of ceremonial of Cornwallis' time. Indeed, Bentinck
tried to open up rigid, caste-bound, British Calcutta, by inviting to formal occasions at
Government House the leaders of Bengali society. Emma Roberts tells us amusingly of the
resulting misunderstandings of conventions, but the tone of Calcutta society about these
things had long been carved in marble: 'The extreme horror which European ladies entertained of appearing to imitate the natives, banished gold and silver from their robes: not
contented with the difference in the fashion of their garments, they refused to wear any
articles of Indian manufacture, careless of the mean effect produced by their fastidiousness . . .
to avoid the appellation of *nautch girls*.'

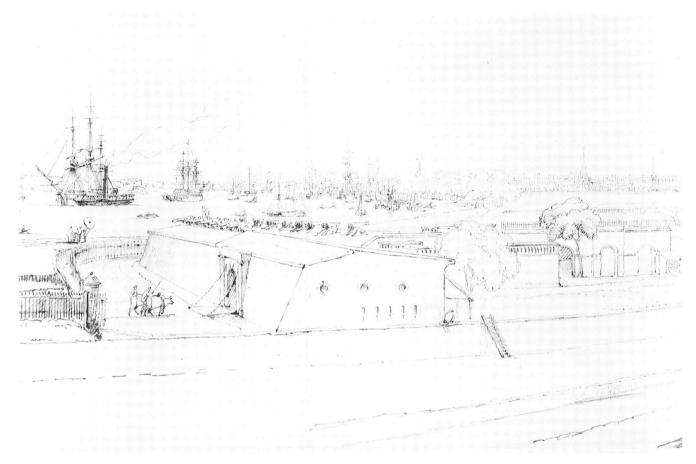

Sarah Amherst tells us more about the south garden (fig.57) in her 'View from our wing of Papa's, with his veranda and part of the dome and veranda of the breakfast room. As this is the private side of the house, there are but few people who have the entrée, a privilege worth having on gala nights – such are the Chief Justice, Members of Council and the Bishop. The circle which is planted with flowers and shrubs, has in the centre a beautiful square basin of white marble from Agra [from the Imperial Baths of Shah Jahan, removed in 1815 by Lord Hastings], and was intended for a fountain, but owing to the muddiness of the river water and the difficulty of raising it, the plan was never accomplished. Therefore since our arrival there have been two arches of iron made to spring from the angles and meet at the top and with creepers planted at the foot it has a very pretty effect. In the distance is part of Chowringhee, which extends a great way further. The house marked No. 1 below it [the left one of the two large ones in the centre, noted by Schalch as the Secret and Political Department] is the ADCs as none of them sleep in the house, there is room for six, the full ADCs, the working ones, the extras and honorarys have mostly houses of their own.' The Amhersts' garden did not survive their departure. As Emily Eden puts it in one of her letters, when writing about her own horticultural attempts, 'Lady Amherst made a magnificent garden round the house ... Lady William Bentinck said flowers were very unwholesome, and had everything rooted out the first week'. Even the circular bed outside the south front did not survive, as it is absent from later views of this side of the house.

We have already met William Prinsep before, in the context of his memoirs, but he was also one of the talented artists surrounding Charles D'Oyly and a pupil of George Chinnery. Among the earliest of his drawings are some albums in the India Office Library of the period 1823-4, depicting among other things the sort of fancy dress balls and amateur theatricals which amused Calcutta society. His earliest topographical drawings are slightly later. A sketch of the view northwards taken in 1828 from the Flagstaff Bastion of Fort William (fig.58) shows the river with on it the steam-tug *Emulous* (sent to Calcutta in 1825 to pull the ships up and down the river) and the ship *Victory*, commanded, so Prinsep's memoirs tell us, by his friend Captain Farquharson. Beside Chandpaul Ghaut is the steam engine, recently installed to pump up water from the river. The *Bengal Hurkaru* of 4 November 1822 tells us that 'on Friday evening about sunset the beautiful steam engine erected at Chandpaul Ghaut for watering the

Fig.58. William Prinsep, Calcutta from Water gate of the Fort William, 1828 (detail). Pencil and pen-and-ink; 23 × 66.5 cm. India Office Library WD 3862.

Fig.59. William Prinsep, Interior of the Arsenal in Fort William, *c.*1830. Pencil, pen-and-ink, and grey wash; 33.5 × 23 cm. India Office Library WD 3860.

The interior of the ARSENAL *Fort William*

streets of Calcutta was put in motion for the first time'. Small masonry aqueducts conveyed the water as far as Park Street (these are visible in fig.80).

Two interior views made by Prinsep about this time are of great interest. His drawing of the interior of the Arsenal in Fort William (fig.59) recalls the inscription over its door: 'Anno Domini 1777. These arms were arranged by order and under the auspices of the Honourable Warren Hastings, Esquire, Governor-General.' Even more interesting is his drawing of the interior of the Chowringhee Theatre, which stood on the corner of Theatre Street and the lower Chowringhee Road (fig.60). It was the principal such place in Calcutta after the closure of the Theatre in Lyon's Range, and was in operation from 1813 until it was destroyed by fire in 1839. The female parts were by this time taken by professional actresses, but those of the men by amateurs, of whom William Prinsep was a prominent example. His memoirs describe his theatrical work in some detail, both as an actor and as a set designer: 'Being myself particularly fond of everything connected with the stage, I was soon enrolled among the dramatis personae, and hard at work in leisure hours in painting scenes and devising costumes,

all the west rows of benches

which being made entirely by native tailors had to be most particularly designed. From that time until the Chowringhee Theatre met the fate of all theatres and was totally destroyed by fire, I was more or less connected with Parker in the stage management as well as the performances, my line being of course comic and in musical representations ... The theatre was a proprietory one, each member, comprising nearly the whole of our society having of course free entrance, and therefore the money taken at the door for performances only once a fortnight never covered the expenses and we were consequently obliged to have frequent recourse to house benefits which deprived the proprietors of their free entrances.'

In 1836 Prinsep was engaged in remodelling the theatre, particularly the ill-contrived stage and scenic arrangements, while a new roof was put on the whole building. This may be the state of the theatre as reflected in this drawing. The inscription states that the theatre holds about 800 persons in the boxes and about 200 in the pit, while the stage is set for the last scene of Prinsep's own set for the play *Blind Boy*. His memoirs also give us insight into the running of the theatre: 'About this time the proprietors of our theatre became so discontented with the ruinous state of their affairs, our expenses being always in excess of our receipts with scarcely one play a week, that they tried to introduce a new system and place legal restraint over us directors, but in vain. If they would have the benefit of our hard work as managers, they must pay the cost whatever it was. The controversy ended in each manager agreeing to get up a favourite play according to his own views and selection of performers for the benefit of the house, the shareholders forfeiting their right of entry for the night ... The returns from my own selection of 'Bluebeard' got up with great splendour were four times larger than the largest yield from the best of the other managers' selections which had only netted 700Rs. The house was so full to see my tamasha that I repeated the performance with equal success and netted 3700Rs! Parker was my Abimeleck and Horace Wilson my Ibrahim, very much to his dislike, but I must mention a little instance of the wonderful energy of this learned professor. I had designed a wonderful march of the Turkish army over the mountains with different sized figures made of pith and painted by an ingenious workman whom I had often

Fig.61. Thomas Prinsep, The
Circular Road, 1826-7. Watercolour;
23 × 33 cm. India Office Library
WD 4192.

Fig.62. Thomas Prinsep, The
steamer *Hooghly* on the river
Ganges, September-October, 1828.
Watercolour; 10 × 14.5 cm. India
Office Library WD 4194.

employed to make masks and other things. He had never failed me and I felt sure of his bringing the whole apparatus in good time. I had set the scenery with great care – the house was crammed – the well known overture was playing but no army appeared – I was in despair and my friend Ibrahim said with a kind of sneer 'Prinsep! You always undertake too much' when in walked my man with 50 coolies carrying my precious battalions on the ends of bamboos to hold behind the art mountains, but alas they were all British soldiers in black hats. We declared this would never do, we sent a gentleman round to the pit to encore the overture, and in that short space of time all the white muslin in the wardrobe belonging to Pizarro's Virgin of the Sun was torn into shreds and made into turbans round their black hats at the professor's suggestion, he himself being the most active in the work. We were amply rewarded by uproarious applause at the beauty of the effect. Our nearest row on the slopes were small Bengalee boys dressed to match our puppets.' Although Prinsep describes this under 1837, in fact Horace Hayman Wilson, the most learned English orientalist in Calcutta at the time and Assay Master of the Mint, and also an accomplished amateur actor, left Calcutta in 1832 for the chair of Sanskrit at Oxford.

William's brother Thomas Prinsep was also present in Calcutta during much of the 1820s. He was the eighth son of John Prinsep and was sent to Addiscombe, the Company's Military Seminary, where he was taught drawing by T H Fielding. Having joined the Bengal Engineers in Calcutta in 1818, he was employed principally on the cutting of canals, and after service in Lord Amherst's war with Burma in 1824 and convalescence at Penang, he was appointed Schalch's successor as Superintendent of Canals in 1826. He was killed in a riding accident in January 1830. A group of his drawings show us various new developments in the city. He was the most talented artist of all the Prinsep brothers, and generally was able to keep free of Chinnery's too pervasive influence, although his unfinished drawing of the Circular Road does in fact still show considerable influence from this source, suggesting a date of about 1826 (fig.61). More characteristic is his lovely watercolour of the Salt Water Lake, about 1827 or 1828, with the city in the extreme distance (plate 21). William Prinsep's memoirs tell us that in 1827, after his brother had unsuccefully proposed to his (William's) sister-in-law, 'he left us in miserable plight to bury himself in the unhealthy employment they had given him of cutting a canal through the Salt Water Lake east of Calcutta, which would improve the navigation and create bunds for keeping the salt water off the neighbouring lands.'

One of Thomas Prinsep's most interesting watercolours shows a steamer on the river Ganges (fig.62). This is from an album including 13 watercolours recording a memorable voyage which Prinsep undertook in 1828. Lord William Bentinck wanted to discover whether steam navigation with paddle-steamers was practicable on the Ganges, in order to cut down the enormous time spent travelling up-country. He arranged an experimental voyage upriver under Captain Johnston using the *Hooghly*, a Calcutta-built wooden paddle-steamer, with a 25 hp steam engine imported from England. It was of course the enormous strength of the Ganges' current which was the principal obstacle, and the rapid transit made by the steamer demonstrated that it could be overcome, for the round voyage of 1000 miles to Allahabad took less than six weeks, compared with the usual three months to get up to Allahabad alone. His brother William noted that 'Tom made a series of most beautiful drawings of the Ganges during the voyage portraying the peculiar colour of the water during the season and the lovely effects of blues over the picturesque fleets of native boats making their slow way against the fierce current'.

The Strand Road north from Chandpaul Ghaut was laid out in the 1820s, reclaiming much land from the river. The old Mint, which was situated on the river between Hastings and Hare Streets, was moved to its new quarters between the northern end of Clive Street and the Strand in 1831, in a building with a Doric portico designed by Major W N Forbes of the Engineers. William Prinsep's memoirs describe, in a letter to his brother James in Benares, the laying of the foundations by Forbes in October 1823. James was the Master of the Benares Mint, and had hopes of succeeding Horace Wilson as Assay Master of the Calcutta Mint. This in fact he eventually did. It was here that the East India Company first started to strike coins in its own name without reference to the Mughal Emperor in Delhi. Tom Prinsep's drawing shows the Mint apparently completed externally, but the drawing cannot be later than 1829

61   a mosque   An unfinished sketch by Tom of the Circular road   a police tannah
                      a hakaree   a kurranchee or hackney coach   or station for chowkeydars

62

James Prinsep. Lithograph by
Colesworthy Grant.

(plate 22). In this same year, Victor Jacquemont describes in his *Journal* his voyage upriver with the Bentincks and the appearance of the Bengali city, with the Mint in its midst, when seen from the river: 'L'aspect de Calcutta, qui s'étend 3 milles environ (une lieue) sur les bords de la rivière, est sale et laid. De misérables habitations en briques, toutes dégradées, et beaucoup de huttes en paille, mais toutes entassées les unes sur les autres, quelques chétives pagodes, deux ou trois clochers, et un seul monument européen, la nouvelle Monnaie, qui contraste étrangement par son immensité, son élégance et son air de fraîcheur, avec les ruines poudreuses et brûlantes de la cité indienne, voilà tout ce que l'on voit sur la rive gauche de l'Hougli.'

The last of this group of drawings by Tom Prinsep is of the famous temple in the Chitpore Road, the 'Black Pagoda' (plate 23). Prinsep calls it the *naubruttun*, a name derived from *navaratna*, nine jewels or pinnacles, with reference to the pinnacles on the subsidiary shrine. The huge main tower with its five pinnacles, as shown in the Daniells' view of 1787 (fig.22), had by this time fallen. The collapse took place some time between 1795 (the temple appears in the distance intact in Solvyns' *Hindoos*) and 1813, the earliest drawing of the collapsed temple so far traced, from an album in the India Office Library drawn in this year by John Elliot, Lord Minto's son and secretary.

From about 1830 comes a splendid view of the whole of Esplanade Row from the Course (plate 24), painted and signed by Shaikh Muhammad Amir of Karraya, who was the most prolific of the Calcutta artists catering for the British in the 1830s and 1840s. His studio turned out an immense number of drawings of sets of 'native types', servants, transport, houses, and animals. In this drawing, which must be one of his earliest, his vision is more personal. Among the inscriptions, the reference to the Bengal Club House serves to date this painting. The Club was founded in 1827, and by July of that year was established in Gordon's Buildings in the middle of Esplanade Row East (the large building with verandahs on three storeys), where Muhammad Amir paints it. About 1830 (the sources are by no means clear) it removed to Tank Square, to a house which had been built upon the land left vacant on the eastern side of the square in front of the Mission Church, and only subsequently did it purchase the house in Chowringhee Road formerly occupied by Macaulay. The painting cannot be earlier than 1828 because of the disappearance of the Amherst plantings in the south garden of Government House under the Bentinck regime, including the circular bed in front of the south portico. The house labelled as the Advocate-General's house, on the western side of Old Post Office Street from the Town Hall, had been until 1825 the residence of Sir Francis Macnaghten, acting Chief Justice, so Lady Sarah Amherst informs us, and was now occupied by the Advocate-General John Pearson. Victor Jacquemont stayed with Pearson when he first arrived in Calcutta in 1829 and writes of him: 'the only lawyer who ever came from England with a great reputation already established. He is ... full of sense and good humour, and a liberal ... which in English means a radical.'

Jacquemont was sent on a scientific expedition by the Muséum d'Histoire Naturelle in Paris, to investigate the natural history of India. He arrived in Calcutta not knowing a soul, but his letters of introduction which he had obtained in London quickly gave him access to all the most notable people there: 'They kept me in the first house I entered; it belonged to the advocate-general of this presidency ... The second person I saw was Lady William Bentinck. Half an hour afterwards she introduced me, without etiquette or ceremony, to her husband, and I was obliged to stay tiffin (a slight meal at half-past one) with them, and then promise to return and take a family dinner. The next day, in a hired carriage, I paid, in the town, which is immense, and in the beautiful country-houses near it, some fifteen visits at least, to judges, members of council, great people, physicians, and merchants, some of them very rich.' His first host was as we have seen the Advocate-General, John Pearson. He forsook his residence on the Esplanade to stay with one of the judges, Sir Edward Ryan, at his house in Garden Reach opposite the Botanical Gardens 'the most magnificent botanical garden in the world. I remained six weeks in his house, crossing the river every morning to have a little botany: being lord and master of this garden, the superintendent of which (a tolerably good Danish botanist [Nathaniel Wallich] with 72,000 francs a year, lodge in a superb house &c) is now in England. I was settled in the magnificent library which the Company have purchased for him;

Plate 17. James Baillie Fraser, *A View in the Bazaar leading to the Chitpore Road*, 1819. Coloured aquatint, engraved by F C Lewis, plate 24 from Fraser's *Views of Calcutta and its Environs*, London, 1824-6; 28 × 42.5 cm.

Plate 18. James Baillie Fraser, *A View of Calcutta from a Point opposite to Kidderpore*, 1819. Coloured aquatint, engraved by R Havell, plate 20 from Fraser's *Views of Calcutta and its Environs*, London, 1824-6; 28 × 42.5 cm.

Plate 19. James Baillie Fraser, *A View of the Botanic Garden House and Reach, 1819.* Coloured aquatint, engraved by R Havell Junr, plate 4 from Fraser's *Views of Calcutta and its Environs,* London, 1824-6; 28 × 42.5 cm.

Plate 20. James Baillie Fraser, *Old Court House Street,* c.1819. Oil on canvas; 58 × 84 cm. India Office Library F 851.

Plate 21. Thomas Prinsep, The Salt Water Lake, c.1827-8.
Watercolour; 17.5 × 32.5 cm. India Office Library WD 4193.

Plate 22. Thomas Prinsep, The New Mint on the Strand, c.1829.
Watercolour; 18 × 25 cm. India Office Library WD 4190.

Plate 23. Thomas Prinsep, The Chitpore Road and the 'Black Pagoda', c.1829. Watercolour; 18.5 × 22 cm. India Office Library WD 4191.

Plate 24. Shaykh Muhammad Amir, Government House and Esplanade Row from the Course, 1828-30. Watercolour; 33 × 74.5 cm. India Office Library Add. Or. 4151.

Plate 25. William Prinsep, Entertainment during the Durga puja, c.1840. Watercolour; 23 × 43.5 cm. India Office Library WD 4035.

Plate 26. William Prinsep, Prinsep's Ghaut and the Water Gate of the Fort from the river, 1841. Watercolour; 23 × 66 cm. India Office Library WD 4027.

Plate 27. Sir Charles D'Oyly, *Custom House Wharf, c.1835*. Coloured lithograph, plate 5 from his *Views of Calcutta and its Environs*, lithographed by Dickinson & Co, London, 1848; 28.5 × 41.5 cm.

Plate 28. Sir Charles D'Oyly, *Calcutta from the Old Course, c.1835*. Coloured lithograph, plate 15 from his *Views of Calcutta and its Environs*, lithographed by Dickinson & Co, London, 1848; 29 × 54 cm.

Plate 29. Sir Charles D'Oyly, *Town and Port of Calcutta, c.1835.*
Coloured lithograph, plate 6 from his *Views of Calcutta and its
Environs*, lithographed by Dickinson & Co, London, 1848; 32 × 53 cm.

Plate 30. Sir Charles D'Oyly, *Esplanade*, from Chowringhee Road,
c.1835. Coloured lithograph, plate 24 from his *Views of Calcutta and its
Environs*, lithographed by Dickinson & Co, London, 1848; 21 × 44 cm.

Plate 31. Sir Charles D'Oyly, *Chowringhee Road from No. XI Esplanade,* c.1835. Coloured lithograph, plate 26 from his *Views of Calcutta and its Environs,* lithographed by Dickinson & Co, London, 1848; 26 × 53.5 cm.

Plate 32. Sir Charles D'Oyly, *Suspension Bridge at Alipore over Tolly's Nullah,* c.1835. Coloured lithograph, plate 20 from his *Views of Calcutta and its Environs,* lithographed by Dickinson & Co, London, 1848; 30 × 41.5 cm.

and there . . . I studied the plants of India which I gathered in the garden.' Of Bentinck and his notorious hatred of pomp and cant, Jacquemont writes: 'The man who, perhaps, does most honour to Europe in Asia, is he who governs it. Lord W Bentinck, on the throne of the Great Mogul, thinks and acts like a Pennsylvanian Quaker. You may easily imagine that there are people who talk loudly of the dissolution of the empire and the world's end, when they behold the temporary ruler of Asia riding on horseback, plainly dressed, and without escort, or on his way into the country with his umbrella under his arm.'

The memoirs of William Prinsep, one of the partners in the great banking firm of Palmer & Company, written admittedly in 1870 and hence full of the benefits of hindsight, are for the years leading up to 1830 full of dire forebodings of the impending great crash. In 1824 the Burmese war opened 'creating a perfect revolution in the money market, which from a complete plethora of unemployed capital became suddenly completely bare. The houses of business [which] had been refusing to take money on deposit even at 3 percent were soon glad to offer 8 percent for it. The Govt. expenditure was so large that their treasuries were soon drained and they opened unsuccessfully at 4 percent loan followed immediately by another at 5 percent. This led to a run upon the houses to invest all loose balances, creating a most inconvenient drain, rendered the more irksome by its suddenness. I attribute to this withdrawal of very large sums from that which was in fact the working capital of the five great banking houses the chief cause of the great breakdown which followed in 1830 to 1833.' Trade was very depressed during these decades, and the house of Palmer was in great difficulties. The crash came in 1830: 'On this day [1 January] the Committee of Merchants . . . sat all day in council in the room over our office to consider whether it was possible by their joint action to stave off the much dreaded calamity. Every member of the other great houses felt that the crisis must reflect most seriously upon themselves, but only one of them all had the boldness to speak out the firm conviction of a well trained judgement. John Smith the head of the firm of Fergusson & Co of equal extent in business with our own, but with a large command of means, stood up and declared that if John Palmer's house was allowed to fall, they would all topple like a pack of cards. Such an opinion was actually hooted down by some of the others who doubtless hoped to benefit by our fall, but this prophecy was speedily fulfilled. First Alexander & Co – then Mackintosh & Co, then Colvin & Co – Fergusson & Co and lastly the smallest of the firms Cruttenden Mackillop & Co, all went through the Insolvent Court within 5 years, involving a total amount of about 12 millions sterling. We eventually paid the largest dividend of 47 percent. One of the others paid nothing – the others had large deficits.' Palmer died in January 1836: 'the bitterness of seeing and hearing of the misery caused by his great failure weighed him down crushingly . . . He was followed to the grave by the whole of Calcutta, for who had not felt, at some time of his past career, some benefit from his kind and generous heart.'

In 1833 there was published in London another extensive series of views of Calcutta, William Wood's *A Series of Twenty-eight Panoramic Views of Calcutta*. This is the first important Calcutta series where the printing process is lithography rather than engraving and aquatinting. The series has a complicated publishing history. Wood was in Calcutta from 1828, helping his brother George run the Asiatic Lithographic Press, and appears to have returned by 1831, the year noted on the earliest dated of the plates, which like most of the others was 'drawn from nature and on stone by W Wood Junr'. Wood's father appears to have been the London bookseller and publisher William Wood, who finished publishing the series in 1833. Unlike later printed and photographic panoramas, Wood's has a moving viewpoint, so that he gives an extremely accurate vista of that part of Calcutta which gave it the epithet of 'City of Palaces'. His views are contemporary with the descriptive sketches published originally in the *Asiatic Journal* by Emma Roberts, and with her description of the view from the Maidan: 'On two sides of this superb quadrangle a part of the city and the fashionable suburb of Chowringhee extend themselves. The claims to architectural beauty of the City of Palaces have been questioned, and possibly there may be numberless faults to call forth the strictures of connoisseurs, but these are lost upon the less erudite judges, who remain rapt in admiration at the magnificence of the *coup d'oeil*. The houses for the most part are either entirely detached

Fig.63. William Wood, Council House Street and Government House, *c.1830*. Lithograph, plate 3 from his *A Series of Twenty-eight Panoramic Views of Calcutta*, London, 1833; 22 × 37 cm.

Fig.64. William Wood, The east end of Esplanade Row and the Dhurrumtollah Bazaar, *c.1830*. Lithograph, plate 6 from his *A Series of Twenty-eight Panoramic Views of Calcutta*, London, 1833; 22 × 37 cm.

from each other, or connected only by long ranges of terraces, surmounted, like the flat roofs of the houses, with balustrades. The greater number of these mansions have pillared verandahs extending the whole way up, sometimes to the height of three stories, besides a large portico in front; and these clusters of columns, long colonnades, amd lofty gateways, have a very imposing effect, especially when intermingled with forest trees and flowering shrubs.'

Wood's first six plates show us views of the buildings along Esplanade Row, forming a complement to the view by Muhammad Amir. The third plate gives us a new view, looking up Council House Street across the grounds west of Government House to the east end of Hastings Street (or Government Place North) where the house of Fergusson & Company and various government offices, such as the Board of Trade, were situated on the north side (fig. 63). The south side of course was still the grounds of Government House. On Council House Street are the Treasury building and behind, the block known as Loudoun Place. We obtain a good view of the new dome of Government House, along with the Britannia or Minerva statue crowning it, all dating from 1824. The next two plates show us the southern end of Old Court House Street, with the jumble of private houses and government offices up to Dacres Lane, and the grandiose Bengal Club House in Gordon's Buildings, whence the Bengal Club migrated to Tank Square at about this time. The sixth plate shows us the crossroads at the north-east corner of the Maidan (fig.64). The Oil Bazaar stood at the top of Chowringhee Road. Opposite, across the Dhurrumtollah Road is 'the extensive but ruinous bazar' noted by Heber above, which was replaced by a mosque in 1842.

Wood then begins a series of 18 plates depicting the buildings along the Chowringhee Road. This area was now expanding so fast that whereas in Schalch's map no substantial houses are marked between the Oil Bazaar and the first side street, Jaun Bazaar Street (subsequently Corporation Street), Wood shows three new ones, one of them still under construction. The buildings along the whole of Chowringhee Road as depicted by Wood amply bear out Emma Roberts' description of them. Government had taken over some of them for official purposes, such as the complex of buildings on the corner of Jaun Bazaar Street, which housed the Secret and Political Department, dealing with relations with the Indian and other foreign states in the region, or the General Post Office on the north side of the corner with Lindsay Street. The stretch between these two official buildings was largely a still vacant garden area, known as the Hydrah Bagaun. Another Government department here was the building in Speke, later Sudder, Street, housing the court known as the Sudder Dewany Adawlut, one of the two courts of appeal, this one for civil cases, for Indians in the presidency outside Calcutta, for whom justice was administered under Hindu or Muslim legal codes as appropriate. The court house in Chowringhee was set well back and invisible in Wood's view: the Indian Museum was subsequently erected in front of it.

At the junction with Park Street, stand the premises of the Asiatic Society (fig.65, right) founded in 1784, under the patronage of Warren Hastings and with Sir William Jones as its first president, the oldest of all the learned societies devoted to the civilizations of Asia. It removed to this house built on ground granted by Government in 1805. Jones declared in 1784 that the bounds of the Society's investigations would be the geographical limits of Asia, and within these limits its enquiries would be extended to whatever was performed by man or produced by nature. Jacquemont gives us an amusing description of it in his *Journal*, nearly 50 years from its founding. 'Elle est composée ... d'hommes habiles en petit nombre qui y sont assez peu considérés, et d'hommes riches ou puissants, mais inhabiles, qui y jouissent de tous les honneurs ... [Elle a] un grand nombre de membres, la plupart employés civils ou militaires du Gouvernement ... La Société se réunit une fois tous les deux mois. Trois jours après mon arrivée à Calcutta, j'assistai à une de ses séances. Il y en avait une autre hier: on l'appela très-nombreuse; nous étions une vingtaine ... Cinq ou six natifs, membres de la Société asiatique, assistaient à la séance. On les appelle *Babou* ou Monsieur; et parlant d'eux, on dit *Gentlemen; a native Gentleman*. Ce n'est pas leur caste qui leur vaut cette appellation polie, c'est leur fortune et leur manière de vivre, moins éloignée des Européens; ils sont tous Hindous ... La maison où s'assemble la Société est fort belle. Le rez de chaussée est une sorte de Muséum où sont exposés, sans ordre et sans goût, des objects d'histoire naturelle et de curiosité ...

63

64

Fig.65. William Wood, The junction of Chowringhee Road with Park Street and the Asiatic Society's building, c.1830. Lithograph, plate 15 from his *A Series of Twenty-eight Panoramic Views of Calcutta*, London, 1833; 22 × 37 cm.

Fig.66. William Wood, Chowringhee Road south of the junction with Park Street, c.1830. Lithograph, plate 16 from his *A Series of Twenty-eight Panoramic Views of Calcutta*, London, 1833; 22 × 37 cm.

Enfin, et je dois supposer que c'est la partie brillante du Muséum de la Société, plusieurs salles et la cage de l'escalier sont ornées d'idoles de toutes espèces, en brique, en porcelaine, en métal, en marbre, en pierre; il y en a de toutes les parties de l'Inde, en deçà et au delà du Ganges. Il y a aussi un grand nombre de pierres couvertes d'inscriptions. Les appartements supérieurs contiennent une bibliothèque dont j'ignore entièrement la richesse en fait de livres et de manuscrits orientaux, mais dont les rayons européens sont assez peu chargées. Un viel Italien, qu'on appelle le Dr Bullini, garde tous ces trésors. Quoique son titre officiel soit celui de bibliothécaire de la Société, ce n'est pas un argus impitoyable. Il y a ici un système libéral, chacun des membres et leurs adhérents emporte chez soi les livres dont il a besoin. Un grand nombre d'examplaires invendus de la collection des Mémoires de la Société ajoutent singulièrement l'ameublement de la bibliothèque. La Société asiatique, comme corps, est absolument nulle. Aucune recherche faite en commun, aucune association de travaux parmi ses membres vers un but commun... Au reste, s'il y a peu de savoir à la Société asiatique de Calcutta, il ne me semble pas qu'il y ait de bien grandes prétentions... Il n'y a de ces discussions familières tournées en conversation, qui rendent souvent si instructives les séances de l'Institut [de France]. Une dignité un peu froide prévaut toujours, et le respect pour les formes fait négliger le fond.' The Society had indeed passed through a fairly lean time in the early 19th century, after the inspiration of Hastings and Jones had faded, but in its lack of communal effort it was no worse, as Jacquemont himself admits, than the vast majority of learned societies. It was, however, soon afterwards to be rejuvenated under the energetic James Prinsep.

Continuing with Wood's panorama, south of Park Street, the General's Tank occupies the Maidan side of the road. The house at what was then No. 33 was occupied from 1834 to 1838 by Thomas Babington Macaulay (fig.66, on the left). He was the Law Member of the Supreme Council, working on the reorganisation of the law in India following the new India Act of 1834 which separated the trading and governmental functions of the East India Company, and forbade their continuing to trade in India at all. Macaulay is also the most famous figure in one of the most heated controversies of British India, over education, whether it should be in English or in the vernaculars with advanced education in Sanskrit or Arabic. Macaulay's famous minute on the subject, pouring scorn on the literatures and religions of the East, although accepted as it stood by Lord William Bentinck, generated more heat than light in this still on-going debate, and by the end of the decade a sensible compromise had been reached. In one of his letters written in 1836, he conveniently sums up the tone of Calcutta society in this decade: 'That tremendous crash of the great commercial houses, which took place a few years ago, has produced a revolution in fashion. It ruined one half of the English society in Bengal and seriously injured the other half. A large proportion of the most important functionaries here are deeply in debt and, accordingly, the mode of living is now exceedingly quiet and modest. Those immense subscriptions, those public tables, those costly entertainments and equipages of which Heber and others who saw Calcutta a few years back, say so much, are never heard of.'

The houses between Chowringhee Road and Russell Street, sparsely indicated in Schalch's map, seem thicker here only a few years later. They are unidentifiable until we come to the Bishop's Palace. This is actually number 5 Russell Street. It served this function from 1825 to 1849, housing Bishops Heber (who had been accomodated first in Government House in the Fort and then the old house of Sir Elijah Impey in Middleton Row), Turner, James and Wilson, the latter of whom built a new Cathedral on the south-east corner of the Maidan and moved the palace to a house opposite the Cathedral across Chowringhee Road. Schalch's map informs us that these grand houses in the lower Chowringhee area are a mix of private residences and Government departments. On the corner of the next cross street, Theatre Road, stands the Chowringhee Theatre (fig.67), which we have already discussed when dealing with the interior view by William Prinsep (see fig. 60). After its destruction by fire in 1839, a temporary theatre was opened on the corner of Waterloo Street and Old Court House Street, until a new theatre, the Sans Souci, was opened in Park Street in 1841. This was plagued by various troubles, and the building was eventually bought by the Jesuits and became part of their school, St Xavier's.

65

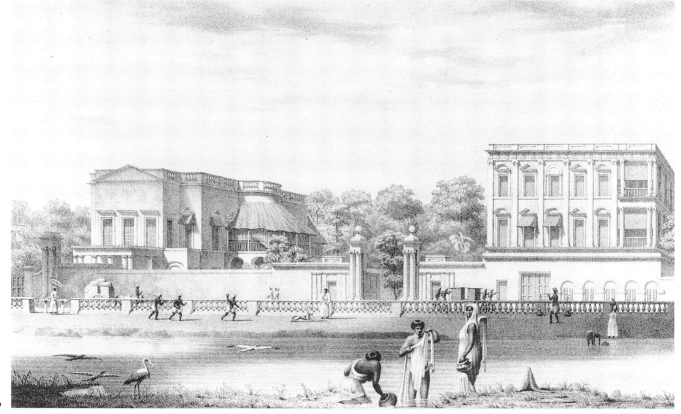

66

Fig.67. William Wood,
Chowringhee Road, and the
Theatre, c.1830. Lithograph, plate
22 from his *A Series of Twenty-eight
Panoramic Views of Calcutta*, London,
1833; 22 × 37 cm.

Fig.68. William Wood, Kidderpore
Bridge, c.1830. Lithograph, plate 26
from his *A Series of Twenty-eight
Panoramic Views of Calcutta*, London,
1833; 22 × 37 cm.

Wood has now practically reached the junction with the Circular Road, and he abandons Chowringhee Road to show us the New General Hospital, a view taken in April 1829. This is the old hospital on the Circular Road, which was enlarged and rebuilt in the 1820s. Wood concludes his survey of views round the Maidan with views of the two bridges which cross Tolly's Nullah to the suburbs to the south of the city, which views are separated by one of Fort William. Kidderpore, Alipore and Bhowanipore are the three suburbs west to east which lie to the south of the Maidan, divided from it by Tolly's Nullah. The Kidderpore Bridge lies at the end of the Course, the main drive across the Maidan, and was erected about 1826; it was the earliest suspension bridge of stone and iron constructed in India (fig. 68). Wood's view of the Alipore Bridge is extremely prosaic when compared with D'Oyly's evocative view published in 1848 (see plate 32).

Wood's view of the Fort is taken from the glacis outside the Chowringhee Gate, which faces towards Park Street (fig.69). Above each of the seven gates is an official residence for one of the senior commanding officers. Above the trees are the towers of the Fort church of St Peter, of which we obtain a good view of the south side from one of Wood's watercolours of the interior of the Fort (fig.70). A church had been planned from the beginning to be included in the Fort, but nothing whatever was done about it until the 1820s. The foundation stone of the church of St Peter was laid in 1822, and its consecration took place in 1828, although it was not finally finished apparently until 1835. It is a rare example of Regency Gothic in India. The artist is looking east across the inner courtyards of Fort William towards the Chowringhee Gate and Chowringhee Road. The Course runs across the Maidan in the middle distance. The building with the pediments is the old Government House in the Fort, southeast of the church, used as such only occasionally. Bishop Heber was first accomodated in it on his arrival in Calcutta in 1823, and describes it as it still is, until a suitable Bishop's Palace was found for him. So too did Wajid Ali Shah, last King of Oudh, who stayed here for three years after his deposition, until his house in Garden Reach was ready. Another view of the interior of the Fort by William Prinsep in the India Office Library notes that the building was the Governor-General's 'house in case of siege', and that the church was built by Captain Hutchinson.

One of William Prinsep's most ambitious watercolours is a picture of a group of Englishmen and women being entertained by a nautch in the courtyard of a great Indian house during the festival of the Durga puja (plate 25). The image of the goddess Durga is enshrined at the back, while on the left a goat is about to be decapitated in her honour. Such houses were found in the northern part of the city, where lived many extremely rich Bengalis, whose wealth was based on immense landholdings in Bengal as well as in some instances the help which they had given the English in the 18th century, as tax-collectors, bankers or merchants. Prinsep, after the collapse of Palmer & Company in 1830, eventually found his financial feet again in a trading and shipping partnership with his friends William Carr and the wealthy Bengali *zamindar* and businessman Dwarkanath Tagore, grandfather of the poet Rabindranath, and the entertainment may have been in his house. Maria Graham describes such an entertainment in one of the grand mansions in north Calcutta, to which she was invited by Maharajah Rajkissen, son of Maharajah Nubkissen. 'The Maha Rajah has a fine house at the end of the Chitpore bazar. The room into which we were ushered was a large square court, covered in for the occasion with red cloth, to which a profusion of white artifical flowers was fastened. Three sides of the court are occupied by the dwelling-house, the walls of which are adorned by a double row of pillars in couplets, and between each couplet is a window. The fourth side is occupied by the family temple, of a very pretty architecture; the arches which support it are not unlike those used in England in Henry VII's time, with cinquefoil heads. A flight of steps leads to the viranda of the temple, where Vishnu [presumably an error for Durga] sat in state, with a blaze of light before him, in magnificent chandeliers. When we entered there were some hundreds of people assembled, and there seemed to be room for as many more. The dancing was begun, but as soon as our host perceived us he led us to the most commodious seats, stationed boys behind us with round fans of red silk, with gold fringe, and then presented us with bouquets of the mogue and the rose, tied up with a green leaf, ornamented with silver fringe. A small gold vase being brought, the Maha Rajah, with a golden spoon, perfumed us with ottur, and sprinkled us with rose-water, after which we were allowed to sit still and look

67

68

Fig.69. William Wood, Fort William
from the east, c.1830. Lithograph,
plate 27 from his A Series of Twenty-
eight Panoramic Views of Calcutta,
London, 1833; 22 × 37 cm.

Fig.70. William Wood, The interior
of Fort William and St Peter's
Church, c.1830. Watercolour;
27.5 × 37 cm. India Office Library
WD 3755.

on. The first dancers were men, whom by their dresses I took for women, though I was rather surprised at the assurance of their gestures, which had nothing else remarkable in them. These gave way to some Cashmerian singers, whose voices were very pleasing . . . I was sorry when they finished, to make way for a kind of pantomine, in which men personated elephants, bears and monkeys. After this some women danced; but though they were pretty, and their motions rather graceful, I was disappointed, after hearing so much of the nautch-girls of India. One of them, while dancing in a circle, twisted a piece of striped muslin into flowers, keeping each stripe for a different coloured flower. The last amusement we staid to partake of, was the exhibition of a ventriloquist (the best I ever heard), although the Maharajah pressed us to remain, saying that he had different sets of dancers, enough to exhibit during the whole night. I was pleased with the attention the Rajah paid to his guests, whether Hindoos, Christians, or Mussulmans; there was not one to whom he did not speak kindly, or pay some compliment on their entrance; and he walked round the assembly repeatedly, to see that all were properly accomodated. I was sorry I could not go to his nautch the next night, where I hear there was a masquerade, when several Portuguese and Pariahs appeared as Europeans, and imitated our dances, music, and manners.' This combination of elements – singing, dancing and pantomine – was the usual entertainment put on at these grand parties given by rich Bengalis, and it was also usual for them to invite English guests on these occasions.

In 1840 there died while on a trip to England James Prinsep, one of the most illustrious of Calcutta citizens, scientist and scholar, Assay Master at the Benares Mint and then at the New Mint in Calcutta, Secretary of the Asiatic Society, and decipherer of the most ancient inscrip- tions of India. William Prinsep tells us that on 30 July of that year 'a great meeting was held at the Townhall, Sir Edward Ryan in the chair, to consider what would be the fittest way for the town to record publicly the loss of so valuable a man as James Prinsep. The natives in the meantime held a meeting among themselves and formed a subscription of their own to build a ghaut to his memory. A site was given them by the Gov. General at the Coolie Ghaut just below the Fort and the erection of a very neat Palladian Porch at the head of a flight of steps was entrusted to our friend Fitzgerald an officer of the Engineers. It is an ornament to the river, and mostly used for the landing of troops arriving by sea which before had mostly to jump out of the boats on to a very muddy shore. It bears the name of James Prinsep on the architrave in four different languages – English, Bengallee, Hindi and Persian. My last act in India was to add 2 stone recumbent lions to slope off the stairs which I got well done at Buxar for 700 rupees, but I did not remain long enough to see them in their place. It is called Prinsep's Ghaut so that our name cannot easily be forgotten in India.' William Prinsep must have drawn this scene shortly before he left Calcutta for the last time in November 1841 (plate 26).

Sir Charles D'Oyly was the most famous amateur artist in India in the first half of the 19th century. An indifferent watercolourist when he first arrived in 1798, he was able to take lessons with George Chinnery, whose figural and landscape style strongly influenced his own. D'Oyly spent most of his career in Calcutta, with the exception of periods at Dacca from 1808-12, and at Patna, 1821-32, until his retirement in 1838. During his last period he seems to have planned to publish a series of views of the city, which eventually appeared as a posthumous publication in 1848 under the title Views of Calcutta and its Environs. He shows far more views of the Indian part of the city than any of his predecessors, but they are mostly picturesque views of small mosques or temples without sufficient identification, and hence add little to our topographical knowledge. Arranging the plates from north to south, we omit those which add little to our knowledge at this stage. A somewhat startling view is entitled a View in Clive Street (fig.71), in which the combination of decaying Palladian buildings and squalid huts seems a rather ironic commentary on what was, and still is, the commercial heart of the city. D'Oyly has one of the most interesting of views of the shipping on the river in his view of Custom House Wharf (plate 27). We read in Lord Valentia's account of Calcutta in 1803 the proposal, and the opposition to it, to erect a wharf by the Custom House in the Old Fort for the easier unloading and loading of goods, and this seems to be it. Indeed, other wharves also have been built a little further upstream. Bishop Heber tells us that 'where the esplanade walk joins Calcutta [that is, at Chandpaul Ghaut], a very handsome quay is continued along this side of the river; resembling in everything but the durability of the material, the quays of

69

70

Fig.71. Sir Charles D'Oyly, *View in Clive Street*, c.1835. Coloured lithograph, plate 13 from his *Views of Calcutta and its Environs*, lithographed by Dickinson & Co, London, 1848; 28.5 × 41.5 cm.

Petersburgh. It is unhappily of brick instead of granite, and is as yet unfinished, but many houses and public buildings are rising on it, and it bids fair to be a very great additional ornament and convenience to Calcutta. Vessels of all descriptions, to the burden of 600 tons, may lie almost close up to this quay, and there is always a crowd of ships and barks'.

On the south side of Tank Square there had been erected in 1824 a portico containing a statue by Chantrey of the Marquess of Hastings, the whole facing the entrance to Wellesley Place and the north entrance to Government House. Portico and statue were later incorporated into the Dalhousie Institute which was built behind it in 1865. D'Oyly's view makes the statue the centre of the picture (fig.72), but beyond the portico may be seen the centre and east end of Writers' Buildings displaying the additional pediments and (in the case of the east end) the portico with which the façade of the building had been decorated in 1821. The west end of course was similarly treated, to disguise a little the gaunt nakedness of the building.

Government House plays a much less conspicuous role in D'Oyly's views than in Fraser's, and the view of it from the north-east by D'Oyly is the only one in which it forms the major subject, apart from the splendid title-page which shows the view through the south-east gate on to the south façade of Government House (fig.73). On the other hand, its setting within Esplanade Row with the Esplanade in front of it and the spires of the churches behind inspired D'Oyly to include three such views within this series. The view entitled *Calcutta from the Old Course* taken in 1838 is almost from the same standpoint as that by Muhammad Amir of eight years earlier, with the same tree and sentry box beside it dominating the composition (plate 28). The Course was the fashionable drive across the Maidan, a continuation of Old Court House Street, straight up which the artist is looking to the Kirk in the distance. Another spire looms up behind the Kirk, belonging to the Catholic Cathedral of the Virgin Mary of the Rosary, which is all, unfortunately, we ever see of it in any of these views of Calcutta. A new laying out of roads on this part of the Maidan had already started, consequent doubtless on the erection in 1838, the year of D'Oyly's departure, of the Baboo Ghaut on the left of this view, to which a new road (subsequently Auckland Road) is curving round. The Baboo Ghaut

Fig.72. Sir Charles D'Oyly, *Statue of the Marquis of Hastings in Tank Square, c.*1835. Coloured lithograph, plate 22 from his *Views of Calcutta and its Environs*, lithographed by Dickinson & Co, London, 1848; 28.5 × 42 cm.

is a colonnade erected at the expense of Baboo Rajchunder Doss at one of the principle Hindu bathing places in the city. The artist is standing nearest the southernmost point of a triangular piece of land known as the 'cocked hat', still enclosed with post and chain fencing, on which the equestrian statue of Lord Hardinge was later erected. Beyond is the plastered balustrade surrounding the south garden of Government House, which the engraver has not understood to be semicircular at its southern end. Fiebig's panoramic view of 1847 shows this layout far more clearly (see fig.83). The area on the left with the carriage was laid out during the period of Lord Auckland (Governor-General 1836-42), as the Auckland Circus Gardens, subsequently the Eden Gardens.

Another tree dominates the view called *Town and Port of Calcutta,* at the end of the Respondentia Walk, which neatly divides the view between the Esplanade with the grand buildings at its northern end on the right, and the river with its shipping on the left (plate 29). An artist is sketching the view. The boy on his pony recalls Emma Roberts's description of this area: 'One of the prettiest spectacles afforded by the evening drive in Calcutta, is the exhibition of its juvenile inhabitants, congregated on a particular part of the the plain between the Government-house and the fort, by the side of the river. This is the chosen spot; all the equipages, a strange grotesque medley, are drawn up at the corner, and the young people are seen in crowds, walking with their servants, laughing, chattering and full of glee, during the brief interval of enfranchisement . . . At day-break, they make their appearance again, in equal numbers; but their gambols are perforce confined to the broad and beaten path . . . Their attendants keep a sharp look-out for snakes.' From further down the river still, at the Water-Gate of Fort William, is a third view, in which the shipping and buildings now form a distant backdrop to the activity on the Strand, which had by this date been extended from Chandpaul Ghaut along the river bank to Fort William and beyond.

Rare among all these views is one of the eastern part of Esplanade Row, which D'Oyly provides us with when viewed across the Dhurrumtollah Tank at the north-east corner of the Maidan (plate 30). Even rarer is his view of the Catholic Church of the Sacred Heart which had

Sir Charles D'Oyly. Engraving after George Chinnery.

Fig.73. Sir Charles D'Oyly, The south-east gateway of Government House, c.1835. Coloured lithograph, from the title-page of his *Views of Calcutta and its Environs*, lithographed by Dickinson & Co, London, 1848; 53 × 37.5 cm (complete).

been built in 1834 just behind the Dhurrumtollah Bazaar on Dhurrumtollah Street, the eastward continuation of Esplanade Row (fig.74). This was begun in 1832 by Mrs Pascoa da Souza, a member of the influential Barretto family, and its position in the heart of British Calcutta no doubt is a consequence of the passing of the Catholic Emancipation Act of 1829. Finally from this corner of the Maidan is the view from No. 11 Esplanade Row (plate 31). Across the Dhurrumtollah Tank may be see our first view of the Ochterlony Monument, a column 152 feet in height erected in 1828 by public subscription in honour of Sir David Ochterlony, Resident in Delhi and Rajputana and victor in the Anglo-Nepalese War of 1814, and one of the last survivors of the era of Warren Hastings. Totally conditioned to Indian ways, he is supposed to have had thirteen wives, and a separate elephant for each of them when he took his evening constitutional.

D'Oyly devotes four plates to the Chowringhee Road area. Moving along Chowringhee Road, although precisely which part of it cannot be determined, is a colourful Hindu procession with floats, which he calls the *Procession of the Churruckpooja*, known to the British as the hook-swinging festival (fig.75). Bishop and Mrs Heber combine to give us a good description of both procession and ceremony: 'As the morning advanced we could see an immense crowd coming down the Chowringhee road... The music consisted chiefly of large double drums, ornamented with plumes of black feathers, like those of a hearse, which rose considerably higher than the heads of the persons who played on them; large crooked trumpets, like the 'litui' of the ancients, and small gongs suspended from a bamboo, which rested on the shoulders of two men, the last of whom played on it, with a large thick and heavy drum-stick or cudgel. All the persons who walked in the procession, and a large majority of the spectators, had their faces, bodies, and white cotton clothes daubed all over with vermilion, the latter to a degree which gave them the appearance of actually being dyed rose-colour. They were also crowned with splendid garlands of flowers, with girdles and baldrics of the same. Many trophies and pageants of different kinds were paraded up and down, on stages drawn by horses, or bullocks. Some were mythological, others were imitations of different European figures, soldiers, ships, &c. and, in particular, there was one very large model of a steam-boat. The devotees went about with small spears through their tongues and arms, and still more with hot irons pressed against their sides... In the evening the Bishop walked to the Boitacon-nah, the part of the city where the trees for swinging are erected; they are not suffered to be placed near the European residences... The victim was led, covered with flowers, and without any apparent reluctance, to the foot of the tree; hooks were then thrust through the muscles of his sides, which he endured without shrinking, and a broad bandage was fastened round his waist, to prevent the hooks from being torn through by the weight of his body. He was then raised up, and whirled round; at first the motion was slow, but by degrees was increased to considerable rapidity. In a few minutes it ceased; and the by-standers were going to let him down, when he made signs that they should proceed: this resolution was received with great applause by the crowd, and after drinking some water he was again spun round.'

Just off the main road, in Kyd Street, D'Oyly has given us a rear view of one of the most interesting houses in the Chowringhee area (fig.76). Built in 1790 as a private house in Speke Street, it was subsequently rented by Government for the use of the Sudder Dewany Adawlaut Court, which gave the name Sudder Street to the street in which it stands. The court had just been transferred to a new building erected south of the Maidan for a Military Hospital, which had been commandeered by Lord William Bentinck for this purpose. D'Oyly calls this building the Sudder Board of Revenue, which function Bentinck must have transferred into the building. In its grounds which stretched southwards to Kyd Street was the Jingerry Talao or Sieve Tank, so called because of the screen which allowed public access to the water of the tank without entry into the grounds of the house. D'Oyly also includes another view of Chowringhee, at the south end of the Maidan, showing what appears to be Elliott's Tank, and then strangely includes a view of the new St Paul's Cathedral. D'Oyly had left India in 1838, retiring eventually to Italy, where he died in 1845. Clearly he cannot have seen the building, but it is possible that he may have seen the architect William Forbes's designs before he left Calcutta, or indeed Forbes may have sent him copies. On the other hand, the composition bears a very close resemblance to the drawing of the cathedral by

VIEWS

OF

CALCUTTA

ENVIRONS

BY

THE LATE SIR CHARLES D'OYLY BART

EAST GATE — GOVERNMENT HOUSE

LONDON

LITHOGRAPHED & PUBLISHED, BY DICKINSON & Cº 114 NEW BOND STREET.

1848.

Fig.74. Sir Charles D'Oyly, *Church Entrance to the Dhurrumtolla*, c.1835. Coloured lithograph, plate 8 from his *Views of Calcutta and its Environs*, lithographed by Dickinson & Co, London, 1848; 30.5 × 42.5 cm.

Fig.75. Sir Charles D'Oyly, *Procession of the Churruckpooja*, c.1835. Coloured lithograph, plate 10 from his *Views of Calcutta and its Environs*, lithographed by Dickinson & Co, London, 1848; 34 × 84 cm.

William Clerihew, who was in India 1843-5. This was published as a lithographic print in March 1845 (see fig.78).

Two of the most attractive plates in this book are of the southern end of the city. The suspension bridge at Alipore over Tolly's Nullah is a little further upstream than the Kidderpore Bridge which we have already seen in Wood's view published in 1833. However, the airy creation of D'Oyly's brush, one of his most attractive compositions (plate 32), bears little resemblance to the more prosaic reality as shown in another one of Wood's views. The lofty scaffolding in the distance is for fire-watching. Looking downriver, from the bend in the river below Tolly's Nullah, D'Oyly gives us an equally lovely view of Garden Reach (fig.77). The domed building on the inner crown of the bend opposite is the house Shalimar, where lived Colonel Robert Kyd, the founder of the Botanical Gardens. On the left we can see part of the dockyard which was first begun by Colonel Henry Watson as early as 1780, before being acquired in 1807 by James and Alexander Kyd, the shipbuilding 'country-born' sons of Robert Kyd.

The Cathedral of St John having proved too small for Calcutta's growing population, Bishop Wilson set about providing a new one. The Government gave the site on the southeast edge of the Maidan, and over half a million rupees were raised from local subscription and from the East India Company and other bodies in England. The design was by Major William Forbes of the Engineers, in a Gothic style. The foundation stone was laid in October 1839, and the building was consecrated on 8 October 1847. A tinted lithograph by T C Dibdin was published in London in March 1845, based on a drawing by William Clerihew the architect, who visited India in 1843-5 (fig.78). This seems to be the origin of the view included in D'Oyly's *Views of Calcutta*. Although laid out in the usual cruciform plan, with the main entrance to the west and high altar to the east, the crossing with the tower and spire above is in fact towards the west rather than the east end. The spire, which had been modelled on that of Norwich cathedral, collapsed in the earthquake of 1897, and the tower was subsequently rebuilt in imitation of the main tower of Canterbury.

Frederick Fiebig was a somewhat mysterious figure who bridged the eras of lithography and photography in Calcutta. His major effort in lithography is a panoramic view of the city of Calcutta published in 1847, while he appears at about the same time to have drawn and published four other tinted lithographs of the city, which are undated. In 1851 he took a whole series of photographs (at least 236) of Calcutta. He was certainly back in London by 1856, as he wrote to the Court of Directors about his photographs from an address in Camberwell. His view of the principal entrance of Government House is taken from Wellesley Place which runs north from Government House to Tank Square (fig.79). The coats-of-arms crowning the northern wings' façades are here missing, having been removed by 1841, presumably on grounds of their decrepitude. In this street was situated the original building of Spence's Hotel, here on the right; one of the views in the D'Oyly sketch book in the Victoria Memorial Hall is taken from it. This was one of the first hotels in Calcutta, opened by 1830, rendered necessary by the growing numbers of transients coming both from Britain and from the provinces, and the decline in the hospitality offered by residents. As Emma Roberts puts it: 'Formerly, strangers visiting Calcutta were dependent upon the hospitality of the residents, or were compelled to take large unfurnished houses, there being neither lodging-houses nor hotels for the reception of guests. But the capital of Bengal has become too large to admit of the continuance of old customs; boarding, and other houses of public entertainment have been opened, and conducted in so respectable a manner, that notwithstanding the great difficulty of subduing ancient prejudices, no person, however fastidious, can now scruple to become an inmate of them ... An enterprising person of the name of Spence, who has set up a splendid establishment of the kind in Wellesley Place, seems to receive all the patronage which he so justly merits.' As Government encroached more and more on the buildings around Government House both for quarters for its servants and officers, and for various departmental offices, Spence's Hotel removed to Old Council House Street, to Loudoun Buildings. These were eventually demolished and an Imperial Secretariat erected on the site later in the century.

Emma Roberts has an amusing passage poking gentle fun at Government House. 'The

74

75

Fig.76. Sir Charles D'Oyly, *Office of the Sudder Board of Revenue from Kyd Street*, c.1835. Coloured lithograph, plate 11 from his *Views of Calcutta and its Environs*, lithographed by Dickinson & Co, London, 1848; 28 × 42 cm.

Fig.77. Sir Charles D'Oyly, *Garden Reach*, c.1835. Coloured lithograph, plate 4 from his *Views of Calcutta and its Environs*, lithographed by Dickinson & Co, London, 1848; 29 × 41 cm.

great objection to it as an Asiatic residence ... is the want of colonnades and porticos. The principal entrances are approached by noble flights of steps; but these, being without shelter, are never used except on state occasions, when a native durbar is held, and the nobles of Hindostan come in all their barbaric pomp to pay their respects at the vice-regal court ... The carriages of the European visitants drive under the steps, and the company enter through the lower regions. The effect upon a stranger ... is very singular. It is scarcely possible for a lively imagination to escape the notion that, instead of being the guest of a palace, he is on the point of being conducted to some hideous dungeon as a prisoner of state. The hall which opens upon the dark cloister formed by the arch of the steps above, is large, low and dimly lighted ... A good deal of rubbish of various kinds, piled confusedly and put out of the way behind rows of pillars, traversing the length of the hall, favours the supposition that it is a place of punishment; for in their shapeless obscurity, these fire-engines, or printing presses, or what-ever they may be, have very much the appearance of instruments of torture. Upon the floor, the spectator, who has imbibed the apprehension that he has been entrapped into some pandemonium of horror, may see the dead bodies of the victims to an tyrannical government thickly strewed around:- human forms apparently wrapped in winding-sheets, and stretched out without sense or motion upon the bare pavement, add to the ghastly effect of the scene. These are the palanquin-bearers, who, wrapped up from head to foot in long coarse cloths, are enjoying the sweets of repose, little dreaming of the appalling spectacle they present to unaccustomed eyes ... Emerging from the damp, darkness, and corpse-like figures of the sleepers, an illuminated vestibule leads to a staircase, handsome in itself, but not exactly correspondent with the size of the building and the halls of state to which it is the approach. It is not until the visitant has gained the altitude of the hall, that the eye is greeted by any portion of the pomp and grandeur associated with our ideas of a court.' The lack of a grand staircase, and its replacement by four staircases at each corner of the central block, was much commented upon, as by D'Oyly in *Tom Raw*:

> In such a palace, one might have expected
> A splendid staircase, as, at home we find,
> In noble edifices, well erected,
> And made, in spacious turns and sweeps to wind;
> But here, forsooth, there's nothing of the kind:
> It certainly a strange and very rare case is,
> One must suppose the architect was blind,
> When there was so much room, and lots of spare places,
> To build four little dingy miserable staircases.

Fiebig's view of the Town Hall shows the bronze statue by Richard Westmacott, of Lord William Bentinck, Governor-General 1828-35, suppressor of Thuggee and Suttee, which faces the entrance, erected about 1838 (fig. 80). He includes another view of St Paul's Cathedral from the south-east, and also a view of Tank Square taken from the steps of the Kirk and looking down Old Court House Street towards the Maidan (fig.81). The spire of the Mission Church protrudes on the left. Some of the principal shops in Calcutta were along the east and south side of the square. Emma Roberts singles out the emporium of Tulloh & Company at the south-east corner of the Square, which had inherited the mantle of Taylor's in the Lall Bazaar lauded by D'Oyly in his *Tom Raw*: 'On the ground floor, a large but by no means handsome hall is set apart for auctions; a pulpit is erected in the centre, and every description of property (houses, horses, carriages, &c. down to thimbles and needles) comes under the hammer in the course of a short time; sales of all kind being very frequent.' To this room ladies were barred entry. 'A broad flight of stairs leads to a suite of apartments above, in which there is a multifarious assortment of merchandize, oddly enough contrasted, the merest trumpery being often placed in juxtaposition with articles of great value. The walls are hung with framed engravings ... and a few bad paintings ... The tables and counters are covered with glass cases, containing various kinds of British and foreign bijouterie; others support immense quantities of China and glass, lamps, lustres, and mirrors; there are quantities of silk mercery and linen drapery, and upholstery of all sorts ... Stuffed Chinese birds, beautifully arranged in

76

77

glass cases, are amongst the rarities of Messrs, Tulloh's emporium; these were reckoned cheap at fifty pounds a case... No abatement whatever is made in the price, in consequence of the delapidations which time may have occasioned; bargains are only to be procured at auctions, and the stock remains on hand during time immemorial, while newer and more fashionable importations of the same nature are knocked down to the highest bidder for any thing they will fetch.' Beyond Tulloh's premises is the grand hotel established as a rival to Spence's under the name of Wilson's, which was changed to the Auckland and then the Great Eastern, which astonished William Russell of *The Times*, when he arrived in Calcutta in January 1858, by its attempts to be a 'Universal Provider', with a multitude of shops within the same building.

Emma Roberts continues: 'The only shops in Calcutta which make much shew on the outside, are those of the chemists and druggists, who bring all the London passion for display to a foreign country; they exhibit splendid and appropriate fronts duly embellished with those crystal vases, in which gems of the most brilliant dye appear to be melted. They are flourishing concerns, and the establishment of manufactories of soda-water has added not a little to their profits... The European jewellers' shops in Calcutta are large and handsome; they do not make any shew on the outside, but the interiors are splendid; the pavement of one or two is of marble, and the glass cases on the various counters display a tempting variety of glittering treasures... The setting of these gems is exceedingly beautiful, and according to the most fashionable patterns of London or Paris, neither of these places boasting a more superb assortment; but the prices are so ruinous, that it is wonderful where sufficient custom can be obtained to support establishments of the kind, of which there are at least four, in addition to the vast number of native artisans, who are not only exclusively employed by their own countrymen, but do a great deal of work for Europeans... Formerly an idea was entertained that European goods could only be obtained in perfection from European dealers; but this notion is now exploded, and it will be seen, in the course of these remarks, that the shop-keepers of both countries obtain their supplies from the self-same source.' Establishments of this sort were Hamilton's further down Old Court House Street, and Twentymen, on the south side of Tank Square beside the Exchange. 'Next to the jeweller's shops, the most magnificent establishment in the city is that of the principal bookseller, Thacker and Co; there are others of inferior note, which have circulating libraries attached to them, but the splendid scale of this literary emporium, and the elegance of its arrangements, place it far above all its competitors... A book which is sold at the publishers at home for a pound, is charged at twenty rupees in Calcutta; and considering the cost of freight and insurance, the perishable nature of the commodity, and the very great care requisite to secure both leaves and binding from being injured by damp, or devoured by insects, the price cannot be considered high. Books intended for sale must be carefully taken down from the shelf and wiped every day, and not only the outside, but the interior also, must be examined; a work of time, which in a large establishment, will occupy a great number of servants... Immense consignments of books sometimes come out to Calcutta, through different mercantile houses, which are sold by auction, and are often knocked down for a mere trifle. American editions of works of eminence also find their way into the market at a very cheap rate; and those who are content with bad paper, worse printing, and innumerable typographical errors, may furnish a library of the best authors at a small expense.'

Fiebig's panoramic view of Calcutta in six plates was published by the Asiatic Lithographic Press, Calcutta, in 1847, with Fiebig again doing the original drawing and also the drawing on stone. The views are taken through 360° from the top of the Ochterlony Monument, and show us the classical city at its most complete. The first view looking towards the south (fig. 82) affords us a rare prospect of the Jail, actually on the Maidan west of the cathedral, which moved here in 1783 from its former home in the Lall Bazaar, and survived on this site until the building of the Victoria Memorial Hall. The Hospital, Sudder Courts and Military Orphanage run along the bottom edge of the Maidan, while the spire of St Stephen's Church, Kidderpore, newly built in 1846, may also be seen. In the second sheet (fig.83) we obtain our first sight of the ground of the Calcutta Cricket Club, on the Maidan between Government House and Fort William, of which the Club had obtained the use in 1825. In 1864 a new curving road from Government House, to the Strand Road above Fort William, was built through this part of the

78

79

Fig.80. Frederick Fiebig, *The
Townhall in Calcutta*. Tinted
lithograph, Calcutta, *c*.1845;
20 × 29.5 cm.

grounds, and the pitch was therefore shifted westward towards its neighbour the Eden
Gardens; gardens and cricket ground have been close neighbours ever since. These gardens
by the river, whose inception is usually attributed to the Misses Emily and Fanny Eden, sisters
of the Governor-General Lord Auckland, were in fact laid out on instructions from the
Governor-General himself. They were planned in 1841 by Captain Fitzgerald, the Civil
Architect (who had designed Prinsep's Ghaut), and were originally called the Auckland
Circus, and then Auckland, Gardens; their name was changed to the Eden Gardens about
1854. The colonnade of the Baboo Ghaut, erected in 1838, and the new road leading to it, are
visible also in one of D'Oyly's plates (see plate 28). The newly erected Bentinck statue stands
in front of the Town Hall. We can now see some evidence of serious planting in the south
garden of Government House, which was the work of the Misses Eden in 1840.

The third plate of Fiebig's panorama (fig.84) gives us the remainder of the Misses Edens'
complicated horticultural arrangements in the south garden of Government House. All their
work went to nought when they returned to England, and it was not until the 1870s that the
permanent garden was established which now surrounds and indeed encroaches on Government House from all sides. This plate centres on Government House, still minus its northern
coats-of-arms. The dome and its statue were both continually struck by lightning over the 20
years since the refurbishment under Lord Amherst, so that the dome again had to be renewed;
under Lord Dalhousie in 1851-2, a new dome of iron was put on a taller pedestal to give it
some greater height, but Britannia was not put up again. A flagstaff and crowning gallery
were erected instead in 1862-4. The tents are doubtless those of some newly arrived troops,
who often used to encamp on the Maidan, before proceeding up-country. Writers' Buildings
may now be seen with all three of its new pediments, added in 1821. The spire of St John's we
have no need to mention at this stage, but the other spires may be confusing. The spires of the
Armenian Church behind Writers' Buildings and of St Andrew's beside the latter are clearly
visible. In the next plate (fig.85), two other spires are visible on the left side, of which the
nearer one is that of the Mission Church, while the far one belongs to the Catholic Cathedral,

Fig.81. Frederick Fiebig, *Tank Square Calcutta taken from the Scotch Church.* Tinted lithograph, Calcutta, *c.*1845; 20 × 29.5 cm.

of which there is no early picture. The colonnaded Gordon's Buildings in the centre of Esplanade Row East, once the Bengal Club, has now been occupied by the Military (subsequently United Services) Club, opened in 1845. The mosque opposite the north-east corner of the Maidan is that built by Prince Gholam Mahomed, son of Tippoo Sultan, opened in 1842, endowed by him 'in gratitude to God and in commemoration of the Honourable Court of Directors granting him the arrears of his stipend in 1840'. It replaced the bazaar seen in Wood's view and mentioned by Heber. On the corner of Dhurrumtollah Street is the Catholic church of the Sacred Heart which appeared in D'Oyly's views.

The last two plates (figs.86-87) show the remainder of the Chowringhee Road. Jaun Bazaar Street is on the left. The still open area is the Hydrah Bagaun leading back to the Fenwick Bazaar, on which ground the new municipal market was opened in 1874. Of the two spires, one is the Free Presbyterian Church in Wellesley Square, opened in 1848, the other (that on the right) St Thomas's in Free School Street, consecrated in 1833 beside the Free School premises. The last plate gives us a distant view of St Paul's Cathedral, right at the end of Chowringhee Road. The other spire is that of St Thomas's Catholic Church in Middleton Row, which was begun in 1841, where the round tank in front of Sir Elijah Impey's house had been, the house itself having become the Loretto Convent. A series of tanks stretches down the length of the Chowringhee Road: the Dhurrumtollah Tank is at the northern limit, the Manohardosss or Colinga Tank with its corner pavilions is opposite Lindsay Street, the General's Tank is opposite Park Street, Elliott's Tank faces Harington Street, and, now invisible behind the Cathedral, is the Birjee Tank.

We have now reached in our survey the middle of the 19th century, and with it a rapid increase in the pace of change, both in the appearance of the city and the technical processes of recording it. We no longer have to rely solely on prints and drawings, since photography was now replacing these arts as the means of recording topography as well as much else. In Calcutta Frederick Fiebig produced in 1851 large numbers of photographs of the city and its buildings and monuments, and each decade that followed added to this store. The other major

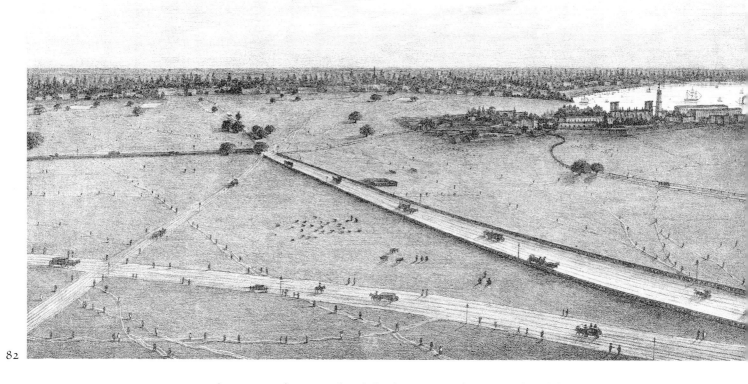

change was of course political, for the Mutiny of 1857-8, which left Calcutta unscathed, had been and gone, and with it went the Company's rule. The Governor-General and Viceroy in Government House now ruled India on behalf of the Crown in Parliament, rather than the Court of Directors in Leadenhall Street.

Photographic panoramas from the top of the Ochterlony Monument taken by Josiah Rowe in 1859 and by Samuel Bourne in 1868-9 may be compared with the Fiebig set of 1847. Little in the way of major change may be seen in Rowe's set, other than the grand new Fever or General Medical Hospital on College Street, opened for the Indian population in 1852, and by its bulk dominating the northern part of the city. The Bourne panorama, however, shows us the beginning of the physical transformation of the city, for the old Supreme Court and three of its neighbouring houses are no more and in their stead is rising the new High Court, in a High Victorian Gothic style. Behind it in Tank Square, renamed Dalhousie Square in honour of the Governor-General Lord Dalhousie (1848-56), the new General Post Office on the site of the New Custom House and hence of the Old Fort, is nearly complete but for its dome. With its building all trace of the walls of the Old Fort disappeared from public view, and Calcutta finally lost sight of the roots from which it had sprung. The European part of the city was now fully occupied, and the provision of larger buildings for government or commercial undertakings increasingly meant the destruction of the old classical houses. Like London until recently, Calcutta paid little attention to its architectural heritage, and tore down and replaced its buildings at will. Ever larger and more inappropriate structures have replaced or hidden the classical houses, and the 'City of Palaces' can no longer impress the visitor with the magnificence of its cityscape.

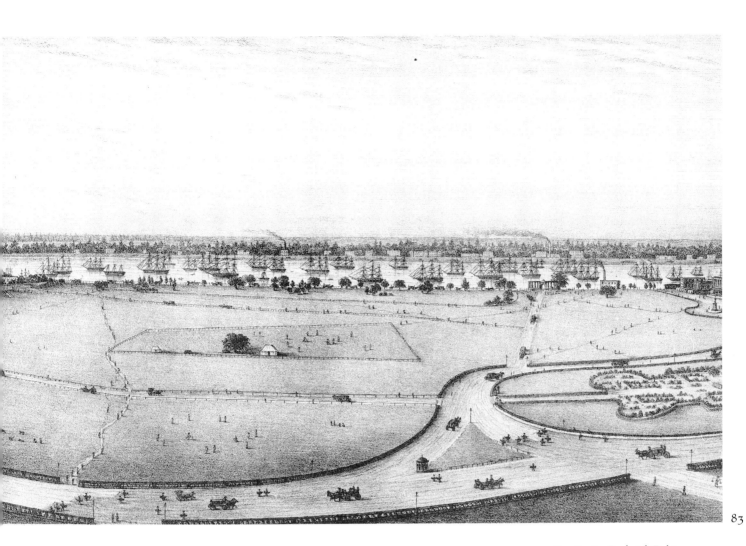

83

Figs.82-87. Frederick Fiebig,
panoramic view of Calcutta from
the Ochterlony Monument, in six
parts. Lithographs, published by
T Black, Asiatic Lithographic Press,
Calcutta, 1847; each 21 × 32.5 cm.

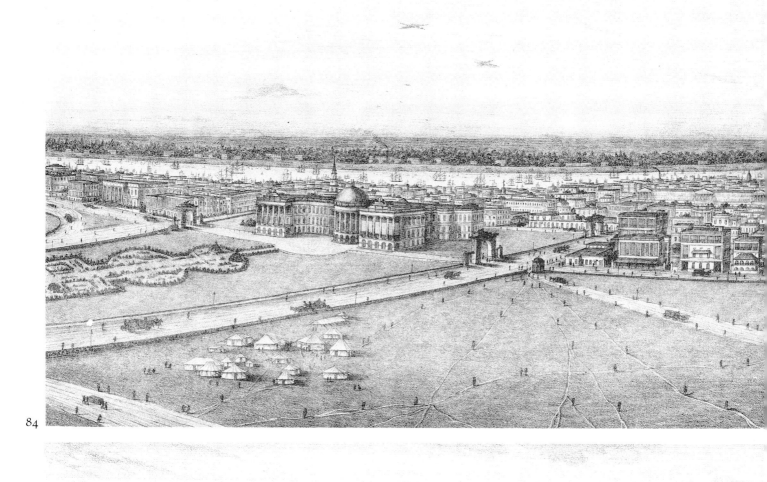

84

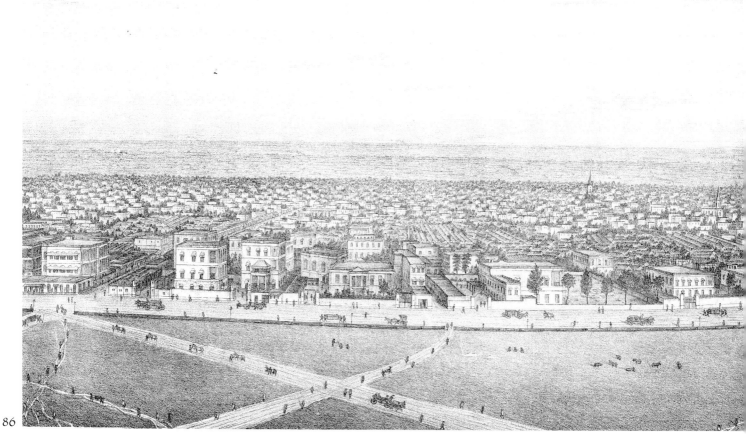

86

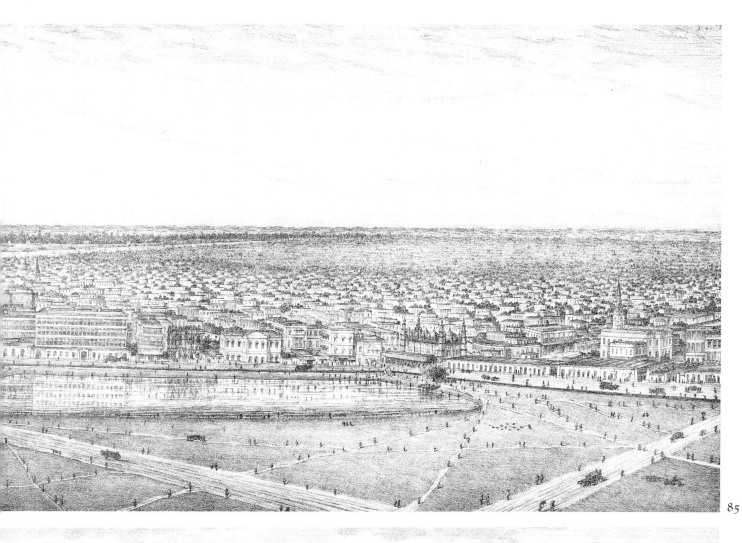

Bibliography

Primary material, printed

Asiaticus, *pseud* [John Hawksworth], *Part the First. Ecclesiastical, Chronological, and Historical Sketches respecting Bengal. Part the Second. The Epitaphs in the Different Burial Grounds in and about Calcutta,* Calcutta, 1803.

Asiaticus, *pseud* [Philip Stanhope], *Genuine Memoirs of Asiaticus,* London, 1780.

Atkinson, James, *The City of Palaces, and other poems,* Calcutta, 1824.

Bevy of Bengal Beauties. A Collection of Poems, London, 1785.

Calcutta: A Poem, London, 1811.

'Calcutta Gazette', *Selections from the* Calcutta Gazettes . . . *1784-1823,* Calcutta, 1864-9.

'Calcutta Journal', *Selections from the Indian Journals, . . . 1818-57,* Calcutta, 1963-5.

Description of a View of the City of Calcutta, now exhibiting at the Panorama, Leicester Square. Painted by the Proprietor, Robert Burford, from Drawings taken for that Purpose by Capt. Robert Smith, London, 1831.

D'Oyly, Sir Charles, *Tom Raw the Griffin: A Burlesque Poem in Twelve Cantos. Illustrated by Twenty-five Engravings,* London, 1828.

D'Oyly, Sir Charles, and Thomas Williamson, *The Europeans in India; from a collection of drawings by Charles Doyley, Esq . . . with a preface and copious descriptions by Captain Thomas Williamson,* London, 1813.

Eden, Emily, *Letters from India,* London, 1872.

Fay, Mrs E, *Original Letters from India,* Calcutta, 1817.

Fenton, Mrs E, *Journal of Mrs. Fenton . . . during the years 1826-30,* ed. by H W Lawrence, London, 1901.

Francis, Philip, *Memoirs with Correspondence and Journals* [incl. A Makcrabie's], ed. J Parkes, London, 1867.

Graham, Maria, *Journal of a Residence in India: Illustrated by Engravings,* Edinburgh and London, 1812.

Grand, G F, *Narrative of the Life of a Gentleman long Resident in India,* Cape of Good Hope, 1814.

Grandpré, L de, *Voyage dans l'Inde et au Bengale, fait dans l'Années 1789 et 1790 . . . orné de belles Gravures,* Paris, 1801.

Grant, Colesworthy, *An Anglo-Indian Domestic Sketch: a Letter from an Artist in India,* Calcutta, 1849.

Hamilton, Alexander, *A New Account of the East Indies,* Edinburgh, 1727.

Hartly House, Calcutta, London, 1789.

Hastings, Francis Rawdon, *Marquis of, The Private Journal of the Marquis of Hastings,* ed. The Marchioness of Bute, London, 1858.

Heber, Reginald, *Narrative of a Journey through the Upper Provinces of India,* ed. Mrs Amelia Heber, London, 1828.

Hickey, William, *Memoirs of William Hickey,* edited by A Spencer, London, 1913-25.

Hodges, William, *Travels in India, during the Years 1780, 1781, 1782, & 1783,* London, 1793.

Holwell, John Zephaniah, *A Genuine Narrative of the Deplorable Deaths of the English Gentlemen and Others Who were Suffocated in the Black Hole at Calcutta,* London, 1758.

Holwell, John Zephaniah, *India Tracts. By Mr. Holwell and Friends,* London, revised edition, 1764.

Jacquemont, Victor, *Letters from India; describing a Journey in the British Dominions in India . . . during the Years 1828, 1829, 1830, 1831,* London, 1834.

Jacquemont, Victor, *Voyage dans l'Inde . . . pendant les Années 1828 à 1832 . . . Journal,* Paris, 1841-4.

Kindersley, Mrs, *Letters from the Island of Teneriffe, Brazil, the Cape of Good Hope, and the East Indies,* London, 1777.

Kipling, Rudyard, *The City of Dreadful Night, and Other Places,* Allahabad and London, 1891.

Life in India: or The English at Calcutta – a Novel, London, 1828.

Orme, Robert, *A History of the Military Transactions of the British Nation in Indostan from the Year MDCCXLV,* London, 1763-78.

Prinsep, G A, *An Account of Steam Vessels and of Proceedings Connected with Steam Navigation in British India,* Calcutta, 1830.

Roberts, Emma, *Scenes and Characteristics of Hindostan, with Sketches of Anglo-Indian Society,* London, 1837.

Roebuck, T, *The Annals of the College of Fort William,* Calcutta, 1819.

Solvyns, François Baltazard, *A Catalogue of 250 Coloured Etchings Descriptive of the . . . Hindoos,* Calcutta, 1799.

Stavorinus, J S, *Voyages to the East Indies,* London, 1798.

Twining, T, *Travels in India a Hundred Years Ago,* ed. W H G Twining, London, 1893.

Valentia, George, *Viscount, Voyages and Travels to India, Ceylon, the Red Sea, Abyssinia and Egypt in the Years 1802, 1803, 1804, 1805, and 1806,* London, 1809.

Vansittart, Henry, *A Narrative of the Transactions in Bengal,* London, 1766.

Williamson, Thomas, *East India Vade Mecum,* London, 1810.

Other early sources include the Calcutta newspapers: *Hicky's Bengal Gazette* (1780-82), *India Gazette* (1780-1843), *Calcutta Gazette* (1784-1815), *Bengal Hurkaru* (1795-1827), *Calcutta Journal* (1813-23), etc.

Primary material, manuscript

Amherst, Lady Sarah Elizabeth: Letter to her brother in England 1824, India Office Library WD 4129-32.

Fraser, James Baillie: Diaries, letters and letter books at Moniack, Inverness.

Prinsep, Henry Thoby: Three Generations in India. India Office Records, MSS EUR C 97.

Prinsep, William: Memoirs. India Office Records, MSS EUR D 1160.

Published original records

Fort William – India House Correspondence 1748 – 1800, New Delhi, 1949-78.

Hedges, William, *The Diary of William Hedges Esq. during his Agency in Bengal, 1681-7*, ed. Col. H Yule, London, 1887-9.

Hill, S C, ed., *Bengal in 1756-7: A Selection of Public and Private Papers dealing with the Affairs of the British in Bengal*, London, 1905.

Long, Revd J, *Selections from Unpublished Records of Government 1748-67 Inclusive Relating mainly to the Social Condition of Bengal*, Calcutta, 1869.

Master, Streynsham, *The Diaries of Streynsham Master 1675-1680 and other Contemporary Papers relating thereto*, ed. R C Temple, London, 1911.

Wilson, C R, ed., *The Early Annals of the English in Bengal, being the Bengal Public Consulatations for the First Half of the Eighteenth Century*, London and Calcutta, 1895-1917.

Wilson, C R, ed., *Old Fort William in Bengal: A Selection of Official Documents dealing with its History*, London, 1906.

Books with plates

Daniell, Thomas and William, *Oriental Scenery, Twenty-four Views in Hindoostan, from the Drawings of Thomas Daniell, engraved by himself and William Daniell*, London, 1797-8.

D'Oyly, Sir Charles, *Views of Calcutta and its Environs*, London, 1848.

Fraser, James Baillie, *Views of Calcutta and its Environs, from Drawings executed by James B Fraser, Esq, from Sketches made on the Spot*, London, 1824-6.

Solvyns, François Baltazard, *A Collection of Two Hundred and Fifty Coloured Etchings Descriptive of the Manners, Customs and Dresses of the Hindoos*, Calcutta, [1796] 1799.

Solvyns, François Baltazard, *Les Hindoûs*, Paris, 1808-12.

Wood, William, *A Series of Twenty-Eight Panoramic Views of Calcutta, extending from Chandpaul Ghaut to the end of Chowringhee Road, together with the Hospital, Two Bridges and the Fort*, London, 1833.

In addition to the above books of plates, and some of the books with engravings in the section on original printed material, other views of Calcutta in this period appear in:

Andrásy, Emanuel, *Graf, Reise des Grafen Emanuel Andrásy in Ostindien, . . . und Bengalen*, Pest, 1859.

Daniell, Thomas and William, *A Picturesque Voyage to India by the Way of China*, London, 1810.

Greene, D Sarsfield, *Views of India*, London, 1859.

Jump. Richard, *Views in Calcutta*, London, 1837.

Orme, William, *24 Views in Hindostan, drawn by William Orme from the Original Pictures painted by Mr. Daniell and Col. Ward*, London, 1802-05.

Salt, Henry, *Twenty-four Views taken in St. Helena, the Cape, India, Ceylon, Abyssinia and Egypt*, London, 1809.

Simpson, William, *India, Ancient and Modern*, London, 1867.

Secondary material, historical

This is a very small selection; much has appeared in recent years of particular relevance to the Bengali city:

Bengal Past and Present, Calcutta, 1907 – (a journal of historical and topographical information, to which I am greatly endebted for a mass of information in articles and notes too numerous to cite here individually)

Blechynden, Kathleen, *Calcutta past and present*, London and Calcutta, 1905.

Busteed, H E, *Echoes from Old Calcutta, being chiefly Reminiscences of the Days of Warren Hastings, Francis, and Impey*, London and Calcutta, 4th revised edition, 1908.

Cotton, H E A, *Calcutta Old and New: a Historical & Descriptive Handbook to the City*, Calcutta, 1907.

Curzon, George, *Marquis, British Government in India: the Story of the Viceroys and Government Houses*, London, 1925.

Firminger, Revd W K, *Thacker's Guide to Calcutta*, Calcutta, 1906.

Ghosh, S C, *Social Condition of the British Community in Bengal, 1757-1800*, Leiden, 1970.

Hart, Revd W H, *Old Calcutta: its Places and People 100 Years Ago*, 1895.

Hyde, Revd H B, *The Parish of Bengal, 1678-1788*, Calcutta, 1899.

Hyde, Revd H B, *Parochial Annals of Bengal: being a History of the Bengal Ecclesiastical Establishment of the Honourable East India Company in the 17th and 18th Centuries*, Calcutta, 1901.

Khan, A M, *The Transition in Bengal 1756-1775: a Study of Sayyid Muhammad Reza Khan*, Cambridge, 1969.

Long, Revd J, *Peeps into Social Life in Calcutta a Century ago*, Calcutta, 1868.

Marshall, P J, *East Indian Fortunes: the British in Bengal in the Eighteenth Century*, Oxford, 1976.

Marshall, P J, *Bengal: the British Bridgehead, Eastern India 1740-1828*, Cambridge, 1987 (*The New Cambridge History of India*, II, 2).

Mukherjee, S N, *Calcutta: Myths and History*, Calcutta, 1977.

Nandy, S C, *The Life and Times of Cantoo Baboo*, Calcutta, 1978-81.

Phillimore, R H, *Historical Records of the Survey of India. Volume I 18th Century; Volume II 1800-1815*, Dehra Dun, 1945-50.

Sinha, Pradip, *Calcutta in Urban History*, Calcutta, 1979.

Sterndale, R C, *An Historical Account of the Calcutta Collectorate*, Calcutta, 1895.

Tripathi, A, *Trade and Finance in the Bengal Presidency, 1793-1833*, New Delhi, 1979.

Secondary material, art-historical

Abbey, J R, *Travel in Aquatint and Lithography 1770-1860 from the Library of J R Abbey*, ed. M Oliver, London, 1957.

Archer, Mildred. *Early Views of India. The Picturesque Journeys of Thomas and William Daniell, 1786-94: The Complete Aquatints*, London, 1980.

Archer, Mildred, and Toby Falk, *India Revealed: the Art and Adventures of James and William Fraser 1801-35*, London, 1989.

Harrold, Pauline, 'The India Office Library's Prints of Calcutta', in *India Office Library & Records Report 1 April 1972 to 31 December 1973*, London, 1975.

India Office Library, London: *British Drawings in the India Office Library*, by Mildred Archer, London, 1969.

India Office Library, London: *Company Drawings in the India Office Library*, by Mildred Archer, London, 1972.

India Office Library, London: *The India Office Collection of Painting and Sculpture*, by Mildred Archer, London, 1986.

Nilsson, S, *European Architecture in India, 1750-1850*, London, 1968.

Pal, P, and Vidya Dehejia, *From Merchants to Emperors, British Artists and India, 1757-1930*, New York, 1986.

Rohatgi, Pauline, and Pheroza Godrej, *Scenic Splendours: India through the Printed Image*, London, 1989.

Victoria Memorial Hall, Calcutta: *Calcutta A Catalogue of objects on Calcutta in the Collection of the Victoria Memorial*, Calcutta, 1976.

Welch, Stuart Cary, *Room for Wonder: Indian Painting during the British Period*, New York, 1979.

Index

Numbers in *italics* refer to the pages on which black and white illustrations are found

Abel, Dr, 95
Accountant-General's office *see* Treasury
Ackermann, R (*fl*. late 18th, early 19th century), 74
Addiscombe Military College, 81, 102
adjutant-birds, *84, 91, 92, 94, 96, 98, 97-8*; pls. 15, 20
Adlard, H (*fl*. mid-19th century), *58*
Agg, Lieutenant James, 56
Agra, imperial baths at, 99
Akbar, Mughal Emperor (1556-1605), 11
Alais, J (*fl*. early 19th century), *48*
Alexander & Co, 88, 105
Alipore, 40, 47, 58, 62, 110
Alipore Bridge, *110, 118*; pl. 32
Alivardi Khan, Nawab of Bengal (1740-56), 28-9, 51
Ambassador's house, 28
Amherst, Jeffrey, 95
Amherst, Countess, 95-6, 98
Amherst, Earl, Governor-General (1823-8), 82-4, 95-6, 98, 102
Amherst, Lady Sarah Elizabeth, 95-6, *97-8*, 98-9, 104
Amratollah Street, 64
aquatint engraving, 44, 48, 81, 105
Arakan, 11, 15
Armenians, 18, 22-3, 31-2, 35, 38, 54, 88
artists, British: amateur, 64, 81-2, 99, 102, 112; professional, 44-5, 48, 81-2; Indian, 42, 48, 81, 104
Asiatic Lithographic Press (*fl*. 1825-1850s), 105, 122, *127-9*
Asiatic Society, 106, 108, *109*, 112
Asiaticus, 54, 56, 66
Atkinson, James, 7, 8, 45
Auckland, Lord, Governor-General (1836-42), 110, 124
Auckland Circus Gardens, 115, 124
Auckland Hotel, 122
auctions, and auction-rooms, 60, 68-9, 86, 88, 89, 94, 120. 122
Aurangzeb, Mughal Emperor (1658-1707), 14-18, 22
Auriol, James Peter, 48, 56
Baboo Ghaut, 114-5, 124, 127; pl. 28
Bacon, John, 96
Bagshaw, Barlow & Co, 81; pl. 13
Baillie, William (1753-99), 36, 37, 47, 64, 65, 66, *67-8*
Balasore, 11, 15
banks, 79, *79*, 88, 94, 105; collapse of, 105
Banksall, 27, 39
banyans, 12, 19, 42
Barlow, Sir George, Governor-General (1805-07), 80
Barrackpore, 40
Barrackpore House and Park, 80-1, *81, 83-4, 83*; Memorial Hall, 83, *83*
Barretto, Joseph, 90, 116
Bartolozzi, Francesco (1727-1815), 33
Barwell, Richard, Member of Council, 46, 48, 50. *57-8, 62, 66-7*
Bazaar, Great or Bara, 18, 23, 32, 35-6
Bellamy, Mr, 28
Bengal, 11, 24; Mughal government of, 12, 14-15; 17-18, 21-2, 33, 35, 46; *divani* of, 35, 46; revenues of, 46; trade of *see* trade, of Bengal
Bengal Army, 36, 66
Bengal Club, 104, 106; pl. 24
Bengal Engineers, 56, 71, 81, 91, 102, 112, 118
Bentinck, Lady, 99, 104
Bentinck, Lord William Cavendish, Governor-General (1828-35), 98, 102, 104-5, 108, 116; his statue, 120, 124, *124, 127*
Best, James (*fl*. 1803), 73
Betor, 11
bihishtis, 42, 86, 87, 94; pl. 14
Bipradas, 16

Bishop's Palace, 108, 110
Black, Thomas (*fl* 1825-1847), *127-9*
'Black Hole', 32, 37, 51, 52
'Black Hole' monument, 37, 39, 50, 51-2, 52, 66, 84, *84*, 87
'Black Pagoda', 23, 36, 48, 49, 63, 84, 104; pls. 3, 23
'Black Zamindar', 18, 23, 48
Blount, Sir Charles, 63
Bombay, 38, 46, 80
Botanic Gardens, Sibpur, 93, 104-5
Botanic Garden House, 93, 104; pl. 19
Bourchier, Richard, 28, 56
Bourchier, Sarah, 56
Bourne, Samuel, 126
Bow Bazaar, 45, 88, *89*
Bowles, John, 21
Boytaconnah Street, 88, 116
Bride, Mr, 53
Brohier, Captain John, 35
Brooke, Captain, 11
Brown, Revd David, 54, 64, 66
Bryce, Revd James, 86
Buckingham, James Silk, 82
budgerows, 20, 30, 55, 79, 80; pl. 5
Bullini, Dr, 108
bungalows, 40
Burke, William, Paymaster-General, 58
Burrell & Gould, 68, 70
Burying Ground Road *see* Park Street
Buxar, battle of, 35
Byrne, William (1745-1805), 45
Bysacks, 11, 15
Calcutta, founding of, 7, 11, 15-16; advantages of site, 15-16; original village of, 16; unhealthy climate of, 16, 38; mortality at, 16. 20. 43-4; renting of, 17, *17*, 21; declared independent of Madras, 18; revenue from ground rents and dues; 18-20, 24; divisions of, 18, 22; population of, 16, 18-20, 38, 76; law in, 18-19, 46, 106; different religions in, 20, 22; bounds of, 20, 22-3, 33, 35; defences of, 23, 24-33, *25, 27, 30-1*; attack on in 1756, 31-3; recapture of, 32, 35; restitution money for the sack of, 33, 35.
— surveys of, 46-7, 64, 94; plans of, 22-4, 23, *25, 26-31, 27, 32, 36, 40, 42, 46-8, 47, 64, 83, 94*; general descriptions of, 7, 20, 37-8, 44-5, 76, 95; general views of, *25, 30-1, 30-1, 36, 39, 48, 118, 124-6, 126-9*; sets of views of, 64, 66-68, 76, 82-3, 105, 112.
— speculative building boom in, 36-7, 40, 47, 50-1, 54, 60, 78, 82, 85, 106; houses in, 17-18, 20-2, 25, 27-8, 29-31, 30-2, 35-8, *39, 40, 44-5, 47-9, 51-2, 52-3, 54, 55-8, 57, 59, 60-4, 61, 65, 68, 68-70, 71, 77, 88, 89-90, 91, 105-6, 107, 108, 109, 110, 114, 119, 124, 126, 128-9*; pls. 1-2, 7-8, 10, 25, 30-1; interiors of houses, 38, 41, 59-60, 62, 74; rent of houses, 27, 41, 43, 49-50, 58-62.
—, British inhabitants of, 16, 19-20, 22, 26, 31, 35, 38, 40-1, 43, 47-50, 56, 59-63, 66, 74, 75, 81-2, 92, 98, 104-5, 110, 112, 115, 118; cost of living in, 20, 38, 41-3, 50, 59-60, 62, 82, 122; Indian inhabitants of, 15, 18, 22, 24, 35, 38, 47, 54, 86, 95, 98, 106, 110, 112, 126; Bengali part of, 'Black Town', 18, 22-4, 32, 38, 46, 48-9, 63, 68, 76, 84, 92-5, 103, 104, 110, 112, 126; pls. 3, 5, 9, 17, 23, 25
camera obscura, 48, 62
canal cutting, 95, 102
Cantoo Baboo, 29
Carr, William, 110
Cartier, John, Governor of Bengal (1769-72), 47, 60
castes, 41-2, 67
cathedrals: St John's, 90-1, 90, 95, 118, 124, 128; pls. 24, 28-9; St Paul's, 108, 116, 118, 123, 124-5, 129; Virgin Mary of the Rosary, Catholic, 22, 88, 90, 114, 124-5, 129; pls. 24, 28
cemeteries: old burial ground, 16-17, 23, 25, 26-8, 30, 31, 37, 39, 44, 55-6; Park St, 43, 43, 44; mausoleums in, 23, 25, 31, 37, 39, 43, 43, 44. 51, 55-6, 91; pl. 6

Chamber of Commerce, 81
Chambers, Sir Robert, Judge and Chief Justice, 46, 48, 58, 61, 66
Chambers, William, 54
Chandernagore, 33, 58
Chandpaul Ghaut, 61-2, 69, 78-80, 79, 91, 94, 99, 99, 102, 112, 115, 124; pl. 7
Chantrey, Francis, 114
chaplains, 13, 19-20, 22, 40, 44, 54-5, 60, 66
Charak puja, 116, 119
Charity School, 28, 49-50, 54
Charnock, Job, Agent in Bengal (1685-92), 7, 11, 14-17, 20; his mausoleum, 17, 23, 55-6; pl. 6
Charters, Samuel, 48
China, 80, 82, 95
Chinnery, George (1774-1852), 81-3, 82, 93, 95, 99, 102, 112, 116
Chinsura, Dutch factory at, 11-12, 13, 21, 54; Governor of, 12, 59-60
Chitpore, 16, 23, 58, 63, 94
Chitpore Road, 23-4, 26, 48, 49, 63, 68-9, 84, 86, 93-4, 104, 110; pls. 9, 17, 23
Chittagong, 11, 15
chobdars, 22, 42, 92, 98; pls. 2, 15
chowkidars 86, 87, 114; pl. 28
Chowringhee, 63, 76, 77, 95, 105, 128-9
Chowringhee Bazaar, 116, 107, 125
Chowringhee Road, 35, 63-4, 76, 93-4, 98, 99-100, 104, 106, 107, 108-10, 109, 111-13, 116, 119, 125, 128-9; pls. 8, 30-1
Chowringhee Theatre *see* theatre, Chowringhee
chunam, 24, 38, 68, 75
church, Armenian, of the Holy Nazareth, 22-3, 22, 26, 35-6, 38, 39, 48, 64, 124, 128; pl. 5
— Greek, 64
— Mission, of Beth-Tephillah, 53, 54, 64, 66, 120, 124, 125, 129
churches, Anglican: St Anne's, 20-2, 24, 25-6, 26, 28-9, 29, 30-2, 35-6, 38, 40; pls. 1-2; St John's chapel 36-8, 39, 40, 50, 51, 51, 55, 55, 64; St John's, 50, 55-6, 60, 61, 69, 84, 85, 86, 90, 94; pl. 6, 12 (*see also* cathedrals: St John's); St Peter's, Fort William, 110, 113, 126; St Stephen's, Kidderpore, 122, 126; St Thomas's, Free School Street, 125, 128
—, Catholic, first, 17, 22; Virgin Mary of the Rosary, 20, 22-3, 22, 26, 35, 38, 40, 64, 88 (*see also* cathedrals: Virgin Mary of the Rosary); Our Lady of Doris, 88, 89; Sacred Heart, 115-6 119, 125, 129; St Thomas's, Middleton Row, 125, 129
—, Scotch, St Andrew's, 50, 83-4, 84, 86, 87, 92, 94, 114, 115; pls. 14, 16, 20, 24, 28; Free Presbyterian, 125, 128
Chutanutte *see* Suttanuttee
Circular Canal, 94-5
Circular Road, 63, 71, 88, 89, 94, 102, 103, 110
'City of Palaces', 7, 8, 45, 80, 105, 126
Clavell, Mr, 12
Clavering, General Sir John, Commander-in-Chief, 46, 54, 62
Clerihew, William (1814?-80?), 118, 123
Cleveland, Augustus, 62
Clive, Colonel Robert, Governor of Bengal (1758-60, 1765-7), 32-3, 33, 35, 46, 58; his houses, 26, 30, 39, 52, 52, 58, 60
Clive Street, 51, 52, 86, 87, 102, 112, 114
coachbuilders, 67
Collector of Calcutta, 18, 28, 48
Collector's offices *see* Cutcheries
College Square, 94
College Street, 94, 126
Collins, Captain, 63
Colvin & Co, 79, 79, 88, 105
Commissioners of Police, 46
Company's House, 25, 26-8, 29, 30, 31, 32; pl. 1
Coote, Sir Eyre, Commander-in-Chief, 60
Cornwallis, Marquis, Governor-General (1780-93, 1805), 35, 58, 98; his statue, 96
Cornwallis Street, 94
Cossimbazar, 14, 19, 29-30, 51
Cossitollah Street, 93, 95; pl. 17
Council, of Bengal (*see also* East India Company: its government in Bengal),

13-14; of Fort William, 18-19, 46
Council Chambers, 12, 75, 96
Council House, old, 64; new, 44, 58-60, 61, 63, 65, 66, 69, 71
Council House Street, 60, 61, 71, 74, 84, 85, 90, 92, 93, 106, 107
Course, the, 38, 40, 43, 96, 98, 104, 110, 113, 114, 126-7; pls. 24, 28
Cricket Club, 122, 127
Croll & Collier, 97, 98
Cruttenden, Edward, 28, 30, 52
Cruttenden, McKillop & Co, 88, 105
customs dues, 12, 14-15, 17-21, 24, 33
Custom Master's house, 36, 39, 50, 51, 54, 55, 64, 66, 67; pl. 10
Customs House, 36, 39, 54-5, 55, 64, 66, 84, 85, 126; at Hooghly, 19
Customs House Wharf, 112; pl. 27
Cutcheries, 28, 54
cyclone, of 1737, 22, 24, 28, 48
Dacca, 12, 14, 10, 112
Dacre, Philip Milner, Member of Council, 48
Dalhousie, Earl of, Governor-General (1848-56), 124, 126
Dalhousie Institute, 114
Dance, Nathaniel (1734-1811), 33
Daniell, Thomas (1749-1840), 49, 51-3, 55, 57, 59, 61, 65; pls. 3, 5-9
Daniell, William (1769-1837), pls. 3, 9
Daniell, Thomas and William, 36, 40, 48-9, 54-6, 58-9, 63-4, 66, 74, 83-4, 91, 104; their *Oriental Scenery*, 63-4, 66; pls. 3, 9
Davis, Samuel (1756?-1819), 80; pl. 12
Dawson, Matthew, 63
de la Combe, E, 94
Devis, Arthur William (1762-1822), 48
Dhurrumtollah Street, 94-5, 106, 107, 116, 119, 125, 129
Dhurrumtollah Tank, 115-16, 129; pls. 30-1
Diamond Harbour, 13, 80
Dibdin, Thomas Coleman (1810-93), 118, 123
Dickinson, Lowes Cato and W Robert (*fl*. mid-19th century), 114-5, 117, 119, 121; pls. 27-32
distillery, 48, 64
Dockyard, 27, 30, 31, 39, 55, 55, 64, 66; Colonel Watson's, 48, 118, 121
Douglas, Ensign Charles, 28, 30
D'Oyly, Sir Charles (1781-1845), 71, 81-2, 93, 96, 99, 110, 112, 114-6 116, 118, 120, 124-5; his *Tom Raw the Griffin*, 71, 73-5, 74, 79-80, 82, 86, 88, 91-2, 96, 120; his *Views of Calcutta and its Environs*, 112, 114-15, 117, 119, 121; pls. 27-32
drainage, 46, 50, 51, 94-5
Drake, Roger, President of Fort William (1752-8), 28-9, 32-3
Driver, Thomas Syars, 90
Duburgh, C (*fl*. early 19th century), pl. 12
Dum Dum, 40
Dunkin, Sir William, Judge, 61, 91
Durga puja, 69, 88, 110, 112; pl. 25
Dutch East India Company, 11-12, 15
earthquake, of 1897, 54, 118
East India Company, 7, 11-12, 14-15, 18-22, 26-30, 40, 46, 56, 60, 66, 71, 73, 76, 78, 85, 94, 102, 104, 108, 125; its charters, 11, 18-19; its factories, 11-18, 21, 33; its monopoly, 14, 80, 88, 108
— its servants, 12-14, 17, 19, 35, 37, 50, 75, 85; their morals, 13, 14; their ranks, 13; their pay, 14, 18-20; its soldiers, 15, 17-18, 20-1, 33, 53, 64, 66, 83, 112, 124; its fleets, 13, 52
— its government in Bengal, 7, 14, 16, 18-19, 22, 24, 26-9, 33, 35, 40, 46-7, 49-52, 54-5, 58-63, 71, 76, 78, 85-6, 88, 95, 98, 104-6, 108, 112, 110, 118, 120
East Indiamen, 13, 80
Eden, Emily and Fanny, 99, 124
Eden Gardens, 115, 124, 127
education debate, 95
elephants, 49, 57. 65, 67, 76, 84, 116; at Barrackpore, 81, 84

Elizabeth, Mrs Gracia, 88
Elliot, John, 104
Elliot's Tank, 116, 125, 129
Elliott, Mr, 24
Ellis, Francis, Member of Council, 17
Ellis, James, 57
epidemics, 44
Esplanade (see also Maidan), 35-6, 39, 40, 44-5, 48, 56, 57, 58, 61, 62-4, 69, 78
Esplanade Row, 35, 44, 45, 58-64, 59, 61, 65, 66, 69, 74, 78, 79, 80, 83, 91, 91, 93, 99, 104, 106, 107, 114-6, 124, 125, 128-9; pls. 7, 12, 24, 28-31
Europe shops (see also shops), 57, 57
Eyre, Sir Charles, President of Fort William (1700), 17-18
Eyre, Edward, Member of Council, 26, 28
Exchange, 49, 84, 85, 86
fakirs, 48, 67, 69
famines, 24, 36, 76
Farquharson, Captain, 99
Farquharson, William, 78
Farrukhsiyar, Mughal Emperor (1713-19), 21-2
Fay, Mrs Eliza, 36-7, 40, 43-4, 48, 48, 76, 86
Fenwick Bazaar, 125
Fergusson & Co, 105-6
Fiebig, Frederick (fl. 1845-55), 43, 90, 115, 118, 120, 122, 124-6, 123-9
Fielding, Thales (1793-1837), pl. 16
Fielding, T H, 102
fire prevention, 118; pl. 32
firmans, 12, 14-15, 17-18
Fitzgerald, Captain William Robert, 112, 124
food and drink, 12-13. 20. 24, 38, 41-3, 56, 76, 88, 104, 108
Forbes, Major William, 102, 116, 118
Forresti, Theodore, 23, 24, 26
Fort St George see Madras
Fort William, old, 17, 20-3, 25, 28, 29-30, 30-2, 35-8, 39, 40, 50-1, 51-2, 54, 55, 64, 66, 67, 84, 126; pls. 1, 2; its fortifications, 17-18, 20-1, 23, 26-30, 32; Factory building, 17, 20-2, 25-6, 28, 29-30, 30, 35-6, 39, 50, 55, 55, 59-60; pls. 1, 2; Long Row, 17, 21-2, 28, 30; armoury and magazine, 20-1, 30; plans of, 21, 23, 25, 27, 32; prison in, 21, 32; warehouses beside, 20, 23, 30, 31, 59, 64, 84, 85; flagstaff in, 22, 29, 30; pl. 2; destruction of, 32, 35
Fort William, new, 35-6, 37, 38, 39, 44-5, 47, 47, 62-4, 75-6, 77, 93, 95-6, 110, 113, 115, 126; fortifications of, 36, 36, 45, 47, 47, 65, 99; pls. 12, 26; Government House in, 36, 39, 47, 47, 108, 110, 113; barracks in, 36, 38, 39, 47, 47, 64, 65; armoury in, 36, 100, 100; church in (see also churches: Anglican, St Peter's, Fort William) 36, 40; views from, 45, 80, 99, 99, 115; pl. 12
Fort William, College of, 84-5, 85
Fortnom, Colonel John, 59-60
fortunes, East India, 19, 33, 35
Francis, Philip, Member of Council, 46-7, 50, 52, 57-8, 58, 62-3
Fraser, James Baillie (1783-1856), 82-94, 96, 114; pl. 20; his Views of Calcutta and its Environs, 82, 83-5, 87, 89-91, 93; pls. 14-19
Free School, 54, 125
Free School Street, 125
French East India Company, 15, 29, 33, 35
Fulta, 32
furniture, 38, 41, 59-60
Ganges, River, 102, 103
Garden Reach, 36. 40, 45, 47-8, 62, 76, 77, 78, 93-4, 104, 110, 118, 121, 126; pl. 19
garden-houses, 38, 40, 42, 44-5, 47-8, 54, 58, 77, 80, 93, 104
gardeners, 42, 96, 97
gardens, 12, 13, 20, 23, 40, 42, 77; of the Seths, 23; of Gobindram Mitter and Omi Chand, 23, 25, 26; of Government House see Government House, new: grounds
Garstin, Colonel John, 82, 91-2
Garstin's Buildings, 82
General's Tank, 108, 109, 125, 129
Gholam Mahomed, Prince, 125
Gobindpore, 11, 15-20, 22-4, 26, 28, 35
Gobindram Mitter, 18, 23, 26, 48, 63; his temple see 'Black Pagoda'

Goldborne, Sophia, 40, 43, 76, 78
Goldsborough, Sir John, Commissary-General and Chief Governor, 17, 21, 22
Goodwin, Mr, 48
Gordon's Buildings, 104, 106, 124, 129; pls. 24, 30
Government House, old, 45, 50, 57-60, 59, 62, 64, 66, 71
Government House, new, 53, 71, 73-6, 73, 80-1, 83, 85, 91-2, 91, 93, 94-5, 97-8, 98, 106, 107, 114, 118, 120, 123, 124, 126, 128; pls. 11, 13, 15- 16, 24, 26, 28-30; its grounds, 71, 74, 92, 93, 95-6, 97-8, 99, 104, 107, 115, 124, 127-8; its gateways, 74, 92, 93, 96, 97, 114, 117; pls. 14-16; its dome, 73, 73, 74, 96, 97, 106, 107, 124; coats-of-arms on, 73, 81, 93, 96, 97, 118; pl. 13; interior of, 74, 75, 95, 98, 120; celebrations in, 75-6, 99
Governor(-General)'s Bodyguard, 22, 92, 96, 97, 98; pl. 15
Governor(-General)'s state, 58, 62, 71, 80-1, 92, 96, 97, 98; pls. 2, 13, 15
Graham, Maria, 69-70, 73-5, 85, 95-6, 110, 112
Graham, Robert, 76
Graham, Thomas, Member of Council and President of the Board of Trade, 76, 78
Graham Street, 76
Grand, Mrs Catherine, 57-8
Grand, Francis, 57-8
Grandpré, Louis de, 36, 49, 53, 58, 66
Grant, Charles, Director and Chairman of the East India Company, 54
Grant, Colesworthy (1813-80), 86, 104
Grant, Harry, 86
Grant, T, 63
Griffiths, Mr, 26, 28, 31, 36
Haileybury College, 85
Hale, Edward, 95-6
Hamilton, Captain Alexander, 16, 19-21, 44
Hamilton, Captain-Commandant Robert, 26
Hamilton, Surgeon William, 21
Hamilton's, jewellers, 122
Hannay, John, 48
Harding, Mr, 57
Hare, Dr James, 86
Hare Street, 27, 56, 82, 102
Harington Street, 76, 125
Harmonic Tavern, 69, 86
Hartly House (see also Sophia Goldborne), 37, 40, 78
Harvey, Mr, Chief at Malda, 14
Hastings, Mrs Marian, 47, 59
Hastings, Warren, Governor-General (1773-85), 29, 33, 35-6, 44-7, 49-50, 55-6, 59, 62-3, 63, 98, 100, 106, 108, 116; his houses, 47-8, 58-9; duel with Philip Francis, 47, 62; his impeachment, 62-3
Hastings, Marchioness of, 92, 94, 98
Hastings, Marquess of, Governor-General (1813-23), 81-2, 82, 83-4, 92, 94, 98; pls. 13, 15; his statue, 114, 115
Hastings Street, 23, 71, 74, 102, 106
Havell, Robert (1769-1832), 85; pl. 18
Havell, Robert, Junior (1793-1878), 83-4, 87, 89, 91, 93; pls. 14-15, 19
Havell, William, 82
Hay, Edward, Chief Secretary, 63
Heath, Captain William, 14
Heber, Bishop Reginald, 83-4, 88, 90, 95, 95, 108, 110, 112, 114, 116, 125
Hedges, William, Agent in Bengal (1682-4), 13
Hickey, Thomas (1741-1824), 50, 63
Hickey, William, 45, 48, 50, 52-8, 60-4, 63, 66, 69, 71, 76, 78, 80, 85-6, 91, 93; his houses, 60-2, 61, 64, 69, 91
Hijili, 15
Hindoo College, 94
Hindus (see also 'Black Pagoda' and Kalighat, temple at), 20, 48, 55, 55, 69-70, 110, 112, 115-16; pl. 25
Hindustani College see Madrassah
Hodges, William (1744-97), 44, 45, 48, 63
Holwell, John Zephaniah, Governor of Bengal (1760), 28, 30, 32, 33, 37, 52
Home, Robert (1752-1834), 75
Hooghly, 11, 14, 16, 19; English factory at, 11-12, 14-15

Hooghly, River, 11, 13, 15, 21, 23, 29-31, 39, 44-5, 45, 47-8, 54-55, 55, 62, 68, 70, 76, 77, 78-80, 79-81, 83, 93-5, 99, 99, 104, 112, 115, 118, 121, 126-9; pls. 1, 5, 12, 18-10. 26 ~ 20; navigation of. 11. 13. 15; its bore, 68; embankment of, 70, 94-5, 102
Hoppner, John (1758-1810), 58
hospitals: first, 20, 23, 28; General Hospital, 78, 78, 110, 122, 126; Fever, 126
Howrah, 48, 64
Humphry, Ozias (1742-1810), 45, 46
Hutchinson, Captain George, 110
Hyde, John, Judge, 46, 58, 61, 91
Hydrah Bagaun, 106, 125, 128
Ibrahim Khan, Subahdar of Bengal, 15, 17
Impey, Sir Elijah, Chief Justice, 42, 46, 50, 58, 61; his house, 41, 42, 44, 61, 108, 125
Impey, Lady, 41, 42
Improvement Committee, 94
interlopers, 14, 16, 18
Jackson, Captain Nicholas, 26
Jacquemont, Victor, 104-6, 108
jail: on Lall Bazaar, 28, 69, 70; on the Esplanade, 28, 122, 126
'James and Mary' sands, 13
Jaun Bazaar, 54, 106, 125, 128
Johnson, Frances, 'Begum', 29, 50, 51, 56
Johnson, Revd William, 51, 54-6, 60
Johnson & Co, 92
Johnston, Captain, 102
Jones, John (1745?-97), 63
Jones, Sir William, Judge, 62, 106, 108
Jukes, Francis, 67; pl. 10
Justices of the Peace, 68; their court, 68, 70, 86, 89
Kali puja, 70
Kalighat, temple at, 16, 23, 69-70; pl. 4
Kedgeree, 80
Keighley, James English, Chief at Cossimbazar, 56
Keir, Archibald, 60-2
Kidderpore, 40, 47-8, 58, 66, 93, 110
Kidderpore Bridge, 110, 111, 118
Kidderpore Nullah see Tolly's Nullah
Kiernander, John Zachariah, 54, 78
Kindersley, Mrs, 37-8, 40-3, 76
Kipling, Rudyard, 7-8
Kirkall, Elisha, 21
Kirkpatrick, Captain William, 64
Kitchin, Thomas (fl. mid-18th century), 25, 30-2
Koila Ghat Street, 59, 64. 84, 85
Kyd, Colonel Robert, 93, 118; his sons, 93, 118
Kyd Street, 116
Lall Bazaar, 23-4, 26, 28, 46, 54, 68-9, 70, 86, 88, 89, 93
Lall Dighi see the Tank
Lambert, George (1710-65), 20-22, 26, 28; pls. 1-2
Larkins Lane, 56
Le Gallais, Francis, 58
Le Maistre, Stephen, Judge, 46, 62
Levett, Mr, 48, 64
Lewis, Frederick Christian (1779-1856), 87, 89-90; pl. 17
Library, the, 57, 57
Lindsay Street, 63, 106, 125
lithographic printing, 105, 118
Littleton, Sir Edward, President of the New Company, 17
Livius, George, 47
Locker, Edward Hawke (1777-1849), 81, 81
lotteries, 94, 91, 94
Loudoun Buildings, 92, 106, 107, 118
Lyon, Thomas, 50, 52, 67
Lyon's Range, 67; pl. 10
Macaulay, Thomas Babington, Law Member of Council, 50, 62, 104, 108
Macdonald, John, 85
Mackintosh & Co, 105
Mackrabie, Alexander, 62
Macnaghten, Sir Francis, acting Chief Justice, 104
Macpherson, Colonel Allan, 48
Macpherson, Sir John, Governor-General (1785-6), 48, 78
Madras, 11, 14-5, 17-8, 24, 32, 38, 46
Madrassah, 45, 46, 94

Mahomed Reza Cawn, Nawab of Chitpore, 58-60, 71
Mahratta Ditch, 24, 25, 26, 28, 35
Maidan, the (see also Esplanade), 48, 63, 74, 76, 77, 78, 78, 95, 98, 105-6, 107, 108, 109, 110, 111, 113, 114-6, 118, 122, 126-9; pls. 24, 28-31
Manohardoss Tank, 63, 125, 129
Marathas, 22, 24, 26, 46, 71
Master, Sir Streynsham, Agent in Madras (1677-82), 12-14
Mayor's Court, 19, 28, 49
M'Clintock, Robert, 95
Mevell, Martin Boutant de, 54
Middleton, Bishop Thomas Fanshaw, 86, 90
Middleton, Nathaniel, 51
Middleton Row, 108, 125
Military (later United Services) Club, 125, 129
Minchin, Captain-Commandant George, 32
Minerva, statue of see Britannia
mint, Mughal (at Rajmahal), 12, 21
mint, old, 33, 79, 102; new, 102, 104, 112; pl. 22
Minto, Earl of, Governor-General (1807-13), 81, 83, 90-1, 94, 98, 104
Mir Jafar, Nawab of Bengal (1757-60, 1763-5), 33, 35, 51
Mir Qasim, Nawab of Bengal (1760-3), 35
Mission Church see church, Mission
Mission Row, 53, 54, 65, 86
Mission School, 54
Moffat, James (1775-1815), 74, 76, 77-9, 78-9, 91, 93; pl. 11
Monson, Colonel George, Member of Council, 46, 62
Mordaunt, Colonel John, 63
morpunkhis, 77, 78
mosques, 32. 103, 106, 125, 129
Mowbray, John, 76
Mughals, 12-13, 13, 14-15, 17-20, 22, 24, 26, 35, 46, 102
Muhammad Amir, Shaykh, 104, 106, 114; pl. 24
Murray, Colonel Peter, 63
Murray, Mr, 48
Murshid Quli Khan, Subahdar of Bengal (1704-26), 21-2
Murshidabad, 14, 21, 29, 33, 58
Muxadabad see Murshidabad
Muslims (see also mosques), 20, 45, 112
nautches, 88, 98, 110, 112; pl. 25
New China Bazaar, 52, 86, 87
Nicholls, Charles George, 76
Norfar, Mr, 53
northwesters, 62, 68
Nubkissen, Maharajah, 49, 55, 110
Nuncoomar, Maharajah, 50
Ochterlony, Sir David, 116
Ochterlony Monument, 116, 122, 126; pl. 31
offices, Government, 50, 55, 58-60, 64, 91, 91, 98, 99, 106, 108, 116, 118, 121, 126
Oil Bazaar, 106, 107, 116, 129
Old Court House Street, 40, 49, 56, 57-8, 57, 60, 71, 74, 81, 92, 93, 94, 97, 100, 108, 114, 120, 125; pls. 13, 15-16, 20, 24, 28
Old Fort Ghaut, 55, 55
Old Post Office Street, 104
Ollifres, John (d.1745), 23, 24, 26
Omi Chand, 23-4, 26, 28, 32-3
Oriental Library, 86, 87
Orissa, 11, 24
Orme, Edward, 50, 74, 80
Orme, Robert, 24, 25, 26, 28, 30, 30-2, 33, 35-6, 42
Orme, William (fl. 1794-1805), 50; pl. 12
Orphanages, Military, 48, 64, 66, 66-68, 122, 126
palaces, 44-5, 71, 76, 80
palanquins, 13, 20, 41-2, 44, 51, 67, 87. 89, 90, 90, 93, 103, 120; pls. 2, 6-7, 10-11, 15, 20, 31
Palmer, John, 82, 86, 88
Palmer, General William, 98
Palmer & Co, 88, 105, 110
parasols, 13, 51, 57, 70, 89; pls. 6-7, 10-11, 24, 31
Park, the, 22-3. 28, 32, 49; pl. 2
Park, the (in Chowringhee), 42, 44, 61
Park Street, 44, 100, 106, 108, 109, 110, 125

135

Parker, Colonel, 48
Parthenio, Father, 56
Patna, 14, 16, 19-20, 112
Paxton, Cockerell & Co, 52, 52
Peachie, Jeremiah, Member of Council, 17
Pearse, Colonel Thomas Deane, 48
Pearson, John, 104
Pellew, Admiral Sir Edward, 81
Petrie, John, 48
Phillips, Thomas (1770-1845), 95
photography, 118, 125-6
pirates, 15
Plaisted, Bartholomew, 26, 31
Plassey, battle of, 33
police station, 86
Polier, Major Antoine (1740/1-95), 36, 39, 44, 54
Portuguese, in Bengal, 11, 15, 22
Portuguese, in Calcutta, 18, 22-3, 31-2, 35, 38, 40, 54, 76, 88, 90
post offices, 49, 106, 126
Pott, Robert, 62
pottahs, 50, 52
powder magazine, 23, 25, 27-8; — yard, 55
Presbyterians, 20, 86
presents, 18, 33, 35
Prinsep, Henry Thoby, 98
Prinsep, James, 92, 102, 104, 108, 112
Prinsep, John, 36, 44, 56, 82, 102
Prinsep, Thomas (1800-30), 84, 102, 103, 104; pls. 21-3
Prinsep, William (1794-1874), 82, 88, 92, 99, 99, 100, 100-1, 102, 105, 108, 110, 112; pls. 25-6
Prinsep's Ghaut, 112, 124; pl. 26
public entertainments (*see also* Government House, new: celebrations in), 49-50, 52-3, 62, 66, 86, 91-2, 108, 110-11
Raban, Thomas, 54
racecourse, 40
Rajchunder Doss, Baboo, 115
Rajkissen, Maharajah, 110, 112
Reid, Mr, 48
Respondentia, 79
Respondentia Walk, 115; pl. 29
Reynolds, Sir Joshua (1723-92), attrib., 33
Rider, Jacob, 63
riding academy, 54
roads, laying out of, 22-3, 40, 46, 49, 53, 56, 71, 74, 94-5, 102, 114, 122, 124; state of, 46, 67
Roberts, Emma, 66, 98, 105-6, 115, 118, 120, 122
Rohilla Monument, 90, 91
Rope Walk, 23, 28, 54
Ross, James, 26
Rowe, Josiah, 126
Roxburgh, Dr William, 93
Rundell, Francis, 53
Russell, William, 122
Russell Street, 108

Ryan, Sir Edward, Judge, 104, 112
Ryne, Jan van (1712?-60?), 28-9, 29, 30
Saadat Ali Khan, Nawab of Oudh (1798-1814), 93
St Andrew's Library, 86, 87
St Xavier's school, 108
salt, 15, 35
Salt, Henry (1780-1827), 76, 77, 80
Salt Water Lake, 15-16, 20, 23, 88, 94-5, 102; pl. 21
saltpetre, 14, 19-20, 38; saltpetre godown, 30, 30
Sanderson, Robert, 58
Satgaon, 11, 15
Savignhac, P (*fl.* 1826-35), 82
scavengers, 76, 94, 96; pl. 20
Schalch, John Augustus, 83, 86, 91. 94, 99, 102, 106, 108
Schuylenburgh, Hendrick van (1620?-89), 12 13
Scott, Colonel Caroline, 27-8
Scott, Samuel (1710?-72), 21; pl. 1
sepoys, 51, 53, 53, 113
Serampore, 80, 82-3
servants, 13, 37-8, 41-2, 41, 68, 76, 96, 104, 120
Seths, 11, 15, 19, 23-4, 30, 33
Seton, John Thomas (*fl.*1761-1806), 63
Shah Alam, Bahadur Shah, Mughal Emperor (1707-12), 18
Shah Alam, Mughal Emperor (1759-1806), 35
Shah Jahan, Mughal Emperor (1628-58), 11
Shaista Khan, *Subahdar* of Bengal, 14-15
Shalimar, 93, 118, 121
Shee, Sir George, 57, 93, 118, 121
Sheldon, Ralph, Member of Council, 18
ships and shipping, 13, 15, 19, 21, 27-8, 29-31, 32, 38, 39, 44-5, 45, 48, 55, 55, 64, 77, 78. 79, 79-80, 88, 99, 99, 102, 103, 110, 112, 114-15, 121; pls. 1, 5, 12, 18-19, 21, 26-7, 29; country-shipping, 19, 39, 79-80, 88
shops, 57, 57, 67, 86, 88, 94, 97, 98, 119, 120, 122, 125; pls. 10, 17, 20
Shore, Sir John, Governor-General (1793-8), 57-8, 71
Short, Charles, 63
Shuja ud-Daula, Nawab Vizier of Oudh (1753-75), 35
Sieve Tank, 116, 121
Siraj ud-Daula, Nawab of Bengal (1756-7), 29-33, 51
Skirrow, William, 76
Sloper, General Sir Robert, Commander-in-Chief, 60
Smith, John, 105
Solvyns, François Baltazard (1760-1824), 48, 67-9, 86, 104; pls. 4, 10
Speke Street *see* Sudder Street
Spence's Hotel, 118, 122
Stables, John, Member of Council, 60

Stackhouse, John, President of Fort William (1731-8), 27
Stark, Mr, 48
Stavorinus, J B, 59-60
steam-engine, at Chandpaul Ghaut, 99-100, 99, 124, 127
steam-boats, 99, 99, 102, 103, 116
Steuart, James, 66
Steuart & Co, 66-7, 86; pl. 10
Stewart, Mr, 48
Strand, the, 94, 102, 112, 114-15, 121; pls. 22. 26-7, 29
street cleaning, 46, 99-100, 124
Stuart, Hon Charles, Member of Council, 58, 63, 71
subscriptions, 49-50, 52, 56, 60, 82, 116, 118
Sudder Dewany Adawlut, Court of, 106, 116, 121, 122
Sudder Street, 63, 106, 116
Supreme Court (*see also* court house), 46, 50. 57, 60-2, 85
Surat, 11
Surman, John, 21, 63
Suttanuttee, 11, 15-18, 22-4, 26, 28, 35-6
Tagore, Dwarkanath, 110
talukdars, 18
Tank, the, 23, 85, 86, 87
Tank Square, 49-54, 51-3, 56, 64, 66, 74, 83-4, 84-5, 86, 87, 90-1, 94-5, 104, 106, 114, 115, 120, 122, 125, 126; pl. 14
tanks, 23, 49. 86, 91, 94-5, 116, 125, 129
Tanna, 15
Taylor & Co, 68, 86, 88, 89, 120
textiles, Bengal trade in, 11-12, 15, 19-20, 88; English market protected against, 19
Thaker (Spink) & Co, 86, 122
theatres: old Playhouse, 28, 30, 31, 53, 54; in Clive Street, 52-3, 52, 86, 100; Chowringhee, 100-2, 101, 108, 111; Sans Souci, 108
Theatre Street, 100
Tippoo Sultan of Mysore (1782-99), 71, 75
Tiretta, Edward, 44
Tolly, Colonel William, 47-8
Tolly's Nullah, 23, 26, 48, 110, 111, 118; pl. 32
Tooke, William, 28, 30
Town Hall, 82-3, 91, 91, 92, 93, 94, 96, 104, 112, 120, 124, 128; pl. 24
trade, of Bengal, 11-13, 15, 17, 19-20, 22, 33, 46, 76, 82, 88, 105, 108, 110; season for, 13; profits from, 17-19, 82, 105; private trade, 14, 19, 24, 35
transport, methods of, 42, 48, 67, 84, 90, 94, 96, 104
Treasury, the, 60, 61, 65, 66, 69, 91-2, 91, 93, 106, 107, 126; pls. 24, 28
treaties, between the English and Mir Jafar, 33, 35; and Siraj ud-Daula, 33; and Shah Alam and Shuja ud-Daula, 35
Tremamondo, Antonio Angelo, 54

Tulloh, Mr, 56
Tulloh & Co, 120, 122, 125
Twentymen's, jewellers, 122
Twining, Thomas, 45, 55, 79-80
Upjohn, Aaron, 24, 40, 64, 94
Valentia, Viscount, 75-6, 78, 80, 112
Vandergucht, Gerard, 21
Vansittart, Henry, Governor of Bengal (1760-4), 42, 44
Vansittart, Henry, 48
verandahs, 12, 35, 40, 49, 54, 60-3, 78, 80, 84, 106
Verelst, Henry, Governor of Bengal (1767-9), 47, 60
Vestry, of the parish of Calcutta, 49-50, 54
Wajid Ali Shah, King of Oudh (1847-56), 110
Wallich, Nathaniel, 104
Ward, Francis Swaine, 50
warehouses, 12, 13, 17, 20, 27, 51, 54-5, 55
wars, between England and Holland, 12, 83; and France, 19, 29, 32-3, 40, 83; and Burma, 102, 105; and Nepal, 116
water, drinking *see* tanks
Watson, Admiral Charles, 32-3, 35; his mausoleum, 56; pl. 6
Watson, Colonel Henry, 45, 48, 118
Watts, William, Member of Council, 28-30, 33, 51
Wellesley, Marquess, Governor-General (1798-1805), 71, 73-6, 75, 79-80, 83- 5, 91, 94, 98
Wellesley Place, 74, 114, 118
Wellesley Square, 46, 94, 125
Wellesley Street, 94
Wellington Square, 94
Wellington Street, 94
Wells, Lieutenant William, 27, 27-8, 30, 49
Westmacott, Richard, 120
Wheler, Edward, Member of Council, 48, 58, 71
Wheler Place, 57-8, 71
Williamson, Mr, 26, 30
Wilson, Bishop Daniel, 108, 118
Wilson, Horace Hayman, 101-2
Wilson's Hotel, 102
Wood, Colonel Mark (1750-1829), 36, 47, 47, 63-4, 94
Wood, William, 105
Wood, William, Junior (1774-1857), 105-6, 108, 110, 118, 125; his *A Series of Twenty-eight Panoramic Views of Calcutta*, 105, 107, 109, 111, 113
Wood Street, 94
Writers' Buildings, 50, 51, 52, 52, 67, 84-6, 84, 87, 114, 115, 124, 128
Wyatt, Captain Charles, 71, 73-4
zamindars, 17-18, 33
Young, Colonel James, 82
Zayn al-Din, *Shaykh*, 41
Zoffany, Johan, 47, 56